Also by David Roberts

On the Ridge Between Life and Death: A Climbing Life Reexamined

The Pueblo Revolt: The Secret Rebellion That Drove the Spaniards Out of the Southwest

Escape from Lucania: An Epic Story of Survival

True Summit: What Really Happened on the Legendary Ascent of Annapurna

A Newer World: Kit Carson, John C. Frémont, and the Claiming of the American West

The Lost Explorer: Finding Mallory on Mount Everest (with Conrad Anker)

Escape Routes: Further Adventure Writings of David Roberts

In Search of the Old Ones: Exploring the Anasazi World of the Southwest

Once They Moved Like the Wind: Cochise, Geronimo, and the Apache Wars

Mount McKinley: The Conquest of Denali (with Bradford Washburn)

Iceland: Land of the Sagas (with Jon Krakauer)

Jean Stafford: A Biography

Moments of Doubt: And Other Mountaineering Writings

Great Exploration Hoaxes

Deborah: A Wilderness Narrative

The Mountain of My Fear

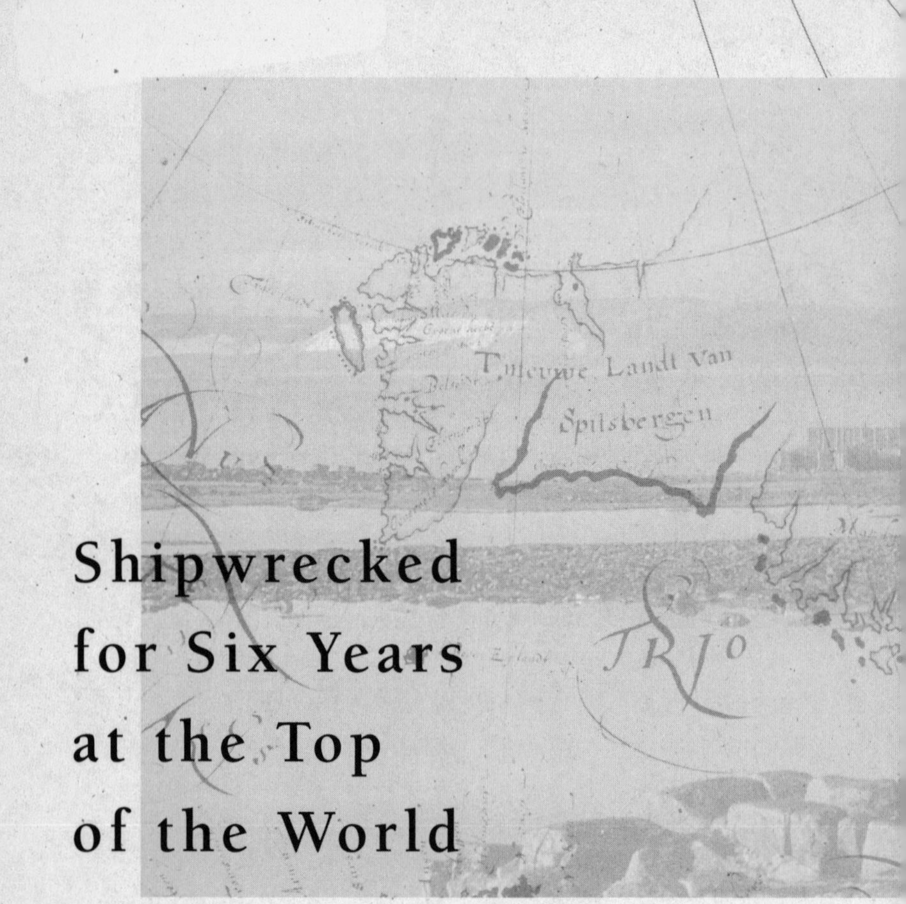

Shipwrecked for Six Years at the Top of the World

Four Against the Arctic

David Roberts

Simon & Schuster Paperbacks
New York London Toronto Sydney

SIMON & SCHUSTER PAPERBACKS
Rockefeller Center
1230 Avenue of the Americas
New York, NY 10020

First Simon & Schuster paperback edition 2005

SIMON & SCHUSTER PAPERBACKS and colophon are registered trademarks of Simon & Schuster, Inc.

For information about special discounts for bulk purchases,
please contact Simon & Schuster Special Sales:
1-800-456-6798 or business@simonandschuster.com

Designed by Karolina Harris
All insert photographs courtesy of author
Maps on pp. xiv, 191 © Jeffrey L. Ward

Manufactured in the United States of America

1 2 3 4 5 6 7 8 9 10

The Library of Congress has cataloged the hardcover edition as follows:
Roberts, David, date.
Four Against the Arctic / David Roberts
p. cm.
1. Edge Island (Norway)—Description and travel. 2. Survival after airplane accidents, shipwrecks, etc. 3. Le Roy, Pierre Louis, 1699-1774. Erzèhlung der Begebenheiten vier russischer Matrosen. I. Title
G787.E33R63 2003
919.8'1—dc21 2003050666

ISBN-13: 978-0-7432-2431-4
ISBN-10: 0-7432-2431-0
ISBN-13: 978-0-7432-7231-5 (Pbk)
ISBN-10: 0-7432-7231-5 (Pbk)

For Vaughn and Michel—

With gratitude for the friendship that only a shared adventure can forge

Contents

"One who furrows the sea enters into a union with happiness—the world belongs to him, and he reaps without sowing, for the sea is a field of hope."

—INSCRIPTION ON A RUSSIAN PROMISE CROSS
FOUND ON SVALBARD, 1869

Four Against the Arctic

SVALBARD ARCHIPELAGO

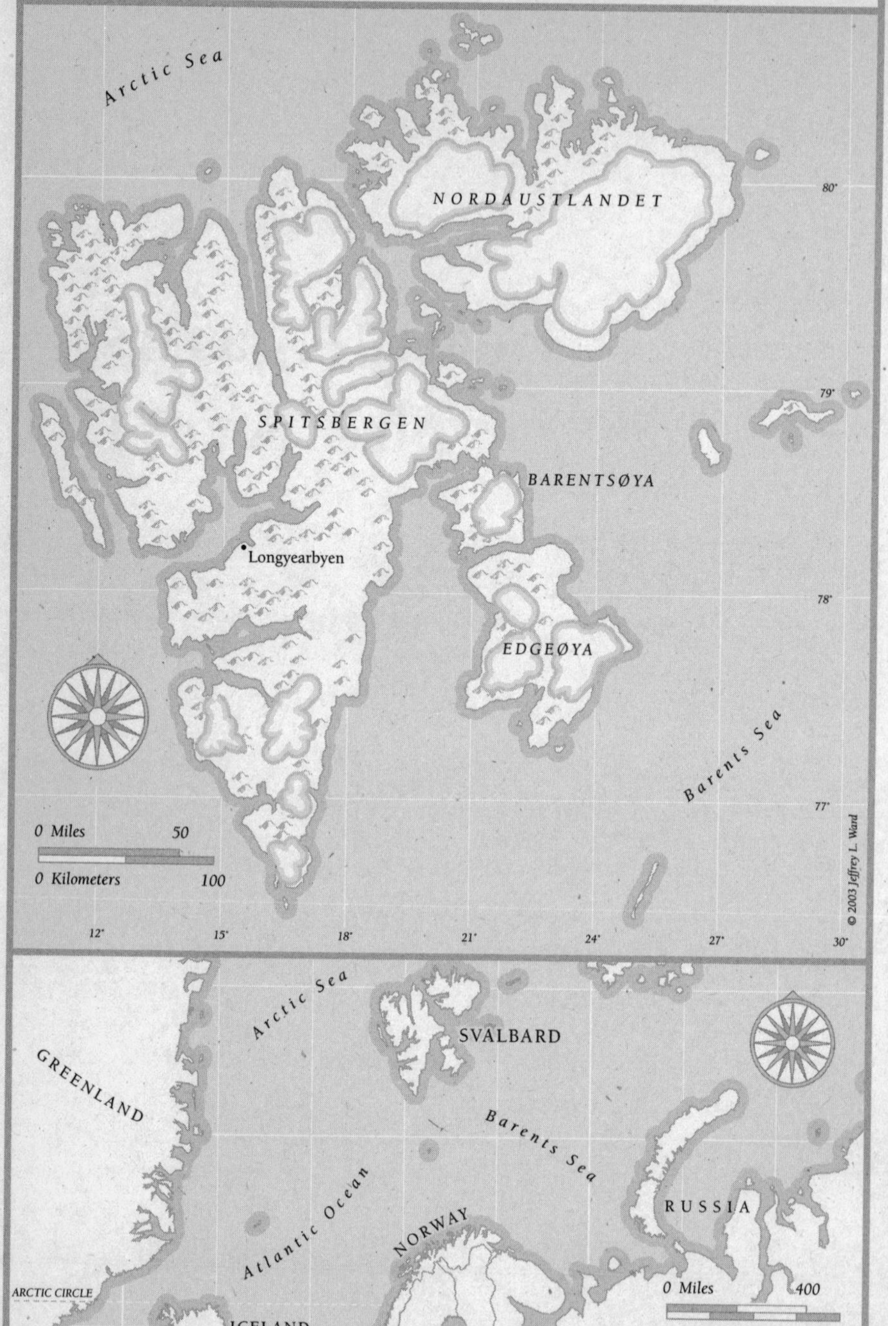

Arctic Sea
NORDAUSTLANDET
80°
79°
SPITSBERGEN
BARENTSØYA
Longyearbyen
78°
EDGEØYA
Barents Sea
77°
0 Miles 50
0 Kilometers 100
© 2003 Jeffrey L. Ward
12°
15°
18°
21°
24°
27°
30°
Arctic Sea
SVALBARD
GREENLAND
Barents Sea
Atlantic Ocean
RUSSIA
NORWAY
ARCTIC CIRCLE
ICELAND
0 Miles 400
0 Kilometers 800

Prologue

For eight days out of Russia, their small wooden ship flew northwest before a favorable wind. They passed beyond the 76th parallel; even at midnight, the sun stood above the horizon.

Then, on the ninth day, the wind changed—and with it, for the men on the ship, the world itself changed irrevocably. An evil gale out of the southwest drove them headlong off course. Helpless to steer their craft, the men tried to ride out the storm. At last they came in sight of land: high, barren plateaus of schist and basalt, lapped by the tongues of vast, half-invisible glaciers. Yet as the ship approached this forlorn shore, sea ice engulfed it. Within hours, the vessel lay trapped in a shifting maelstrom of broken floes.

It was May 1743. The fourteen men aboard the imperiled ship were Pomori—literally "seacoast dwellers," though the term carries the weight of an ethnographic distinction. These hardened, resourceful sailors, born and bred in the Russian north, were virtually a separate race from their more urbane countrymen in St. Petersburg, Moscow, Kiev. At least four of the fourteen came from Mezen, a small town only fifty miles south of the Arctic Circle, situated on the east bank of the river of the same name, upstream from its delta. For centuries, Mezen sailors had launched fearlessly out in their hand-built boats onto the little known Arctic Ocean. In this wilderness of fickle ice, uncharted seas, and bleak, uninhabited islands, the Pomori were as comfortable as any men alive.

Their ship was a *kotch,* a vessel of indigenous design that had evolved among the boatbuilders of the Russian north since the eleventh century. Because the tides at the deltas of such rivers as the Dvina, the Mezen, and the Pechora are so extreme, the Pomori had learned to affix one plank to another not with nails or wooden pegs, but with lashings of juniper root. Somehow without leaking, these "sewn boats" flexed and warped to resist the tide rips that battered them.

On the open sea, a sturdy *kotch* could sail for days at a time at a steady six or seven knots. The ship's chief drawback was that it was almost impossible to steer in heavy winds. With its pair of square sails, its six thick-handled, thin-bladed oars, the ship responded poorly to efforts to tack aslant the prevailing wind. It took two men to handle the heavy rudder; in a storm, the Pomori roped the rudder in place rather than wrestle against its violent veerings.

The fourteen men were walrus hunters. It was their intention to spend the summer along the west coast of Spitsbergen, the main landmass in the Svalbard archipelago, a collection of islands lying far to the north of Norway, between 76½° and 80½°N—one of the most northerly landscapes on earth. With muskets, lances, and axes, they would slay the great sea mammals, the ivory of whose tusks was among the most precious of substances on earth, exported as far as India.

Within a decade after its discovery (or rediscovery) by the Dutch sailor Willem Barents in 1596, Svalbard had become the most active whaling ground in the world. In the early sixteenth century, it was chiefly the Dutch and the English who chased whales there, sometimes firing upon or pirating each other's ships. The master whalers, however, were Basques, most of whom hired out as specialists on Dutch and English expeditions. The favorite resort of the hunters was the west coast of Spitsbergen, whose waters, warmed by the Gulf Stream, were usually ice-free all year round, teeming with an unfathomable multitude of whales.

So fugitive are the records, no one knows when the Pomori started coming to Svalbard. In Dutch and English chronicles, there is no mention of Russian competition before 1697. Some scholars, however—they happen to be Russian—argue that the Pomori reached Svalbard in the thirteenth century, and raise the possibility that the archipelago was known to these intrepid mariners as early as the eleventh. As yet, there is no hard archaeological or historical evidence for this claim.

By 1743, when the *kotch* with its fourteen sailors was driven off-course to the northeast, the Russians were making regular voyages to Svalbard. Their chief interest, however, was not whaling, but hunting: the Pomori went after not only the amphibious walrus, but land animals—the polar bear, the fox, and the reindeer.

The shore off which the ice-locked *kotch* now hovered was the south coast of Edgeøya, third largest of Svalbard's four main islands. On the map, Edgeøya looks like a tooth, the twin fangs of its roots pointing south from its squarish cap. Seventy miles long from north to south, forty-five miles from east to west, the island is a far less hospitable place than the nestling fjords of west Spitsbergen. Fully a third of its surface is covered by an icecap, the sprawling, shapeless Edgeøyjøkulen. Unlike the whaling waters off Spitsbergen's west coast, the seas surrounding Edgeøya are crowded with ice pack for as much as eleven months each year. The unfortunate Pomori in their runaway *kotch* had run smack into the leading edge of the massive Arctic pack that drifts relentlessly each year down the east side of Svalbard from the north.

The men on the ship were terrified that the grinding floes might wreck and sink their vessel. In this crisis, however, the pilot, a man named Aleksei Inkov, about forty-four years old, stepped forward. Inkov told his shipmates that he recalled the expedition of a number of fellow Mezen men some years before, which had deliberately wintered over on Edgeøya. To accomplish this feat, in a clime where no trees (nor even bushes) grow, the Mezeners had brought on board a kind of prefabricated log cabin; having carried the timbers ashore, they had assembled them to erect their hut. Inkov believed that the place these men had overwintered lay nearby.

It is highly unlikely that the sailors on the *kotch* possessed even a rudimentary map of Spitsbergen, let alone of Edgeøya. How Inkov had kept his bearings while the ship was driven before the gale, one can only guess. But in the eighteenth century, when Pomori came back from the Arctic, they spent hours and hours recounting to fellow sailors in their hometowns just what they had done. They drew maps in their heads, which their eager listeners memorized.

Inkov now volunteered to go ashore to search for the hut. Three other Mezen men offered to go with him. They were Khrisanf Inkov, Aleksei's godson (and perhaps cousin), a fit young man of some twenty-four years; Stepan Sharapov, aged about thirty-six; and Fedor Verigin, a rather portly fellow, age unknown. Should this foursome find the hut, unlikely though the search might seem, it promised to offer a haven for the crew, an alternative to the besieged *kotch.* If worse came to worst, and the ship remained frozen in the ice through the summer, the fourteen men, having carried the expedition's gear and food to shore, holing up in the hut, might just survive the winter. Despite his youth, Khrisanf Inkov had already spent one or more winters in Svalbard, in Russian quarters on the west coast of Spitsbergen.

Theirs, however, was a terribly dangerous assignment. Some two miles of shifting floes and pressure ridges stretched between the *kotch* and shore. To trek across that half-frozen sea was to invite death by sudden plunge through a hole or a skin of thin ice, followed by immersion in the 32° water. To reduce the risk, the four men went as light as possible. Besides the clothes on their backs, they carried only a musket with twelve balls and twelve charges of black powder, a single knife, a single axe, a small kettle, twenty pounds of flour in a bag, a tinderbox and a little tinder, a pouch of tobacco, and one wooden pipe each.

After a halting passage performed almost on tiptoe, the men sighed with relief as they stepped on solid earth. They hiked inland. The ship behind them disappeared from sight.

Somewhere between two thirds of a mile and a mile from shore, astoundingly, the men came upon the hut. The seasons since it had been abandoned had taken their toll, leaving gaps between the logs, but the basic structure of the building stood intact. Worn out, the men bivouacked in the hut, struggling to sleep as a high wind whistled through the holes in the walls. Early the next morning, the two Inkovs, Sharapov, and Verigin hastened back to the shore to tell their comrades the good news and to begin the job of unloading the ship.

The shock of the sight that greeted them lies almost beyond comprehension. Gone from the sea before them was every last chunk of floating ice, and the ship as well. The gale in the night had apparently driven the ice far out to open sea. The sailors knew from other Arctic sojourns that no *kotch* could have survived such a cataclysm: the crashing floes must have crushed its hull, taking the boat and its ten doomed Pomori to their grave deep in the unfathomed waters. (No trace of the men, nor any identifiable piece of floating wreckage from the ship, was ever found.)

The four survivors stared into one another's eyes, transfixed with horror. Despite the visit of their fellow Mezeners some years before, ships almost never deliberately coasted the shores of Edgeøya, if for no other reason than the sea ice that so fiendishly blocked access year after year. The sum of the men's possessions was the paltry kit they had carried on their overnight foray; their only food, those twenty pounds of flour. With no alternative, they turned inland once more to trudge back to the hut, appalled by the certainty, foremost in each man's mind, that whether they managed to hang on for weeks, months, or even a winter, they would never again leave this desolate island on which they had been marooned by pitiless fate.

1: Driftwood

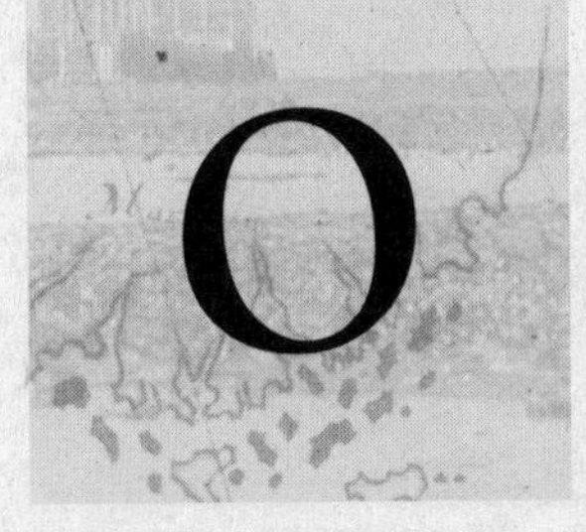

On a fresh spring day in 1997, I was in Chamonix, France, a happy and somewhat inebriated guest at a book party in the offices of Editions Guérin. The year before, I had first met Michel Guérin, head of one of the more eccentric presses in business today. In our youth, Michel and I had both been passionate mountain climbers; now, in middle age, we remained devotees of its literature. Michel's firm, founded only a couple of years before, specialized in reprints of classic mountaineering books in deluxe, illustrated editions.

Now, in the midst of the babel of voices filling the office, Michel was asking me if I'd ever heard of some Russian named Albanov. It seemed that Michel's next publication would deviate from his mountaineering formula to delve into Arctic exploration. A friend of Michel's since boyhood, Christian de Marliave, had become one of France's leading experts on polar exploration. As assiduous a connoisseur of Arctic and Antarctic literature as Michel was of mountaineering writing, Christian had tipped off his friend to a lost classic of Arctic survival, written by a Russian named Valerian Albanov. Michel would soon be publishing *Au Pays de la Mort Blanche (In the Land of White Death)*.

Over the din of the party, my ear caught scraps of the story. Something about twenty-four men on a ship heading off north of Siberia in

1912. Trapped in the ice, they drift for a year and a half. Half the party abandons ship, to trudge with homemade sledges toward Franz Josef Land. Only two survive. The book is eventually written by one of them: Albanov.

Since the age of eighteen, I had read many of the classic polar narratives—Scott, Shackleton, Cherry-Garrard, Mawson, Nansen, Stefansson, Rasmussen . . . I thought I had a pretty good overall grasp of the Golden Age of Arctic and Antarctic Exploration (roughly 1890 to 1920). It took me aback, then, to recognize that not only had I never heard of *In the Land of White Death,* but that I was utterly ignorant of the tragic expedition it chronicled.

Back home in Cambridge, Massachusetts, I followed up on Michel's lead. In Harvard's Widener Library, I found a copy of the 1928 French edition of Albanov's book (originally published in Russian in 1917). The old due date slip glued inside the back cover was blank: in the sixty-eight years the book had gathered dust in the stacks, it had never been checked out.

Reading the first few pages, I was struck by a bolt of lightning. Not only was Albanov's narrative extraordinary, but it was unique in the polar literature, so far as I knew: a combination of plain but vivid detail with hallucinatory, poetic passages that, taken all together, somehow captured the fevered tedium of being driven to the very edge of survival. Inquiring further into the book's history, I was stunned to learn that the account had never been published in English.

I marveled over everything in Albanov's story, even its slightly anticlimactic ending, as he and co-survivor Alexander Konrad limped back to Arkhangel'sk aboard the disintegrating ship that had fortuitously rescued them. But one paragraph, some three quarters of the way through the tale, plunged me into a hectic incredulity. I read it over and over, trying to penetrate the mystery of its unlikelihood.

By July 1914, Albanov and Konrad have reached Franz Josef Land, but most of their comrades are dead or missing. Down to a pitiful minimum of gear and food, Albanov tries to imagine whether he and his teammate can make it through the winter, if no help comes. Then he writes:

> I was reminded of the story about a team of Russian seal hunters who had been shipwrecked on one of the many islands of the Sval-

bard archipelago. They, too, had no weapons. Like the Swiss Family Robinson, they lived for seven years on that island, relatively happy and content. They fed and clothed themselves by hunting with bows and arrows. They built all sorts of traps that they put to good use. They were finally picked up by a ship that happened to call at the island.

Staring at the page, I thought: *Seven years? It's not possible! It's a myth. And if it's not. . . .*

So began, for me, a long lesson in humility. Whatever I thought I knew about the parameters of survival, those six dry sentences of Albanov seemed to contradict. The passage was already lodged beneath my skin, like a splinter broken off on entry. It would take more than a year of scratching and gouging to work its tantalizing sting back toward the surface.

What haunted me in Albanov's bland résumé was the image of modern men reverting, as it were, to a Stone Age life as hunters with bow and arrow. Moreover, I could not imagine how the Russian sailors could have concocted such a weapon, for I knew that on Svalbard not a single tree grew, not even thickets of scrub willow or dwarf birch.

I e-mailed Christian de Marliave. He knew the bare bones of the 1743 story, and he did not seem to think it was an apocryphal tale. He referred me to an old book called *Histoire des Naufrages* (*History of Shipwrecks*). Back in the Widener stacks, I found a copy of the book, its pages liver-spotted with age. An *omnium gatherum* of hoary survival epics assembled by one Desperthes (first name unspecified), it had been published in Paris in 1826.

Desperthes gave me sixteen large-type pages about the Mezen sailors in 1743. Clearly he was paraphrasing a fuller account by one Pierre Louis Le Roy, an academician from St. Petersburg who had interviewed two of the survivors four months after their return to Russia. I went back to Harvard in search of this primary source, finding it at last in the Houghton Library of rare books. The English edition of Le Roy, published in London in 1774, had a wonderfully long-winded title page: *A Narrative of the Singular Adventures of Four Russian Sailors, Who Were*

Cast Away on the Desert Island of East-Spitzbergen. Together with Some Observations on the Productions of that Island, etc. By Mr. P. L. Le Roy, Professor of History, and Member of the Imperial Academy of Sciences at St. Petersburg. Translated from the German Original, at the Desire of Several Members of the Royal Society.

Later I would sort out the tangled publishing history of Le Roy's work. A Huguenot whose family had fled France after the revocation of the Edict of Nantes in 1685 (which stripped French Protestants of all civil and religious freedoms), Le Roy was educated in Germany at the universities of Frankfurt and Halle. In 1731, at the age of thirty-two, he was invited to St. Petersburg to become the tutor of the sons of the Graf von Biron, the chief advisor and lover of the Empress Anna, who ruled Russia from 1730 to 1740. Seventeen years later, he became tutor to the children of Count Petr Shuvalov, a favorite of the new Empress Elizabeth, who had put him in charge of the whale fishery in the Arctic. By all accounts an undistinguished academician, Le Roy could boast the useful talent of being fluent in French and German.

On August 15, 1749, a Russian ship blown off course as it neared Svalbard came in sight of the coast of Edgeøya. From the ship the mariners saw a strange sight: a signal bonfire sending skyward a column of smoke, and men frantically running along the shore waving a flag that, it turned out, was made of reindeer hide. Six years and three months before (not quite the seven years Albanov had indicated), these castaways had suddenly found themselves the sole survivors of the crew of fourteen aboard the *kotch* that had been blown off course in May 1743, then sunk in the thrashing sea ice. Apparently no other ship had passed by their refuge in all that time.

Now, in 1749, the errant vessel plucked the castaways off their island and headed back to Arkhangel'sk, where it arrived on September 28. The story the survivors had to tell was so outlandish they were not at first believed. Instead, they were cross-examined like criminals, asked again and again to retell their tale, as dubious auditors sought to catch them up in self-contradictions.

The fuss in Arkhangel'sk reached the ears of Count Shuvalov in St. Petersburg, who summoned Aleksei and Khrisanf Inkov to the great city to examine them himself. Shuvalov put the interrogation in charge

A

NARRATIVE

OF THE SINGULAR

ADVENTURES

OF

Four Ruſſian Sailors,

Who were caſt away on the deſert Iſland of EAST-SPITZBERGEN.

TOGETHER WITH

Some OBSERVATIONS on the Productions of that Iſland, *&c.*

BY MR. P. L. LE ROY,

Profeſſor of Hiſtory, and Member of the Imperial Academy of Sciences at St. Peterſburg.

Tranſlated from the GERMAN ORIGINAL,

At the deſire of ſeveral MEMBERS of the ROYAL SOCIETY.

Title page of the English edition of Le Roy's *Narrative*. (Houghton Library, Harvard University) of Pierre Le Roy, whom he had hired as his children's tutor only the year before.

In the Houghton Library, as I read Le Roy's *Narrative* for the first time, my astonishment clashed with annoyance. The details of the Mezen men's ordeal were mind-boggling, but they had to be filtered through Le Roy's pompous academic style, his habit of veering from the story to deliver digressions (on the nature of reindeer, for example, or the various ways American Indians lighted fires) that were little more than set pieces of scholarly pretension. Le Roy's account was as maddening as it was intriguing, and from that first reading on I sensed that it had to be taken with a large dose of salt, that there were many matters on which the academician was unreliable.

I soon learned that Le Roy had written two original versions of his narrative, one in French (published in St. Petersburg in 1766), the other in German (published in Riga, Latvia, in 1768—from which the English version was translated four years later). It would take me almost two full years to find a copy, in the British Library, of the exceedingly rare German original. But at Harvard, right away I found the French *Relation des Avantures Arrivées à Quatre Matelots Russes . . .* on microfilm. The two versions dovetailed closely; whole paragraphs seemed virtually identical; yet there were also odd discrepancies between the two, as well as piquant details in the French that were missing in the English. One of the first questions that occurred to me was to wonder why it had taken Le Roy so long to publish. He had interviewed the sailors for several days starting on January 8, 1750. One might imagine that everyone in Russia was eager to hear their story. Yet it had taken the academician sixteen years to convert his notes into a written text. Was he a classic procrastinator, or were there other reasons for the delay?

As I later learned, Le Roy did not even get the sailors' names right. He calls the Mezen pilot and his godson Alexis Himkof and Iwan Himkof, respectively. It would take a twentieth-century Russian scholar, poring through obscure census records, to restore the men's identities as Aleksei and Khrisanf Inkov. The other two sailors' names Le Roy came closer to getting right: he calls Stepan Sharapov "Stephan Scharapof," Fedor Verigin "Feodor Weregin."

Despite my annoyance with and distrust of Le Roy, I read his seventy-five-page *Narrative* in a trance of bewildered admiration for the four sailors. After six pages of preliminary throat-clearing, Le Roy finally gets down to the story. In straightforward terms, he narrates the *kotch*'s headlong flight before the gale out of the southwest, its imprisonment in the ice, Aleksei Inkov's volunteering to take three men to search for the remembered hut, their discovery of the building and bivouac therein, and the return to the shore to tell their friends the good news. "I leave my readers," writes Le Roy, "to figure to themselves the astonishment and agony of mind these poor people must have felt, when, on reaching the place of their landing, they saw nothing but an open sea, free from the ice, which, but a day before, had covered the ocean." Le Roy adds, "This melancholy event depriving the unhappy wretches of all hope of ever being able to quit the island, they returned to the hut from whence they had come, full of horror and despair."

Certain that they were doomed, the sailors nonetheless determined to survive for as long as they could. At this point in the narrative, I asked myself what was the first thing I would have done in their predicament. I glanced back at the lamentably short list of objects the men had carried ashore to sustain their two-day reconnaissance: "a musket, a powder-horn containing twelve charges of powder, with as many balls, an axe, a small kettle, a bag with about twenty pounds of flower [*sic*], a knife, a tinder-box and tinder, a bladder filled with tobacco, and every man his wooden pipe." I would probably have used up a good portion of the flour, splurging on a steaming batch of biscuits, a bellyful of consolation in the face of impending starvation. Since they were smokers, however, no doubt the first thing the sailors did was to fill their pipes and light them, puffing away as they ruminated on their destiny.

According to Le Roy, "Their first attention was employed, as may easily be imagined, in devising means of providing subsistence. . . . The twelve charges of powder which they had brought with them, soon procured them as many reindeer; the island, fortunately for them, abounding in these animals." Here was my first inkling of just what resourceful survivalists these four Pomori must have been. Twelve shots with an eighteenth-century musket, twelve dead reindeer. As I would eventually learn firsthand, Svalbard reindeer are curious about human visitors, allowing hikers to get surprisingly close before trotting off in skittish avoidance. Still, it seemed impressive that not a single animal had required two balls to finish off.

Although the abundance of reindeer was a blessing for the sailors, the presence of another mammal was not—or not, at least, in a way they could immediately foresee. The men had had the bad luck to be cast away by their lost ship on a shore that, then as now, is home to one of the greatest concentrations of polar bears in the world. In other parts of Svalbard, white bears are rarely seen, but the whole of Edgeøya lies smack on a major migration route for *Ursus maritimus*. The threat posed by the polar bears profoundly changed the daily existence of the Pomori, for in addition to the challenge of staying warm and well fed, they dared not relax their constant vigilance for a single waking moment. The men could not afford to take the most casual stroll along the beach without peering in all directions, checking every few minutes for the telltale speck of white in the distance. Having no natural enemies except other bears, these great carnivorous mammals were more likely to run toward the anomaly of an upright, two-legged creature than to take flight.

With their twelve reindeer, the men at least had a good supply of meat. Next, they set about repairing their hut. Le Roy offers an admirably detailed description of the structure, albeit a somewhat puzzling one. It stood, he says, thirty-six feet long by eighteen feet wide by eighteen feet tall. Reading these dimensions, I was struck at once by the large size of the hut. Of course, the original Mezen expedition that erected the hut might have been a sizable party. What made no sense to me was the height of the building. Eighteen feet amounted to a solid two stories. In Arctic and Antarctic regions, Europeans almost never built their huts tall: the roof was kept low, the structure squat, to conserve heat and to withstand the tempests that swept the naked landscape.

The hut, says Le Roy, had two rooms: an outer vestibule, "about twelve feet broad," and a larger inner living room. The vestibule made sense, an old design to keep the sleeping quarters as warm as possible, by providing a buffer against the outside air.

I had more difficulty picturing the "earthen stove, constructed in the Russian manner," that according to Le Roy provided the heat: "a kind of oven without a chimney, which serves occasionally either for baking, for heating the room, or, as is customary amongst the Russian peasants, in very cold weather, for a place to sleep upon." In the absence of a chimney, Le Roy goes on to explain, the upper regions of the living room's interior filled with black smoke, but only down to the level of the windows, which could be opened to let the fumes escape. These windows, Le Roy remarks, are "each a foot in [length], and about six inches [high]: they are cut out of the beams whereof the house is built; and by means of a sliding-board, they may, when occasion requires it, be shut very close." The windows were placed about the height of a man sitting down (as most windows in most houses are). Lest the reader find the Mezeners' hut rude and barbaric, Le Roy hastens to add that in his day most houses "inhabited by the lower class of people in Russia are seldom built otherwise," and that the whole setup worked just fine, as "persons may continue in the room, without feeling any great inconveniency" from the smoke.

The hut was constructed of logs already shaped to fit in Russia; they may even have had numbers painted on them to indicate where each was to go in the building erected on the Arctic shore. By the time Inkov's party came upon the hut, it stood in disrepair. Nowhere does Le Roy indicate how much earlier the structure had been built: "some time before" is his vague formula. There were gaping cracks between the timbers where they had sagged, through which the wind whistled, but the wood itself was still sound. Using their axe, the four refugees trimmed the logs and fit them back together, chinking the seams with moss that grew in abundance all over the island. Le Roy adds an editorial encomium at this point: "Repairs of this kind cost the unhappy men the less trouble, as they were Russians; for all Russian peasants are known to be good carpenters: they build their own houses, and are very expert in handling the axe."

By now the sailors had a snug, ample hut and a supply of meat that should last for a while. Yet was all this any more than a thumb in the dike of the sailors' hopeless plight? With the firing of the twelfth ball and the twelfth charge of powder, the musket was useless. What hope was there of long-term survival? What plan could the men concoct to outface the winter that lay just around the bend of the calendar they read in the sun's slipping lower and farther south each day?

A person unfamiliar with Svalbard might well wonder what good a stove might be in a country where no trees grow. The answer derives from a geographical quirk, upon which the sailors' survival completely depended. The coasts of Svalbard are covered with driftwood. We know today that these uprooted trees—mostly larch, fir, and pine—come from the Russian interior: they are borne north on the floods of great rivers, spilled into the Arctic Ocean, then carried by the prevailing currents more than nine hundred miles to the shores of the barren archipelago that stretches north from latitude 76½°.

A hut, an abundance of firewood, and four months' worth of meat—still no formula for long-term survival. Without some dramatic turn of events in the near future, once the reindeer meat was gone, the four men would inevitably begin to starve to death.

By the time I had finished my first reading of Le Roy's *Narrative*, I had decided that the sailors' saga was the most astounding survival story I had ever read or heard about.

But how did I know it was a true story?

In Russia no less than in England and France, the eighteenth century was at once a skeptical and a credulous age. Two of the most popular literary genres of the day were the travel narrative and the *voyage imaginaire*, the thin line between which was wickedly exploited by the great satirists. The names of Daniel Defoe and Jonathan Swift did not appear on the title pages of the first editions of *Robinson Crusoe* (1719) and *Gulliver's Travels* (1726). The books were passed off instead as true accounts of the experiences of the shipwrecked sailors Crusoe and Lemuel Gulliver, written by themselves.

There were two different ways in which Le Roy's narrative might turn out to be fiction. The first is if the academician himself had pulled off a *voyage imaginaire*, making up the story out of whole cloth. It did not take me long to discount this possibility. Nothing in the sketchy account of Le Roy's life that I pieced together over the following weeks hinted at the wit of a Swift or Voltaire: the Huguenot looked like a classic academic drudge. Moreover, several more percipient investigators than he, including his colleague at the Imperial Academy, the polymath Mikhail Lomonosov, independently expressed great interest in the sailors' story.

The second possibility was that the sailors themselves had perpetrated a hoax. Wherever they might have whiled away the more than six years of their absence from Russia, by this scenario they would have conspired to make up a tale of survival on Edgeøya that was unprecedented in Arctic annals.

Le Roy himself was skeptical when he first heard the details of the story. "I must confess," he writes on the second page of his narrative, "that I myself was, in the beginning, at a loss what opinion to form, when Mr. Vernezobre, Director of the whale-fishery, transmitted to me the first account of them from Archangel." He was not alone in his dubiety—whence the several occasions on which the sailors were made to repeat their story over and over, in hopes of catching them up in some criminal self-contradiction. Le Roy's initial interviewing of Aleksei and Khrisanf Inkov was anything but friendly: "I examined them with all the circumspection and care I was master of; proposing to them such questions as I thought necessary to satisfy me of the truth of this relation." Gradually Le Roy was convinced of the sailors' honesty.

A skeptic myself, I had taken a keen interest over the years in exploration hoaxes, having written a book and a novella about the subject. Almost from the start, I was convinced that the sailors' tale was a true story. There was too much that was plausible about it, however extraordinary the feat of survival. In an odd way, the several veins of Le Roy's account that made little sense or that seemed internally contradictory added to its plausibility. Hoaxers tie up their loose ends. Eventually I came across a very brief testament by the captain of the ship that had rescued the sailors, which perfectly corroborated their account (of the rescue, at least). As I pushed my inquiries further, I found that none of the experts who had showed an interest in the story, including Christian de Marliave and the two Russian scholars who had studied the tale most carefully, doubted its fundamental veracity.

What drove me to distraction was how much Le Roy failed to explain, how many pages he wasted showing off in his learned digressions. There was almost no sense in the *Narrative* of the day-by-day process of this ordeal by monotony and terror; no real differentiation among the characters of the four sailors; only two sentences from Aleksei Inkov's mouth by which to sample the sailors' own voices; no account of the survivors' later lives; no insight into what it was like to sit through three months of winter darkness and Arctic cold without going crazy.

For weeks I ransacked Harvard's libraries, hoping to find some other avenue into the story. It was fruitless: all roads led back to Le Roy. In Le Roy's own account, however, there was the promise of three other lines of primary research—each with a rich potential to become an extended wild-goose chase.

The first offered the prospect of a lost second original source, in all likelihood a more accurate one than Le Roy. In the first pages of his narrative, the academician acknowledges that source: "As soon as the unfortunate sailors arrived at Archangel, Mr. Klingstadt, chief Auditor of the Admiralty of that city, sent for and examined them very particularly concerning the events which had befallen them; minuting down their answers in writing, with an intention of publishing himself an account of their extraordinary adventures. This Gentleman, some time after, came to Petersburg, and seeing the Narrative which I had drawn up, he was pleased to say, that he preferred it to his own, and therefore gave up all thoughts of publishing one himself. But he was so obliging as to favour me with a sight of his manuscript, in order that I might insert (as I actually have done) some particular incidents, which the sailors had omitted to inform me of, but had related to him."

Three things in this paragraph made me salivate. Klingstadt (or Klingstedt, as I would learn his name was more usually spelled) had interviewed the sailors at once, not four months after their return, so there was less chance the tale had been corrupted in the frequent retelling. The man had questioned the sailors "very particularly . . . minuting down their answers"—which promised a richly concrete manuscript. And he had only "favoured [Le Roy] with a sight of" that manuscript, raising the chance that he had kept possession of it after the academician had ransacked it for what he wanted.

Might Klingstedt's notes and/or manuscript still exist, in some archive or library? What I would not give to lay my hands on them!

Secondly, the Pomori had arrived in Arkhangel'sk with a rich collection of artifacts—tools and weapons they had ingeniously crafted on their island, together with the spoils of six years of hunting. Most of these goods the sailors had offered as gifts to Count Shuvalov. In St.

Petersburg, the tools and weapons had been wondered over and admired by many a learned savant. Might they still exist in the storage chambers of some archive or museum? It would seem a heartless act for some curator simply to chuck the stuff out as old junk. Was there the slightest hope of someday holding in my hands the bow and arrows the sailors had manufactured out of the most unpromising materials? Yet 250 years was a long, long time, and I knew from other archival research just how fugitive once precious objects could prove.

Finally, there was a tantalizing passage in Le Roy, in which he discussed his queries to the sailors about the nature of the island where they had spent their six years. Le Roy had the excellent contemporary map of northern Europe drawn by the great Dutch cartographer Gerard van Keulen, which plainly displayed Edgeøya, and had laid this chart before the Inkovs. "In this," he later wrote, "they had pointed out the place of their exile, shewed the very spot where they conceived their hut to stand, and had marked it with the stroke of a pen."

It was perhaps too much to hope that that very copy of van Keulen's map still existed, with its telltale stroke of the pen. But might it be possible to find the coastline where the sailors had survived their incomparable ordeal? Even in ruins, might something of the hut still stand? For the first time, I fantasized about a trip to Edgeøya—still today one of the most remote places on the surface of the earth.

At this point, sanity would have dictated laying the sailors' story back on the shelf, grateful to have stumbled upon a marvelous but half-mythical parable, about which I could not hope to learn much new. But I had become obsessed with the tale. As I tried to fall asleep at night, my mind gnawed away at Le Roy, trying to bite through the *Narrative*'s impermeable skin to the sweet juice of some new understanding.

It was the beginning of September 2000. I had scheduled a month in Europe to work on a pair of magazine assignments. I decided to tack on a week in Russia, where I might make a very tentative reconnaissance of the crooked path that already seemed to wind into my future like some fool's errand into the lost and forgotten.

Supplying much of the motivation for my quest was my awareness that, in pursuing this fugitive tale, I was rubbing shoulders with men who were downright geniuses at survival. Sometime after the end of their first summer, in September or October of 1743, I guessed, the

Mezen men had performed the deed upon which all their future hopes hung. To my mind, that deed emerged as the single most astonishing episode in Le Roy's consistently astonishing narrative.

By that point, the sailors were almost out of reindeer meat. With no remaining musket balls or black powder, they were powerless to kill more game. Then one day, as they combed the beach of their island, the men discovered several boards among the driftwood that had five- to six-inch nails driven through them, as well as a long iron bolt. These boards, says Le Roy, must have been "the melancholy relicks of some vessels cast away in these remote parts." To the four survivors of their own shipwrecked *kotch,* the debris of another shipwreck would thus provide a miraculous deliverance.

2: Two Lances and a Lamp

Christian de Marliave put me in touch with Victor Boyarsky, the director of the Arctic and Antarctic Museum in St. Petersburg. Boyarsky had become something of a celebrity in Russia after 1989–90, when he was part of an international team led by Will Steger and Jean-Louis Etienne that made the first unsupported traverse of Antarctica, in an epochal 3,741-mile dogsled journey that lasted 220 days.

Over the phone from Cambridge, my first words were, "Do you speak English?"

"But of course!" boomed the distant voice. Boyarsky proceeded to demonstrate his mastery of our tongue in a series of vivid but distinctly idiosyncratic outbursts. His manner was hearty, yet constantly distracted: I pictured a succession of aides thrusting urgent polar memoranda across his desk as he talked to me.

I asked Boyarsky if he knew the tale of the shipwrecked sailors from Mezen.

"Of course!" he exclaimed. "Is famous story in Russia." As I would soon learn, however, Boyarsky knew only the vague outlines of the tale, perhaps in the same way that the average American grasps the doings of, say, Daniel Boone. He had apparently never read Le Roy's account, which was first published in Russian in 1772 and reprinted three times in the twentieth century. Nonetheless, when I came to St. Petersburg, Boyarsky promised, he would put himself entirely at my disposal.

I was worried about language. The sum total of my command of Russian, cribbed during an Antarctic cruise aboard a former Soviet research vessel converted to tourism in the hard times after the demise of the Evil Empire, amounted to *da* and *nyet, spasibo* ("thank you"), *pozhaluista* ("please"), and *pivo* ("beer"). I asked Boyarsky if it would be hard to get by with such limitations.

"Is five million people in St. Petersburg!" he bellowed. "Is four million speak English!"

I had never been to Russia. Until I had read Albanov's *In the Land of White Death,* in fact, with its bland paragraph about the shipwrecked sailors, I had no thought of ever traveling to that vast, inchoate land.

In early October 2000, however, after four weeks in France and Italy pursuing my magazine assignments, I flew from Paris to St. Petersburg. I was met at Pulkovo Airport by one of Victor Boyarsky's young charges, who steered me past the tourist taxis and into one that charged Russian rates. Within an hour, I was sitting at a table inside the Arctic and Antarctic Museum, housed in three drafty floors cobbled into the interior of a ramshackle Baroque church, sharing a lunch of salad, blinis, caviar, and vodka with Boyarsky's entourage.

All of them greeted me warmly, and they expressed a kind of puzzled interest in my quest. It was great, they seemed to think, that I had fallen under the thrall of the old tale of the Russian sailors, but to come all this way from America . . . ? One of the scientists, who would become my closest friend in St. Petersburg during the coming year, was Masha Gavrilo, a tall, striking black-haired biologist who had studied nesting birds in Svalbard. She too knew the story of the Mezen sailors, but only in the same vague outline that amounted to Boyarsky's comprehension of the tale. At lunch in the museum, I said to her, "This is the most amazing survival story I have ever heard."

"We are Russian," Gavrilo answered promptly. "We have many stories like this." I blinked skeptically. "In Russia," she went on, "life itself is about survival."

I would begin to understand what she meant a few days later, when I invited Gavrilo to a nice restaurant for dinner. The bill, she let me know without embarrassment, amounted to four times her monthly salary.

I had brought with me a copy of the 1933 edition of Le Roy's account in Russian, which I had found at Harvard. Though I could not read a word of it, I had managed to sound out the name of the editor and annotator, V. U. Vize—and with that decipherment, watched a starburst of connection flower in my brain. For the very same Vize, then a young geographer, had been a member of Sedov's expedition attempting to reach the North Pole in 1912, and whose ship, the *Saint Foka*, on its way back to Russia in 1914, had rescued Albanov and Konrad from Franz Josef Land.

Now Gavrilo told me that Vize had become the leading polar scholar of his day in Russia. The last several pages of Vize's edition of Le Roy appended thirty-two endnotes to the text: these, I sensed, would be critical for my search. But when Gavrilo skimmed the notes and, almost at random, read one of them out loud to me in spontaneous translation, I groaned with dismay. For weeks I had hung my fondest hopes on the passage in Le Roy in which he had thrust van Keulen's map before Aleksei and Khrisanf Inkov. "In this," Le Roy wrote, "they had pointed out the place of their exile, shewed the very spot where they conceived their hut to stand, and had marked it with the stroke of a pen."

Now, according to Gavrilo, in endnote 14, Vize dryly commented, "The author has in mind the map of Spitsbergen by Gerard van Keulen and published around 1710. Van Keulen's map as corrected by Johann Petersen Stuurman [as specified by Le Roy] is completely unknown to this editor."

After lunch, Boyarsky began calling around St. Petersburg to set up visits for me at other important institutions. A fit, red-bearded man in his forties, Boyarsky was at his most animated on the telephone, cracking jokes with his interlocutors, winking at me as I sat before his desk like a schoolboy awaiting his punishment in the principal's office. Boyarsky evidently relished such work, but the upshot of his efforts turned out to be negligible. So-and-so was away in the country for a week; someone else would be glad to help, but the American ought really to talk to X, whose current whereabouts were unknown; to enter such-and-such an archive, I needed written permission from Y, but not until after filling out forms that had to be fetched through the something-or-other ministry, which unfortunately was closed for the week. During those minutes in Boyarsky's office, I got my first taste of the infamous Russian bureaucracy, which in the upcoming months I would grow to know and despise all too well.

Boyarsky had assigned a pale, sober-minded young research assistant named Veronika to help me with my research. Unfortunately, Veronika spoke no English, so I had to hire another woman, one Irina, to translate. On my second day in St. Petersburg, our threesome set out to assault the fortress of the National Library.

The look of the place was shocking. The library was evidently vast and full of books, but its sprawl and chaos, I imagined, approximated what Widener Library at Harvard might have looked like in 1930 if the building had recently been deluged by a flood. Forget climate control: the very shelves exuded must.

My modus operandi, I had to admit, was woefully naive. When at last we located the various catalogues, I simply asked Irina and Veronika to look up names: Le Roy, Klingstedt, Vernezobre (head of the blubber trade—a literal translation—in Arkhangel'sk, and the man who had first brought the sailors' remarkable story to Le Roy's attention). Except for the obvious—copies of the twentieth-century editions of Le Roy, which Veronika had already found in the Arctic and Antarctic Museum—we struck out.

Only one name produced bounty: that of Count Petr Shuvalov, favorite of the Empress Elizabeth and the most important man in St. Petersburg in 1749. Shuvalov was an important lead to track down, for it was he who had summoned the Inkovs to St. Petersburg to tell their story, and it was to him that the sailors had given, as presents, the tools and weapons from Svalbard that they had brought back to Russia with them. But here the catalogue pointed us toward literally a dozen Shuvalov archives, in Moscow as well as St. Petersburg, each of which, I was beginning to think, would take several days just to get in the front door.

During my week-long reconnaissance of the St. Petersburg research facilities, another name came up again and again. M. I. Belov, who had edited the most recent edition of Le Roy in 1975, had studied the tale more perspicaciously than anyone else. A great scholar and archaeologist, Belov had been for decades on the staff of the Arctic and Antarctic Museum (the older savants in Boyarsky's crew remembered him well). Toward the end of his life, alas, Belov had become a bit fuzzy-brained, publishing conjectures that as a younger man he would have scoffed at. I should, however, talk to Belov's widow, who, though in her eighties, had worked elbow-to-elbow with her husband and might well have a vivid recall of the fruits of his wormlike borings into the core of the Mezen sailors' saga. Then someone remembered that Madame Belov was traveling—God knows where—and would not be back in St. Petersburg until after the New Year.

During that October week, I did not spend all my time chasing will-o'-the-wisps with Irina and Veronika. I was staying at the Hotel St. Petersburg, a grim, Stalinist blockhouse of a hostelry whose rooms nonetheless commanded stunning vistas over the River Neva. I had planned to spend some downtime taking in the usual tourist sights: the Peter and Paul Fortress, the Winter Palace, above all the Hermitage, one of the great art museums in the world. I should have known better. When obsessed with a hunt, with a research problem as knotty as the one I was now in the grips of, I have no energy left for museums and sights.

I did, however, walk the streets for hours, getting oriented as I correlated my map with the vast boulevards that grid the city Peter the Great created out of nothing after 1703. During my week I had no hope of learning much Russian. But it seemed incumbent at least to get a handle on the Cyrillic alphabet, which I had crammed up on with my Berlitz phrase book on the plane from Paris to St. Petersburg. Now, as I walked the streets, I practiced speaking out loud every other sign or billboard. This exercise bore quick dividends. The frequently seen **ресторан** revealed itself not, as at first blush I sounded it, "pectopah," but "restaran." Likewise **шоколад**, announcing the sale of cartons of "shokolad." My knowledge of French and German sometimes helped, as when **аптека**, or "apteka," clearly proclaimed a pharmacy, or the more prosaic **магазин**, "magazin," a store.

So I walked the streets, mumbling strange words to myself. Sounding out the Cyrillic was critical to my navigation, for my map bore the street names in the Latin alphabet, whereas the corners of a building at my favorite part of town revealed that I was at the junction of **Невский Проспект**, Nevskiy Prospekt, and **Гостиный Двор**, Gostiniy Dvor. I had a real breakthrough when I deciphered the store window sign, **джинсbl**, sounding out "dzheenz-ў" (the "y" indicating a plural). Sure enough, the shop was hung with racks of Wranglers and Levi's.

I was impressed with the monumental austerity of St. Petersburg: only the Baroque churches burst through the universal massiveness with their flamboyant domes and turrets. When I strolled along the Neva, on the shore of Vasilevskiy Island, with the Kunstkamera and the Academy of Sciences at my back, I realized that many of the surrounding buildings had stood as early as 1749.

Thus I tried to imagine the dazzlement Aleksei and Khrisanf Inkov must have felt when they had been summoned to what was then the capital of Russia in January 1750. It would undoubtedly have been their first and only visit: Pomori ordinarily had only the most tenuous of connections with the interior of the continent to the south. The journey from Arkhangel'sk—seven hundred or eight hundred miles by coach or on horseback—must have taken most of a month.

Le Roy, of course, makes no mention of how the "simple sailors" (his epithet) responded to the capital. Surely they sensed that their interrogation was as much a trial of their veracity as a celebration of their remarkable feat. Nor does Le Roy indicate how long the two men lingered in St. Petersburg before heading home, riding back north into the obscurity of their rugged way of life.

By early that first autumn on Edgeøya, in 1743, the four sailors were in trouble. Their reindeer meat had almost run out. The cold and the dark were just around the corner. Then they found the driftwood boards with the five-inch nails and the iron bolt driven through them.

The plan the Pomori now carried out was an entirely premeditated one: no doubt they had brooded for weeks upon such an eventuality. Nonetheless, it reads, in Le Roy's deadpan account, like a prodigy of resourcefulness driven by desperation.

The men softened the bolt over a fire, then drove a nail through "a hole it happened to have about its middle" about two or three inches wide, and worked the nail to enlarge the hole. Eventually they were able to thrust a driftwood stick into the hole, creating a handle. "A round button" at one end of the bolt served as a head: the sailors had manufactured a hammer.

Now, using a sea cobble for an anvil and reindeer antlers for tongs, the men heated a pair of nails and used their hammer to flatten the points. These they sharpened by rubbing with stones until they had created wedge-shaped blades. Next they took a pair of straight driftwood poles "about the thickness of a man's arm" and bound the blades to the ends with thongs of reindeer skin. (Wet rawhide constricts as it dries, affording as tight a clasp as the sailors could have wished.) In this way, the men had improvised a pair of homemade spears or lances.

All this ingenious craft was bent toward a specific goal. The men had no trouble locating the nearest polar bear (their efforts to date had been geared toward avoiding these dangerous beasts). Armed with their two lances, the sailors deliberately attacked the great mammal. Of all the understatements and outright lacunae in Le Roy's maddening text, the single sentence that details this unthinkable battle takes the cake. "After a most dangerous encounter, they killed the formidable creature," writes the academician.

I tried to read between Le Roy's lines, imagining the terror and savagery of this battle. Even a bear shot from a distance with a high-powered rifle can take a long time to die. To thrust their spears home, the sailors must have danced within a foot or two of the beast's ferocious paw swipes. And if the spears failed, breaking on impact, at least one of the sailors would have paid with his life. I tried to hear the bear's outraged roaring, I saw torrents of blood matting its white fur, I envisioned the Pomori feinting and retreating, the two men without weapons trying to distract the animal from the two who hoped to slay it. Even so, the nightmarish combat remained beyond my ken.

In early autumn Svalbard polar bears weigh between 600 and 1,300 pounds. With their desperate triumph, the sailors had instantly replenished their food supply. Says Le Roy, "The flesh of this animal they relished exceedingly, as they thought it much resembled beef in taste and flavour."

But meat was not the point of the killing. Skinning the huge mammal, the sailors extracted its tendons. They had already found among the driftwood "the root of a fir-tree, which nearly approached to the figure of a bow," and with their knife they had further whittled this curved branch into shape. Now they supplied a bowstring made of polar bear tendon.

After reading this passage for the third time, it occurred to me to wonder why reindeer tendons would not have served as well to make a bowstring. And if not, how did the sailors know this? Le Roy implies that the polar bear attack was devised in order to make the bow and arrow possible. Yet his pseudo-explanation of this gambit raises more questions than it answers: "The tendons they saw with much pleasure could, with little or no trouble, be divided into filaments, of what fineness they saw fit. This perhaps was the most fortunate discovery these men could have made; for, besides other advantages, which will be hereafter mentioned, they were hereby furnished with strings for their bow."

As craftsmen, the Pomori were now on a roll. Using smaller nails found among the driftwood, they made arrowheads, which they bound to fir sticks with bear tendon; then they fletched their arrows with "feathers of sea-fowl." "Their ingenuity, in this respect," comments Le Roy, "was crowned with success far beyond their expectation; for, during the time of their continuance upon the island, with these arrows they killed no less than two hundred and fifty raindeer, besides a great number of blue and white foxes."

For months I pondered this brief but pivotal passage in Le Roy's account, trying to flesh out the extraordinary drama it implied. What did it mean to hunt reindeer and foxes with a homemade bow and arrows? Surely each arrow was precious: did the men retrieve every missed shot, and what did they do when an arrow merely wounded its prey, as they watched the reindeer or fox flee with an irreplaceable dart dangling from its bleeding hide? (In the American Southwest, in Anasazi country, I had found many a stray arrowhead made of chert, agate, or flint, some broken, some intact, all testimony to the pitiless vagaries of the hunt.)

For the sailors, their bow and arrows made long-term survival thinkable for the first time. There remained one essential, however, that they could by no means take for granted. That was fire.

• • •

In October 2000, I had hoped to make my way to Arkhangel'sk and Mezen. The latter village, however, was so remote that I had to give up that ambition. No one in the Arctic and Antarctic Museum had ever been to Mezen, despite the fact that the old town had been a gateway to the northern seas for centuries. Victor Boyarsky, who ran a travel business to supplement his niggardly salary as the museum's director, told me that I might just luck out and snag the rare airplane flight from Arkhangel'sk to Mezen, but I could well find myself stranded there for weeks awaiting a return flight. Better to come back next summer, when the schedule was more reliable.

Boyarsky sold me a discount round-trip ticket to Arkhangel'sk, where I would spend a single day. On a gloomy, overcast morning, I boarded a battered-looking Aeroflot prop plane that droned slowly north through a soup of clouds. Two hours later, we landed on a bumpy runway in the middle of nowhere. There were no taxis at the airport, but I guessed that several drivers loitering next to their run-down Ladas were perhaps for hire. Boyarsky's insistence that 80 percent of the St. Petersburg populace spoke English had been, as I suspected, wildly over-optimistic. In Arkhangel'sk, as I soon learned, virtually no one understood a word of my mother tongue. I approached the nearest driver and managed to utter, "Hotel Dvina, *pozhaluista*?"

At three in the afternoon, the sun seemed about to set. We drove for miles across a taiga plain, passing ruined factories and oil rigs belching black smoke. A few curling yellow leaves clung to the branches of birch trees otherwise stripped bare.

Arkhangel'sk was a genuine city, albeit a hideously ugly one. Its outskirts conjured up Orwellian nightmares of Soviet industry. As we penetrated the suburbs, one dilapidated, cheerless apartment building after another, I found it impossible to conjure up the blithe maritime port the town must have been in the eighteenth century—the Bristol of the Russian north.

Yet as we approached the historic waterfront center of Arkhangel'sk, the place relented and a buried charm surfaced. The Hotel Dvina was prettier inside than out, my $10 room considerably more comfortable than the $77 cell I had inhabited at the Hotel St. Petersburg. And in the lobby, to my vast relief, I found a woman waiting patiently for my arrival—Tatyana, a translator Victor Boyarsky had lined up for me.

Tatyana's English was only about as good as my Italian, which is to say, minimal at best. But without her, I would have been reduced to stumbling mute about the city, snapping pictures on my point-and-shoot, fumbling with my Berlitz when I struggled to buy toothpaste or beer. Tatyana took me for a short walk at dusk past the Maritime Museum, now closed, where I would meet the assistant director the next day. Just around the corner stood a winsome, diminutive Russian Orthodox church, whitewashed with gold-and-blue trim. I pondered the spray-paint graffiti on the adjoining building: a silhouette of a haloed basketball player about to drive the lane (a Russian homage to Michael Jordan, I wondered?), and the emphatic assertion **чикита!**, which I was pleased to decipher as "Chiquita!"

We passed a restaurant whose unvarnished wooden doors promised homey premises. I asked Tatyana how the food was. She seemed scandalized. "Only for rich people!" she declared. Later, for 350 rubles (about $13), I dined on red caviar with brown bread, boiled beef with horseradish, and a solid fifty centiliters of excellent vodka.

The next morning I went to the Maritime Museum, where I met Ljudmila Feneva, the assistant director. With Tatyana translating, I perused the small but excellent displays. There were accurate scale models of a *kotch* and a *lodja,* the sewn boats in which the Pomori had traveled to Svalbard in the eighteenth century to hunt walrus and whale. Feneva explained the need for craft that flexed with the waves. "White Sea is closed basin with big tides," she said. "Even one hundred kilometers upstream, villagers see tide. If they use nails, hulls get destroyed. They sew boards together with juniper root." One case displayed a ship's compass made entirely of wood, except for the magnetized needle.

On exhibit there were also muskets and harpoons from the eighteenth century, as well as all kinds of fishing gear. When I mentioned the sailors' feat of bagging twelve reindeer with twelve shots, Feneva added a piece of local lore: "Idea was always to shoot at eye of animal."

There was a dull, rusty axe that conjured up my image of the most precious possession the Mezen sailors had carried on land with them. There were delicate birds of paradise carved out of wood—a favorite northern souvenir for centuries. "They are made only with knife,"

Feneva said through my translator. "They boil wood first to make soft." I murmured my admiration. "The craftsmanship is not surprising," Feneva added sternly. "In those days, knife was main tool here."

A map on the wall fascinated me. It showed the four principal islands of Svalbard, linked to the Arctic coast of Russia by a series of tendentious arrows. Even without being able to read the Russian legends, I could see that the map argued that Pomori had discovered the archipelago after the eleventh century. There was nothing conjectural about those arrows: undocumented early voyages were presented as fact.

"How do we know this?" I asked Feneva.

"Belov proves in his book," she answered, "that Russian sailors came there long before Dutch."

By "his book," I learned, Feneva meant Belov's unfinished four-volume masterpiece, the ambitiously titled *History of Discovery and Exploration of the Northeast Passage*. But when I finally tracked down the passage in question, I was disappointed to find that Belov's "proof" amounted to little more than haughty propaganda:

> Geographical literature almost unilaterally concludes that Spitsbergen was discovered by Russian sailors. For example, the Norwegian explorer Keilhau says that Russian sailors appeared in Spitsbergen in the thirteenth century.
>
> In a monograph about Spitsbergen published in 1943 in Paris, V. Romanovsky says that Russians discovered Spitsbergen in the tenth century. This author rejects the flimsy thesis that Spitsbergen was supposedly discovered by Scandinavians in the twelfth century. Everybody knows the fact that Russians were the first on Spitsbergen. They were the first to hunt and fish there. And this fact is questioned only by a small number of American and Norwegian geographers.

I mentioned Klingstedt's notes, hoping that Feneva might recommend some local repository where those precious pages might be gathering dust. When she instead pointed me toward another pair of Moscow institutions, the Kremlin Archive and the State Historical Museum and Archive, I groaned inwardly.

Just the same, Feneva made a phone call to the Arkhangel'sk Area Archive, where a Dr. Filippov was in charge. Nobody answered. (I would spend months trying to raise this phantom personage via fax and phone from the States, only to learn that he had retired a few weeks before Feneva tried to call him.)

There was one moment of happy corroboration for me in Arkhangel'sk. I mentioned to Feneva the Russian scholar's correction of the names of the two sailors who had been summoned to St. Petersburg: they were Inkovs, father and godson, not Himkofs, as Le Roy had called them. "That makes sense," she said. "We do not have this name Himkof around here. But I know name Inkov was common in Mezen area."

All too soon, I had to catch my plane back to St. Petersburg. This proved a minor ordeal. At the dingy airport, I drank Coke and ate stale biscuits while I waited to board. There was no bathroom in the building—only a foul outhouse in a shack outside. Flights to Murmansk and Kirov came and went. There was no announcement of St. Petersburg. The time of my scheduled departure slipped by. I tried to peer out the windows for my missing aircraft, but the runways were not visible from the terminal. Thrice I made my way toward the security door, thrusting my incomprehensible ticket toward its guardian, only to have three different heavy, frowning women shake their fingers scoldingly and point me toward the wooden bench outside. At last I encountered a Finn who spoke both English and Russian. There was fog on the ground at St. Petersburg, he told me, delaying all arrivals.

"But we'll get off today, don't you think?" I bleated. My flight to the States was scheduled for the morrow.

"Maybe today," he laughed. "Maybe tomorrow. Maybe next week. This is Russia!"

Back in Cambridge, I took a deep metaphorical breath and assessed my prospects. In a week in Russia, I had learned almost nothing tangibly new about the Mezen men's ordeal in the Arctic. Yet I felt as though I had made a visceral connection, not only with Russia, but with the world of the four Pomori, who had, before my trip, flitted only as ghostly silhouettes in my imagination. Why, I had walked the very harbor where the sailors, after six years and three months of the most harrowing exile, had been restored to the community of the living on September 28, 1749.

The frustration of my first feeble stabs at research had, paradoxically, only deepened the old tale's hold on me. Not a day passed that I failed to ponder some puzzling aspect of Le Roy's account. Strangers I met on airplanes or in cafés were forced to endure my breathless résumé of the doings on Edgeøya. Yet those strangers' responses—the incredulous exclamations that attended my recital of the deed of killing a polar bear with two homemade lances—encouraged my suspicion that the story had universal resonance.

I was not ready to file and forget the tantalizing saga from the Russian north. But if I were to continue to try to probe its mysteries, I needed help. I needed, in fact, a translator and research assistant right away.

Through the Slavic Languages and Literatures Department at Harvard, I contacted a graduate student named Julia Bekman Chadaga, whose area of specialization as she pursued her Ph.D. happened to be the eighteenth century. Julia and I hit it off from our first moments over lunch at Casablanca, the venerable basement restaurant in Harvard Square. Short, with straight brown hair, parted in the middle, hanging loose about her face, Julia had brown eyes and delicate features. Though she looked twenty-two, she was about to turn thirty, and was going through all the agonies of a Keats or Schubert *manqué* about the upcoming milestone.

Julia had been born in Minsk, so her first language was Russian. After her parents moved to New York when she was eight, she learned English like every other kid in public school.

Completely bilingual, at home in academe, Julia was thus the perfect person to aid my difficult search. At the moment she was teaching a Russian literature tutorial for undergraduates while she wrote her dissertation, a potentially mammoth opus centered on Mikhail Lomonosov, Le Roy's colleague at the Imperial Academy of Sciences and the Ben Franklin of his day in Russia.

Although Julia knew next to nothing about the Arctic, I thought it auspicious when I learned that Lomonosov had been born in 1711 in the countryside only fifty miles from Arkhangel'sk, and that all his life he retained a keen interest in northern exploration. It was even on record that the academician had expressed great curiosity about the Mezen sailors' outlandish story. He had almost certainly met and talked with Aleksei and Khrisanf Inkov when they had been summoned to St. Petersburg in 1750.

In no time at all, Julia was up to speed on the Pomori's story. She bit off huge chunks of scholarly incunabula and deftly summarized them for me in English. She skimmed vast Russian tomes to extract the page or two that was relevant to my quest. She manipulated the interlibrary loan system to come up with texts whose existence I had not even suspected.

Thus the sailors' story was starting to take over my life. The trouble was, by late November it was starting to take over Julia's as well. At Harvard, graduate study is taken so seriously that it would not have been wise for her to confess to her advisor that a wild story about sailors hanging on in the Far North was beginning to rival Lomonosov for her attention.

I had begun to fantasize about a return trip to Russia, with Julia as my hired gun, the Sundance Kid to my Butch Cassidy, as we hunted down the cowardly obscurities hiding behind the skirts of Russia's bureaucracy-riddled archives. Along with translating and library research, Julia began to write letters for me that I faxed to various authorities in Russia. You did not, I learned from her, just haul off and address a dignitary in the old country with "Dear Mr. Filippov." The greeting had to say, "Esteemed Edward Vasilievich!" Because of this requirement, it was vital to know the name and patronymic of every person with whom you dared correspond.

As November slid into December, it became increasingly unlikely that Julia could actually become my Sundance Kid, knocking off the banks of Russian archival bureaucracy with me. There was too much going on in her grad school life. But I already owed her a great debt. Until I had hired her to help me with my research, I was struck every other day or so by the fear that I was hung up on a tale so fugitive and obscure that only an obsessive romantic could love it. Masha Gavrilo's "We are Russian—we have many stories like this" had daunted me more than I liked to admit.

Now, however, Julia's own fascination with the sailors' saga validated my own. If someone as smart and serious as she could grant that my preoccupation with the Pomori on Edgeøya was indeed worth the candle, then I needn't worry about wasting my time. Julia had given me the heart to push my quest into another whole year of searching.

With their killing of the polar bear with a pair of homemade lances, the sailors on Edgeøya had turned a crucial corner in their effort to survive. The bow and arrows they concocted out of driftwood, polar bear tendons, flattened nails, and bird feathers brought a nearly limitless supply of reindeer and fox within their grasp. But as the days shortened in the autumn of 1743, fire became the men's most pressing concern.

Le Roy's discussion of fire is one of the most problematic passages in his whole account. Among the items in the paltry list of gear he records the team as carrying ashore were "a tinder-box and tinder." The German original calls these items *"Feurzeuge"* and *"Stück Feurschwamm,"* which means a "lighter" and "kindling." Le Roy's French text, on the other hand, refers to *"un fusil à battre du feu"* and *"un morceau d'amadou"*—terms that are problematic for modern translation. The first phrase implies something that sparks a fire; perhaps, as the German has it, a "lighter." The latter reads literally "a piece of tinder." During the eighteenth century, explorers sometimes carried as tinder a substance made from a fungus that grows on birch trees. Yet later, as he explains the problem of fire for the sailors, Le Roy says, "if it should unfortunately go out, they had no means of lighting it again; for though they had steel and flints, yet they wanted both match and tinder."

I would puzzle for months over these contradictory inklings. My guess is that Le Roy—no woodsman himself—did not quite understand what the Inkovs were telling him. The academician is evidently troubled by the questions he so confusedly raises concerning fire, for they nudge him into one of his more extended digressions, about the bow-and-drill apparatus for starting fire among American "savages" and the natives of Kamchatka, as gleaned from the reports of other travelers.

One of Le Roy's most annoying tendencies is his unfailing condescension toward the Pomori whose story he purports to tell. No matter how brilliantly they survive, Inkov and his comrades remain Le Roy's social inferiors. They are always referred to as "our unfortunate sailors," "the unhappy wretches," and so on. Even in the last line of the French version, the two Inkovs and Sharapov are deigned "our poor, miserable, and hardy Russians." Perhaps the core of the condescension lies in that oily pronoun "our."

Having treated the reader to his learned digression on bow-and-drill fire-starting among the New World Indians, Le Roy clucks, "It is not to be presumed that our unfortunate sailors were acquainted with this American practice; they knew, however, that by rubbing together two dry sticks, the one hard, the other soft, the latter would take fire." The problem, Le Roy goes on, was that all the driftwood the men could find was too waterlogged to catch fire, no matter how vigorous the friction applied to it. Though he does not say so, another problem may have been that pine, fir, and larch are all soft woods: there was no hardwood among the drift debris.

We must remember that, months into their stay on the island, the sailors had used fire to forge the bolt and nails into a hammer, spear points, and arrowheads. Had they kept a driftwood fire going from the second day of their captivity? Le Roy's phrase, "though they had steel and flints, yet they wanted both match and tinder," is truly puzzling. My best guess is that the men had carried a limited supply of tinder onto shore with them—the *"amadou"* of the French text, perhaps the very fungal stuff from birch trees. They may also have used some of their black musket powder to start their first fire or fires. But at a certain point, both powder and tinder were gone, and nothing they could find on the island would serve in their place—not even branches whittled with their knife down to dry, curling shavings from the heart of the wood. They could make a spark with steel and flint, but they could not get the spark to catch fire to any substance they could gather on shore.

The driftwood in the vicinity of the hut was plentiful, but not limitless. Le Roy says that there was not enough of it for the men to maintain two fires, one in the earthen stove for warmth, the other outside the hut to cook their meat on. In any event, the days were shortening as autumn waned. Khrisanf Inkov had overwintered before on Svalbard; he knew what to expect of the cold and darkness of December and January. To lose their fire would spell death for the Pomori.

"After revolving this hard problem in their minds," the sailors devised an answer. "In their excursions through the island," Le Roy indicates, "they had met with a slimy loam, or a kind of clay, nearly in the middle of it." The men gathered up some of this clay and fashioned it into a lamp. They filled it with reindeer fat and made a wick out of a twisted piece of linen. To their mortification, however, as soon as the flame melted the reindeer fat, it leaked through the clay and destroyed the lamp.

They tried again, shaping a second lamp, air-drying it, heating it red hot, then quenching it in their kettle full of water. In that kettle, they had boiled some of their flour (of which they had by then eaten half the twenty pounds) down to the consistency of starch. Somehow this pasty admixture made all the difference: "The lamp being thus dried and filled with melted fat, they now found, to their great joy, it did not leak." To make the vessel even more leakproof, the men dipped linen rags in their flour paste and coated the outside of the lamp with them. As soon as they had made the first lamp, the sailors crafted several others as backup. Rather than eat any more of their flour, they saved it for lamp-making. For wicks, the sailors used oakum and hemp found among the driftwood, and eventually sacrificed every last thread of their own clothing, tailoring replacement garments (even shoes) out of reindeer and polar bear hides. For more than six years, the Mezeners thus kept a continuous flame going in their lamp inside the gloomy hut.

Though I had climbed in Arctic Alaska, I had never spent time there in the dead of winter. I had experienced not a single day of the perpetual darkness that reigns in the far north—in Svalbard, for more than three months, from November to February. Obsessed more than ever by the sailors' tale, I often brooded on its details late at night as I tried to fall asleep, in the civilized winter of Cambridge, where the turn of a switch produced light whenever I wanted it. Often the last image before my eyes as I drifted off to sleep was that of a small clay lamp burning with a smoky orange flame, while four men stared into it for long, silent hours, as cold and darkness constricted the Pomori's universe to the vulnerable sanctum of their hut, and they awaited, beyond hope, the fresh tribulations of tomorrow's monotonous, meaningless day.

3: No Man's Land

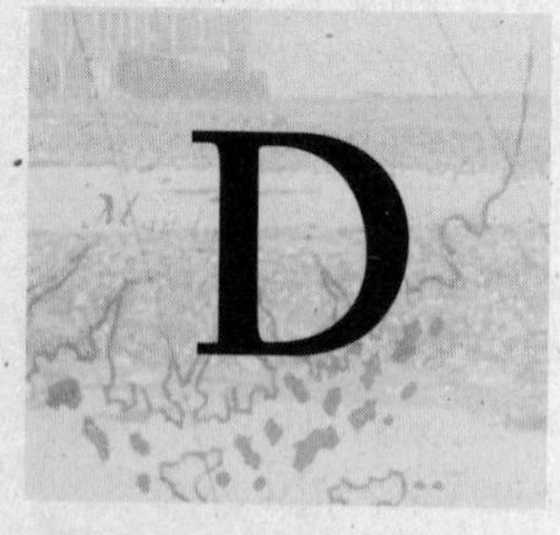

Despite the wishful speculations of the Russian scholar M. I. Belov, most authorities credit the discovery of Svalbard to a Dutch expedition led by Willem Barents in 1596. Like a number of explorers before him, Barents was attempting to sail the Northeast Passage, the long-postulated shortcut to China that coasted Siberia on the north. The Dutch, in fact, had begun to bend their efforts toward the passage only after the English had given up on it, at the end of twenty-seven years of provocative failures. By 1596, Barents himself was making his third voyage in search of the Northeast Passage.

His two previous journeys, like the boldest of the English attempts, had been thwarted by the treacherous Kara Sea, the body of water that lies between the Yamal Peninsula and the islands of Novaya Zemlya. Almost perpetually ice-choked, the Kara Sea had already proved a graveyard for ships. It was in the Kara Sea that the Russian vessel the *Saint Anna* had frozen fast in October 1912, leading to the year-and-a-half-long drift northward and the desperate retreat from the doomed ship that Valerian Albanov had chronicled so movingly in *In the Land of White Death*.

After his second failure, Barents decided that he ought to attempt the passage farther north. All previous voyages had rounded the northern coast of Scandinavia on their way toward Russian waters; now, at the end of May 1596, Barents reached North Cape in Norway and headed straight north. On June 9, the party discovered the isolated Bear Island, which they named in honor of a great white beast that it took several men, armed with muskets, axes, and hatchets, a solid two hours to vanquish. Continuing north, the expedition's two ships sailed across open seas past the eightieth parallel, into waters never before navigated. Barents, in fact, came close to missing Svalbard altogether on the west, but on June 17, as the vessels headed back south, they came in sight of "high land and entirely covered with new snow." It was the northwest corner of the island of Spitsbergen proper.

After considerable difficulty with coastal ice, the expedition made a landfall. Barents thought he had rediscovered Greenland, not some new archipelago, but he claimed the territory for Holland all the same. On shore, the men gathered stones for ballast and many eggs of the barnacle goose, thus disproving a superstition to which a good part of the team subscribed, that these all-but-apocryphal red goose eggs grew on trees in Scotland. The sailors also had another epic battle with a polar bear.

Barents tried to push even farther north, but ice defeated him. On the way south, at Bear Island, the two ships parted ways. The men who had had enough of northern waters headed home under the command of Jan Cornelis Ryp, while Barents himself sailed east for another try at the passage. By the end of August, Barents's sailors had failed to turn Novaya Zemlya on the north, only to find their ship caught in an ice trap. Full of foreboding, they built a big hut of driftwood and prepared to winter over—the first party of Europeans, so far as we know, ever to do so in the Arctic.

Only one man died during the winter, but Barents fell seriously ill with scurvy. By the next summer, the ship had been so damaged by ice that the men had to abandon it. In a pair of open boats, alternately rowing and sailing, they made their painful way south along the coast of Novaya Zemlya. On June 20, Barents died, and his men buried him on the spot. (His pioneering deeds in the Arctic are commemorated in the name of the Barents Sea, the sizable ocean that occupies the void between Svalbard and the Russian coast. It was Barents, moreover, who named Spitsbergen, in allusion to the many sharp peaks with which the country abounds.)

After an odyssey of 1,600 miles by open boat, Barents's surviving men reached the Kola Peninsula, not far from present-day Murmansk, where they ran into three Dutch ships, one of them, surprisingly enough, captained by Jan Cornelis Ryp. Whether Ryp had returned to Holland in the interim or spent the thirteen months wandering around Arctic seas, the historical record is too sketchy to indicate. Ryp carried the twelve survivors home to Holland.

Whether or not Pomori from Mezen and Arkhangel'sk had beaten Barents to the discovery of Svalbard by some four centuries, as Belov would have us believe, there is another band of claimants for the prize. In his comprehensive history of early Arctic exploration, *In Northern Mists,* the great Norwegian explorer Fridtjof Nansen noted that six different manuscripts of the seminal *Icelandic Annals* mention the discovery of "Svalbarð," all assigning it to A.D. 1194. The Old Norse name means "cold edge or side," presumably alluding to a "cold coast." There is no further explanation of the discovery in the *Annals.* As Nansen wryly commented, "Surely no great geographical discovery has ever been more briefly recorded in literature."

The *Landnámabók,* or Book of Settlements, an early Icelandic gazetteer-cum-genealogy, goes further, to assert that "from Langanes on the north side of Iceland it is four doegr's sea to Svalbard on the north in Hafsbotn." A doegr's sea is 120 miles, so this notice would place the remote archipelago at a distance of some 480 miles from the northeast coast of Iceland. In actuality, Svalbard lies nearly a thousand miles as the crow flies from Iceland.

The crucial question, of course, is whether the "Svalbarð" of the *Annals* and the *Landnámabók* is the same land as modern-day Svalbard. Other candidates for the fugitive terrain advanced by scholars include the northeast coast of Greenland, the far more southerly island of Jan Mayen, and even the Arctic coast of Russia. Nansen casts his vote for a bona fide Viking discovery of Svalbard, but he may be swayed by a Norse chauvinism akin to Belov's partiality for the Pomori. Indeed, Nansen goes on to dismiss any pretensions by the Russians to have penetrated far into the Arctic by the sixteenth century with the rather circular argument that the boats and navigation methods the Pomori employed at the time of their first contact with Norwegian ships would have been inadequate to the task.

Summing up the question from a neutral perspective in 1920, the English historian R. N. Rudmose Brown dryly editorialized, "If [the Vikings] discovered Spitsbergen they clearly thought little of it."

For the past five decades, a scholarly debate launched by two Scandinavian archaeologists has cast an entirely new light on the question of Svalbard's discovery. In a 1970 paper titled "Stone Age Finds from Spitsbergen," Hans Christiansson, of Uppsala University in Sweden, and Povl Simonsen, of Norway's Tromsø Museum, summarize their case. The pair claim to have found on Svalbard's shores or located in various museums a large number of stone tools—scrapers, slate knives, boring tools, pounding stones, chipped cores, worked flakes of flint, even a broken arrowhead—dating back as early as 2500 B.C. This assemblage of "110 artifacts, of which at least 45 are undoubtedly made by man," proves to Christiansson and Simonsen the presence of humans on Svalbard by the early Neolithic.

The problem here, as with so many Early Man sites, lies in distinguishing naturally fractured stones from those worked by hunter-gatherers. Within the last decade, experts have increasingly expressed their doubts about Christiansson and Simonsen's thesis. Yet the two scholars make an intriguing argument for the plausibility of Stone Age men finding their way to Svalbard and eking out a living there during a millennium or two.

The reindeer found on Svalbard, which are smaller than those found elsewhere in the world, with relatively short, round heads, belong to a subspecies unique to the archipelago and to Franz Josef Land. This fact in turn argues for a very early date of arrival, giving the animals time to mutate into their own distinct subspecies. Christiansson and Simonsen believe that reindeer must have ventured onto sea ice from northern Russia, only to be trapped on floes that drifted north and west. Presumably Novaya Zemlya and Franz Josef Land were stepping-stones on the way to the animals' eventual migration to Svalbard. In modern times, in fact, branded reindeer have been found on Svalbard: these must have been floe-trapped refugees from herds tended by Lapps and Samoyeds on the European mainland.

The two scholars make the telling point that "if man has not followed the reindeer to Franz Josef Land and Svalbard it would be the only place in the world this has not happened." Christiansson and Simonsen picture Neolithic hunters following the reindeer along the edge of the sea ice, in a long crescent originating in Russia, traversing the skinny length of Novaya Zemlya, leapfrogging from east to west across the myriad islands of Franz Josef Land, and so to Svalbard. Throughout most of this route, there are small islands located no more than fifty miles apart, each one visible from the preceding. The problematic gap is a 170-mile islandless stretch between the northern tip of Novaya Zemlya and the southernmost point of Franz Josef Land. In somewhat procrustean fashion, Christiansson and Simonsen argue that it may just be possible to sight land to the north from the summits of 3,500-foot peaks on Novaya Zemlya, and that reindeer are known to be able to smell land over huge distances if the wind is right. "The Stone Age hunters," the scholars write, "who saw the herd go on to the ice and disappear, have undoubtedly known the reindeer so well that they have understood that the reindeer knew about food on the other side of the ocean."

It would seem at first blush that Svalbard, with no trees or bushes, would prove too inhospitable a place for Stone Age humans to survive. Yet in a comparatively short time, following the musk ox and the caribou, the polar bear and the seal, the Inuit spread all the way from the Bering Strait to northern Greenland, which has, if anything, an even more rigorous climate than Svalbard's. At the time of first contact by the Vikings, as early as the beginning of the eleventh century, the Inuit were flourishing all along the west and north coasts of Greenland. Christiansson and Simonsen point out the advantages of Svalbard from a Neolithic hunter's point of view: an abundance of game far richer than obtains today; plenty of flint, hornstone, and slate for making tools; a supply of driftwood much greater than that with which the Inuit make do on Greenland.

The debate over whether Svalbard has a true prehistory is unresolved. Perhaps only such indisputable evidence as the discovery of an ancient campfire that could be radiocarbon-dated would settle the question. In any case, Christiansson and Simonsen concede, humans had vanished from Svalbard by the time of its modern discovery, whether by Vikings in 1194, by Russians at some indeterminate date, or by the Dutch in 1596.

• • •

Barents himself seems not to have recognized that his discovery at 80° N might bear practical fruit. Svalbard went unvisited for the next eleven years after his epochal landfall. Only in 1607 was the island group rediscovered more or less by accident by Henry Hudson, sailing for England, which, newly interested in the Northeast Passage, had sent the veteran navigator off to find it. In the grips of a theory of the day that the worst ice was to be encountered at the latitude of the Arctic Circle—around 67° N—and that beyond that, the farther north one sailed, the more open the sea, Hudson headed straight north, veered east away from Greenland, and blundered upon the west coast of Spitsbergen not far from where Barents had struck the archipelago. What Hudson noted that Barents did not was that these waters teemed with seals, walruses, and above all whales.

Before 1607, the prime whaling ground in the world was the Bay of Biscay. Basques, who by then had pushed the hunt as far as Newfoundland, were the virtuosi of the industry ("harpoon" is a Basque word). The Biscay whale was, by definition, the "right" kind of whale to hunt, because it yields the greatest quantity of oil and because it has baleen instead of teeth in its upper jaw. By the beginning of the seventeenth century, right whales had become immensely valuable. The oil they produced was the chief European fuel for lamps, as well as being rendered into soap; the ambergris was transformed into perfumes and aphrodisiacs; and the baleen furnished the ideal material for the stays that shaped the corset, the torturous woman's undergarment that had become de rigueur in the salons of the Renaissance.

It turned out that the polar whales discovered by Hudson were close cousins of the Biscay whale, although considerably larger. Thus began one of the most intense rivalries in oceangoing history. Basing their claims to Svalbard on Barents and Hudson respectively, Holland and England set out to monopolize the polar whale hunt. France and Denmark also entered the fray. As historian Jeannette Mirsky writes in *To the Arctic!*, "The nation that controlled the Spitsbergen waters was . . . at once the leading plant furnishing light, the foremost distributor of lubricating oil, the largest manufacturer of soap, and the source whence derived the vast trade of cosmetics." Not to mention corsets.

The hunt off the west coast of Spitsbergen did not become lucrative, however, until after the Dutch and the English hired Basque whalers to teach them how to carry out the complicated business of killing, dragging to shore or ice floe, and flensing and reducing an aggressive sea mammal weighing up to 120 tons. During the first years, the fleets brought all their cumbersome equipment with them, packing up the gear to take home at the end of the season. Eventually they hit upon the expedient of leaving much of the equipment in a camp to which the whalers would return the following year, but this labor-saving gambit presented strong temptations for pilferage by other crews.

It is something of a wonder that Holland and England did not go to war over the Spitsbergen whale hunt. Several times, the whole summer's catch of one nation's fleet was commandeered by the other's. Envoys traveled between Amsterdam and London seeking redress. Sometimes rival captains, acting upon their own authority, met on shipboard and divvied up the nearby harbors, agreeing to stay clear of each other's whaling grounds, producing thereby a summer's uneasy truce. But in 1618, a genuine naval battle erupted. The English lost not only several men dead, but the spoils of an entire summer, whose value, in an official petition to King James I, was reckoned at £22,536.

At the height of the whaling boom, in the 1630s, the Dutch sent as many as three hundred ships and eighteen thousand men to Svalbard in a single year. On Amsterdam Island, at the very northwest corner of the island of Spitsbergen, they built Smeerenburg—literally, "Blubber Town." A dense slum of hastily erected wooden buildings, Smeerenburg had no fewer than twenty cookeries, some two stories tall and a hundred feet long, in which the dead whales were reduced to oil and ambergris and baleen. There were also roomy warehouses for gear and shipbuilding, and the excellent natural harbor was packed with boats. The huts in which the men lived—quaintly called tents—were as large as eighty by fifty feet, with attics full of bunk beds.

There were liquor shops in Smeerenburg not unlike the saloons that would spring up 250 years later in the American West. There were bakeries: a horn that could be heard all over town sounded whenever hot rolls were ready for sale. There was a church, and a fort whose cannons were primed to fire upon Danish interlopers. There were even houses of prostitution. The population was rumored to range up to ten thousand, although the best twentieth-century authority reduces that number to about 1,200. As Jeannette Mirsky conjures up the place,

"Out of whalebone and whale blubber this town had been built; the stink and grease of dead whales touched everything."

Yet so daunting was the prospect of winter at 80° N that even in its heyday, Smeerenburg was occupied for only six weeks at the height of summer. During the other ten and a half months of the year, the town was deserted.

During the first thirty years of the hunt in Svalbard, nearly all the activity focused on the west coast of Spitsbergen, where the Gulf Stream nourished a seemingly infinite supply of right whales. At the same time, Dutch and English navigators were aggressively exploring the rest of the archipelago. We have only the most fugitive glimpses of these findings, however, because commercial rivalry dictated secrecy. As Mirsky puts it, "Discovery was a trade secret to be guarded jealously from eager followers; discovery was a scout opening up new whaling-grounds; discovery was discreetly kept dark, lest any information prove useful to competing nations."

For this reason, we cannot be sure which navigator made the discovery of Edgeøya, the third largest of Svalbard's islands, where the Mezen sailors would endure their six years of exile after 1743. The ice-capped island, which forms the southeast corner of the archipelago, is named after Thomas Edge, a gifted but shadowy merchant and sailor from Lancashire, who died in 1624.

Edge apparently discovered the forlorn island that would bear his name in 1616. But Sir Martin Conway, whose 1906 book, *No Man's Land*, remains the best history of Svalbard published in English, argues convincingly that two years earlier an equally shadowy, one-legged Dutch sea pilot, one Joris Carolus, sailed within sight of the two prominent capes, Hvalpynten and Negerpynten, that thrust south from the tooth-shaped bulk of Edgeøya, and also came very close to Halfmoon Island, the crescent-shaped four-mile-long satellite that stands just off Edgeøya's south shore. The proof, for Conway, inheres in the shapes of the sighted lands marked on Carolus's own chart, an exceptionally rare document the English scholar came across in The Hague Archives.

In any event, Edgeøya played almost no part in the whaling craze that occupied most of the seventeenth century off the west coast of Spitsbergen. There were indeed whales to be found along Edgeøya's shores, but not in the abundance around Smeerenburg. In addition,

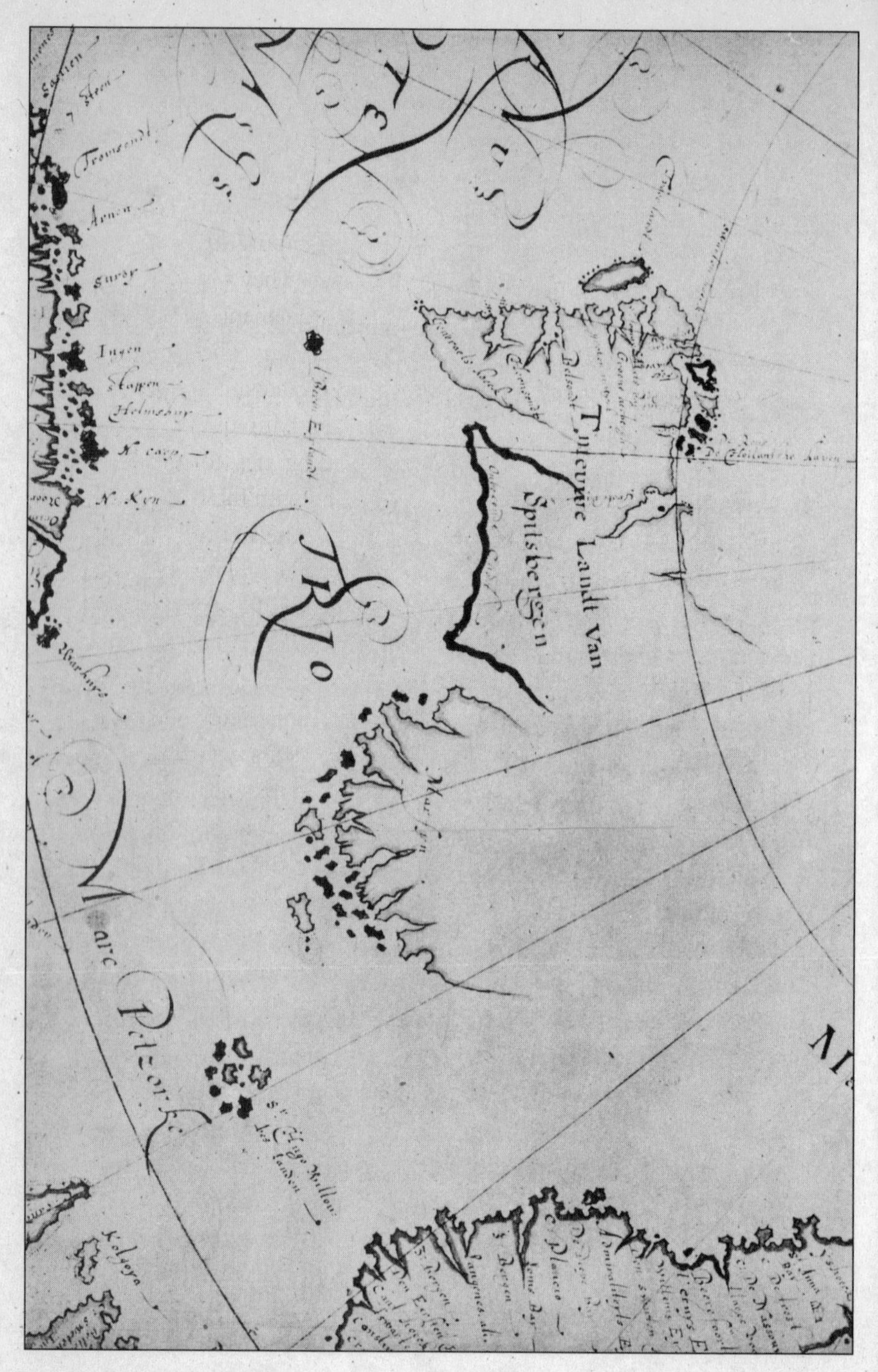

Joris Carolus's map, proving the Dutch navigator's discovery of Edgeøya in 1614 (Harvard Map Collection).

sea ice blocked access to Edgeøya for as much as eleven months of the year, as it never did in west Spitsbergen. It would not be until the Russians got into the game, toward the beginning of the eighteenth century, that Edgeøya became the locus for a whole new hunt.

With no grand ramshackle town like Smeerenburg to anchor their whaling, the English hit upon another approach. They would hire men to winter over, thereby establishing a semipermanent settlement to ground a claim of all of Svalbard as an English colony. The trouble was, no sailors were willing to overwinter on the desolate archipelago, even after being offered handsome inducements. The Muscovy Company, a consortium of London merchants with trading ties to Russia that stretched back into the sixteenth century, toyed with the idea of hiring Lapps from the Kola Peninsula to do the job (the notion of the day being that these reindeer herders were almost a separate species of humans, constitutionally better equipped to endure the cold). The company obtained a license from the tsar of Russia to this end, but nothing came of the scheme.

Finally, the Muscovy Company recruited a small band of London criminals who were under sentence of death. They were offered not only building materials, warm clothing, and ample provisions for a northern winter, but the promise of full pardon for their crimes on completing their stint in the Arctic. These men sailed to Svalbard and settled in at the designated site (whose location has not come down to us). As autumn neared, however, they lost their nerve. To a man, they told their wardens that they would rather be taken back to London and hanged than have to spend a winter in such a godforsaken place. The men were shipped home. Thanks to the intercession of the Muscovy Company, whose merchants took pity on the criminals, they were pardoned anyway.

The first known overwinterers on Svalbard, then, were eight English sailors who were accidentally left on shore in the autumn of 1630. At the end of a profitable summer of whaling, three Muscovy Company ships were heading for a rendezvous at Bell Sound, a major fjord on the west coast of Spitsbergen. The captain of one of the ships sent eight men on shore to hunt reindeer to bolster the crew's provisions. These hunters had no trouble slaying fourteen of the over-curious animals, but when they returned to the shore, they found that their ship had headed out to sea to avoid an ice floe that had drifted tight to the land.

There followed a series of minor fiascoes, as the eight sailors tried to reach Bell Sound in their shallop, or small boat: they got lost in the fog, quarreled over the geography of the coastline, and finally reached the rendezvous point one day after the fleet's scheduled departure for England, only to find the harbor empty of ships and men. It may seem incredible that the captain of the expedition was unwilling to delay his return by a single day to wait for the missing sailors, but in Renaissance voyaging human lives were regarded as fairly expendable.

Thus began the ordeal. Thanks to the literary endeavor of one of the survivors, a sailor named Edward Pellham, we have a vivid account of the first Svalbard overwintering. Pellham's thirty-page treatise bears the wonderfully baroque title *God's Power and Providence: shewed in the Miraculous Preservation and Deliverance of eight Englishmen, left by mischance in Green-land, Anno 1630, nine moneths and twelve dayes . . .* ("Greenland" was often used at the time to refer to Svalbard, for by 1630 it was still not certain that the two landmasses were distinct.) As Pellham's title suggests, rather than being consumed with indignation at the captain and crew that had abandoned him and his seven shipmates, he is full of gratitude—not only toward God, but toward the Muscovy Company, to whom he dedicates his chapbook. On that dedicatory page, he salutes the "brave adventurers," meaning, in that classic Renaissance epithet, not the men with whom he endured a winter's darkness and cold at 78° N, but the London merchants who had dared to invest in the expedition.

At first, Pellham and his companions were sure their abandonment was a fatal sentence: "Wee thought that no other thing could be looked for but a miserable and a pining death, seeing there appeared no possibility of inhabiting there, or to endure so long, so darksome, and so bitter a winter. . . . Well wee knew that neither Christian or Heathen people had ever before inhabited those desolate and untemperate Clymates."

A forced overwintering at such a latitude was inevitably a desperate proposition. Yet Pellham and his compatriots were by no means in as dire a predicament as the one the Mezen sailors would face 113 years later. The Pomori in 1743 had only a ruined hut. Pellham's men had the accumulated debris of more than fifteen years of assiduous whaling, by both Dutch and English, in the excellent harbors of Bell Sound. After the initial shock of finding themselves abandoned, the eight sailors took stock. "Shaking off therefore all childish and effeminate feares," writes Pellham, "it pleased God to give us hearts like men, to arme our selves with a resolution to doe our best for the resisting of that monster of Desperation."

Four days later, even before the men had secured their lodgings, they set out to hunt reindeer, hoping to lay in a supply of venison for the winter. Camping in a "tent" jury-rigged out of the shallop's sail and oars, they killed nineteen deer and four polar bears in two days. Surprisingly, through all their tribulations the men had kept two dogs with them, which were immensely helpful in the hunt. In nearby Green Harbor the sailors salvaged a second shallop that belonged to the Muscovy Company. They loaded their meat in one boat, and a vast supply of whale bones in the other—the discarded wreckage of the summer's catch ("which wee there found in heapes flung upon the ground"), to which scant morsels of meat and gristle were still attached.

Back in Bell Sound in early September, the sailors set to work on their winter "tent" or hut. Fortunately, the Dutch had built a huge building, eighty feet by fifty, for their barrel-makers to work and live in. Ingeniously enough, the English scavenged wood and bricks from another nearby Dutch structure and erected a smaller hut inside the large one. They were even able to make mortar for the bricks out of quicklime and sand. In short order, the men had raised a twenty-by-sixteen-foot interior hut. With no windows and a chimney that simply expelled smoke into the larger hut, the refuge must have been a claustrophobe's nightmare. But it was warm, for, as Pellham happily noted, "not the least breath of ayre could possibly annoy us."

Next the sailors laid in a supply of firewood. There must have been a scarcity of driftwood on shore, for Pellham reports that the men, perusing a large number of shallops left in the camp over the years, "found seven of them very crazie, and not serviceable for the next yeare." These they broke up into planks and stored in their hut. They also converted old barrels into firewood.

On September 12, the sailors killed a pair of "Sea-horses" (seals or walruses) they found asleep on a drifting floe. As the days grew shorter and colder, the men despaired of killing more game. The sea froze fast on October 10. For three months the sailors rationed their supply of meat, eating only one meal a day, fasting every Wednesday and Friday, and trying to allay their hunger by gnawing the "Frittars" off the whale bones ("a very loathsome meate").

Pellham's account of the winter of 1630–31 serves to flesh out the psychology of the ordeal the Mezen men would undergo in the next century, the details of which Le Roy hardly bothers to contemplate. By late October, there was little for the men to do but sit inside their snug, gloomy hut and wait. In an eloquent passage, Pellham captures the tedium of that vigil. With "nothing now to exercise our mindes upon, our heads began then to be troubled with a thousand sorts of imaginations."

> Then had wee leisure (more than enough) to complaine our selves of our present and most miserable conditions. Then had wee time to bewaile our wives and children at home, and to imagine what newes our unfortunate miscarriages must needes be unto them. Then thought wee of our parents also, and what a cutting Corasive it would be to them, to heare of the untimely deaths of their children.

As winter wore on, Pellham adds, "that hideous monster of desperation began now to present his ugliest shape unto us; hee now pursued us, hee now laboured to seize upon us." The men prayed constantly.

At some point during the winter, the refugees discovered that their whale "Frittars" had become moldy and spoiled by moisture, and their supply of bear and reindeer meat inadequate for their five-meal-a-week diet. They rationed themselves even more rigorously. "We for foure dayes in the weeke fed upon the unsavory and mouldie Frittars," writes Pellham, "and the other three, we feasted it with Beare and Venison."

The sun first failed to rise on October 14; not until February 3 would the men see it again. Pellham and his companions, one suspects, must have been devout Puritans. In a telltale passage, the chronicler recounts how, during the darkest months, men would "sometimes in impatient speeches . . . breake forth against the causes of our miseries." But a little reflection invariably resulted in "our consciences telling us of our own evill deservings." Their ordeal, the men decided, was "a punishment upon us for our former wicked lives." Should they be spared, it would be evidence of "God's mercie in our wonderful deliverance." Thus railing against fate devolved into praying on hands and knees, two or three times a day.

The men greeted the return of the sun on February 3 with an outpouring of joy. Yet the cold was at its worst during this month. When the sailors ventured out of the hut to gather water, which they found unfrozen in a beach pond under a surface layer of ice, "the cold would nip us in such sort, that it made us as sore as if wee had been beaten in some cruell manner."

At about the same time, the men calculated that they had food remaining for only six weeks, even on their three-meals-a-week starvation diet. God, however, provided, sending a veritable parade of bears past their hut. Of the forty they saw in the late winter and spring of 1631, they managed to kill seven. The meat was a delicious luxury for the sailors, though, like other Arctic explorers before and after, they suffered poisoning from overdoses of vitamin A when they ate the bears' liver. "Our very skinnes peeled off," notes Pellham.

With the return of sea fowl in March, the foxes came out of their dens to prey upon the birds. The sailors made fox traps baited with the skins of dead birds they found on the snowbanks, and caught fifty foxes altogether. They also gathered the eggs of the "Willocks . . . a Fowle about the bignesse of a Ducke."

In view of the fate of so many subsequent overwinterers in the Arctic, one wonders how Pellham's crew managed to avoid scurvy. Perhaps by eating every scrap of the reindeer, bears, and foxes they hunted, they ingested adequate doses of vitamin C. Over the centuries, the Inuit had learned that scurvy could be warded off on an all-meat diet so long as one ate fat along with lean, as well as the intestines, kidneys, and brains that squeamish European palates eschewed.

With their replenished larder, the men ate far more heartily through April and May than they had in the months before. By May, they had adopted the daily practice of climbing to the top of a nearby hill to stare out to sea in hopes of seeing a "water sky"—the miragelike reflection of open sea beyond the landfast ice. On May 24, they saw water sky for the first time. The very next day, a gale broke up the ice and drove it out to sea.

Astonishingly, on May 25, the first day it was possible for ships to enter Bell Sound, two vessels out of Hull penetrated the fjord. Along with intending to pursue their usual whaling business, the ships' crews were on the lookout for the eight castaways, though they harbored scant hopes the men could be still alive. At that pivotal moment, however, Pellham and his companions were busy praying inside their hut.

The Hull sailors came upon one of the two shallops, which showed evidence of recent use, then marched along the shore toward the huge Dutch building. They shouted out the customary nautical salutation, "Hey!" When one of the refugees, who had left the prayer session on an errand inside the outer "tent," heard the call, he instinctively called back, "Ho!"—"which sudden answer," Pellham writes, "amazed them all, causing them to stand still halfe afraid at the matter." Within seconds, however, the overwinterers burst out of their refuge, "all black as we were with the smoake, and with our clothes tattered with wearing." The Hull men, "with joyfull hearts embracing us, and wee them againe," came inside the sailors' hut. "Wee showed them the courtesie of the house," records Pellham, "and gave them such victuals as we had; which was Venison roasted four monthes before, and a Cuppe of cold water, which, for noveltie sake, they kindly accepted of us."

Though the overwinterers were compelled to linger through the summer of 1631 to aid their countrymen in another season of whaling, they returned home at the end of August, full of pious gratitude toward the Almighty.

Despite the tribulations detailed so vividly by Pellham, the lesson learned by the whaling companies of the day seems to have been an ambiguous one. The overwinterers themselves had despaired of ever seeing their loved ones again, but in the end, all eight had survived. Only two years later, shortly after the Dutch had left for the season, a band of Basque privateers looted the whaling station on Jan Mayen, an island at 72° N, roughly halfway between Iceland and Svalbard. In response, the Noordsche Company, the Dutch equivalent of London's Muscovy Company, recruited whalers to guard their stations, men who (unlike the English criminals) were willing to winter over. In the autumn of 1633, seven were left at Smeerenburg, seven at Jan Mayen. The men at Blubber Town passed the winter without succumbing to cold or scurvy. To be sure, they were surrounded by a sizable village full of stored goods of all kinds; but the key to the team's survival lay not only in hunting reindeer, birds, and foxes, but in collecting as much scurvy grass as they could find. This tiny plant with white flowers, known to botanists as *Cochlearia officinalis,* is rich in vitamin C, and its effectiveness as an antiscorbutic was well known by the seventeenth century. The guardians of Smeerenburg kept a twenty-four-hour watch over their precious town, hatching elaborate plans for defending it against attack, but no pirates bothered to show up. For the seven Dutchmen, it must have been a dull winter.

The men on Jan Mayen Island, however, all died, evidently of scurvy. Nevertheless, the Dutch made one more attempt at overwintering in 1634–35, leaving another garrison of seven at Smeerenburg. Unlike their resourceful predecessors, these men got lazy, counting on a supply of salted meat left by the summer whalers to tide them over, hunting only desultorily and neglecting to collect scurvy grass. All seven died. The pitiful entries found the next spring in the diary of one of the victims give glimpses of their agony. As scurvy began to set in at the end of November, the men decided to eat their meals in isolation, out of fear that the malady was contagious. The first man died on January 14. By late February, the wretched diarist wrote, "Four of us that are still alive lie flat upon the ground in our Hutts," and, "No Body is able to stir for Pain." The last entry was recorded on February 26. At the end, wrote the chronicler, "We spend our time in constant prayers, to implore God's mercy to deliver us out of this misery."

In May 1635, the first Dutch whaler to enter the dead men's hut stumbled in the darkness across their bodies. He found three in coffins their friends had managed to cobble together, two in separate cabins, and two lying on the floor, their knees drawn up to their chins.

In the wake of the two Dutch catastrophes, both the Noordsche and Muscovy companies abandoned the ambition of securing their stations with winter guards. Unless some doomed castaways have escaped the historical record, for at least the next seventy years not a single person attempted to spend the winter on Svalbard. It was only early in the eighteenth century that the Russian Pomori, with their contempt for hardship, their willingness to risk all for a small economic gain, began to specialize in overwintering north of the 77th parallel.

Well into the 1630s, the abundance of whales off the west coast of Spitsbergen seemed limitless to the Dutch and English sailors. By mid-century, however, the catch had seriously declined. It was not simply a question of overhunting: whales, being intelligent creatures, had learned to shun the waters where, throughout eons, their kind had frolicked without any fear of predators. The whalers took notice. As early as 1640, one of them recorded, the great sea mammals had become "shy of the Cookeries and the anchorages of the ships shallops." In 1669 the last English whaling ship visited Spitsbergen. By then, Smeerenburg was a ghost town, its once proud buildings starting to collapse into ruins.

The great lacuna in the early history of Svalbard surrounds the Russian presence in the archipelago. Part of the problem stems from the usual condescension toward and ignorance of Russian matters on the part of American and western European chroniclers—the same bias that left such a classic survival narrative as Albanov's *In the Land of White Death* virtually unknown outside of Russia throughout the twentieth century. Jeannette Mirsky, for example—otherwise a judicious and evenhanded historian of the Arctic—smugly pictures the Pomori's thrust toward Svalbard at the beginning of the eighteenth century as a fleet of "large cumbersome boats manned by Russian peasants who were ignorant of compass, clock, sounding-line, and the simplest kind of nautical observation." (As well as condescending, Mirsky is simply wrong on this point.) The Russian fox hunters, according to her, were "huge bearded men" whose "thick, clumsy fingers somehow knew the art of setting delicate snares." Mirsky conjures up these trappers in a sentence that is as patronizing as it is vivid: "When they went out [from their huts], the hunters fortified themselves with glasses of raw vodka, and on their return they again needed vodka to forget."

Another otherwise evenhanded historian, R. N. Rudmose Brown, summarizes a century and a half of Pomori exploration on Svalbard thus: "The Russian trappers added nothing to the map of Spitsbergen. They were practically all illiterate men, unable to record what they found and saw. Theirs was the dark age in the history of Spitsbergen."

Yet the Dutch and English whalers were fully as illiterate as their Russian counterparts, and their captains, for reasons both of indifference and of commercial secrecy, kept their own geographical discoveries to themselves. Even today, such legendary explorers as Henry Hudson and John Cabot remain shadowy figures. That we know what we do about their voyages and discoveries owes everything to chroniclers such as Richard Hakluyt and Samuel Purchas, who assiduously sought out and published first-person accounts of Renaissance journeys that nobody else at first seemed to care about (except the "brave adventurers" in London who had bankrolled them). The Dutch had their own Hakluyts, historians such as Hessel Gerrits, whose 1613 *Histoire du pays nommé Spitsberghe* is the most important early work about Svalbard.

Alas, in the eighteenth century, vis-à-vis Svalbard, Russia had no Hakluyt or Gerrits. It would be left to such twentieth-century scholars as M. I. Belov to dig into the frozen ground of the forgotten Arctic past. Given the chaotic state of Russian archives today (due not only to the country's perpetual poverty, but to the upheaval of the 1917 communist revolution), the challenge is a virtually insurmountable one. Yet there may well exist documents—in some musty compartment, for instance, in the Solovetski Monastery, a hermitage founded around 1425 in a then impossibly remote quarter of Russia near the White Sea, whose monks were vitally concerned with Arctic voyaging—that testify to Russian deeds in Svalbard long before the turn of the eighteenth century.

In 1964, a Russian scholar named Sergei Obruchev published a slim but fascinating volume called *Russian Pomors in Spitsbergen in the Fifteenth Century.* His argument hangs by the thinnest of threads. Obruchev had come across a letter written in 1493 by a doctor in Nürnberg, Germany, to King Juan II of Portugal. The physician, one Hieronymus Münzer, was attempting to persuade the king to send expeditions to the far north. (In the fifteenth century, with navigators such as Bartolomeu Dias and Vasco da Gama, Portugal was in the forefront of world exploration.) Münzer used flattery to bend the royal ear: "You are already revered as a great ruler by the Germans, the Italians, the Poles, the Scythians, and by those who live beneath the grim star of the North Pole. In the same way the great duke of Moscow is revered, for some years ago, beneath the grimness of the said star, the large island of Grulandia was recently discovered, the shore of which reaches on for 300 leagues, and on which there is a large settlement of people under the rule of the said duke."

It is a considerable stretch to make this evanescent allusion "prove" a Russian discovery of Svalbard, but Obruchev advances a cogent argument to that effect. "Greenland," "Grulandia," and "Grumant" would become common appellations for Svalbard, but those names equally referred to Greenland proper. It is possible that Münzer had caught the distant echo of the Viking colonization of Greenland in the eleventh century, but if so, he confused its perpetrators with the "duke of Moscow." (Russia never had anything to do with Greenland.) Even more improbable than a Russian discovery of Svalbard in the fifteenth century is the notion of a "large settlement of people" on its shores by such an early date. So far, no archaeological evidence has been unearthed to support a fifteenth-century occupation of Svalbard by anyone; but archaeology in that remote archipelago is still in its infancy.

There is, however, a startling possible corroboration of the claim for Russian precedence, in an obscure and overlooked passage in a sailor's diary. Theanisz Claesz was a common seaman aboard the ship of Jan Cornelis Ryp, second-in-command on Barents's voyage. In June 1596, as the two ships first sailed into sight of the unknown land in the high Arctic, Claesz jotted down, "Thereupon we sailed once more in a northerly direction from the equinoctial line up to 81° to Greenland [i.e., Svalbard] which country was never visited by any man as we and it is to be feared that after our visit nobody will ever come there."

Yet in almost the next breath, Claesz adds, "We saw some walruses without their heads floating and also a few dead whales. We were astonished seeing these walruses without their heads as the Russians use to make train-oil out of the fat."

Neither Barents's own diary (brought back to Holland after his death by the survivors), nor Jan Cornelis Ryp's affidavit of the expedition, nor Hessel Gerrits's definitive *Histoire du pays nommé Spitsberghe* records this extraordinary observation. Yet how, and why, could an otherwise unsophisticated sailor have made it up? Beheaded walruses floating in the sea could not have testified to the carnage of predator whales or polar bears: they must have been, it would seem, the detritus of human hunters who sought the ivory of the mammals' tusks. That very fact may explain Barents's and Ryp's silence, for to admit to having discovered such a thing would have been to forsake any claim that these Dutch commanders had discovered an unknown land.

It is all the more striking that, a century before any Dutch or English source would note the presence of Russian vessels in the waters around Svalbard, a common sailor knew enough to equate beheaded walruses with Russian hunters. Finally—and most astonishingly—Claesz's observation would seem to imply not only that Russians had got to Svalbard before the Dutch, but that even as Barents coasted the northwest shore of Spitsbergen, there were Russians ensconced somewhere on land carrying out their trade. Whether or not these hunters had founded a genuine colony (as Obruchev believes) or only a summer camp, they would seem to have been so familiar with Svalbard by 1596 as to have practiced an ongoing industry on its shores.

In any event, with the decline of the whale fishery toward the end of the seventeenth century, the eagerness of various nations to claim Svalbard as their territory waned. Bizarre though it may seem, in an age when every tiny island in the South Pacific was claimed for Spain or Holland or England by whichever mariner first stumbled across it, the question of the ownership of Svalbard went unresolved through the seventeenth, eighteenth, and nineteenth centuries. (This oddity explains the title Sir Martin Conway chose in 1906 for his comprehensive history of the archipelago, *No Man's Land.*)

It would not be until 1925, with the signing of the Treaty of Paris, that by international agreement Svalbard was conceded to Norway. Norway is, after all, the closest European country to Svalbard (Greenland, then a Danish colony, is closer), yet as an independent nation of its own, Norway has a relatively short history. The Treaty of Kiev in 1814 formally prized it free from the clutches of the Danes, who had held it in their grasp since the Middle Ages, but for another century Norway struggled to disentangle itself from an alliance with Sweden that gave most of the benefits to the latter country. Modern, autonomous Norway dates only from 1905.

By that date, Svalbard had long since reawakened the interest of competing nations. Coal had been discovered there, and an American entrepreneur, John Munroe Longyear, spurred a kind of mini-Klondike coal rush with the opening of mines in 1906. Today's capital city, Longyearbyen, not only sits on the site of those abandoned mines, but bears the American's name. By 1925, certain travelers had begun to envision mass tourism descending upon the archipelago. Five years earlier, peering through rose-tinted glasses, Rudmose Brown had written of the "matchless scenery" and "invigorating climate" of Svalbard: "If our insular prejudices against new ideas and novel conditions disappear, the day is not distant when Spitsbergen will be a great holiday centre and health resort, in both respects far superior and more comfortably accessible than the Swiss Alps or the Italian Tirol."

At the end of the seventeenth century, needless to say, no one envisioned Svalbard as a tourist destination. The archipelago was still uninhabited, in the sense that no year-round residents lingered on its shores. While the English had turned their backs on the place, the Dutch continued their whaling efforts, albeit on a vastly reduced scale. It was the Dutch who discovered that though the whales had ceased to frequent the fjords on the west coast of Spitsbergen, they still could be found in considerable numbers off other Svalbard coasts. In 1700, for the first time, a Dutch source records the taking of whales off the southern shore of Edgeøya, the ice-locked island where the Mezen sailors would find themselves stranded forty-three years later.

The first certifiable recorded mention of Russians in Svalbard occurs only in 1697, in the notes of a Dutch captain named Cornelius Gisbert Zorgdrager, who, listing the catches of various countries' ships that summer, laconically adds, "There also came in and joined us several Russian vessels, to take advantage of our convoy." As Sir Martin Conway cannily notes, these unknown Russians are alluded to "casually and not as a novelty"—implying that Russian ships had probably been carrying sailors to Svalbard for some time. Conway goes on to observe that a list of numbers of whales caught in 1697 by each nation gives no total for the Russians. From this at first perplexing fact, Conway arrives at the shrewd conclusion that the Russians were not after whales, but walruses.

It is a measure of the poverty and disorganization of Russian archives that even so chauvinistic a scholar as M. I. Belov must rely on western European sources to document these early Russian incursions. Yet even in the secondhand testimony of those Dutch, English, and French documents, there is a vividness of rumor and folktale that itself hints at a rich history of Russian efforts in Svalbard.

The craze for baleen, blubber, and ambergris had blinded the Dutch and the English to the possibilities of the hunt for other animals. Yet the body of a walrus contains a considerable amount of blubber in its own right; the ivory of its tusks is the finest in the world, superior to that of elephants; and though in the water a walrus can be a formidable antagonist, it is easier to kill than a whale.

On Svalbard, there exist only three land mammals—the polar bear, the reindeer, and the fox. The Dutch and English had hunted reindeer when they needed extra food, and fought off the attacks of bears. But it was the Russians who first realized the potential of hunting those three land animals as an end in itself—furs having a commercial value not greatly inferior to that of train oil or walrus ivory. To prosecute that hunt to the fullest, the Pomori were tempted to winter over, for two simple reasons: polar bears are easier to kill on land than in the water (where they tend to frolic during the summer), and foxes' coats turn white, and thus much more valuable, in winter.

After the catastrophes of 1633 and 1634, the Dutch and English had quailed at the prospect of overwintering on Svalbard: to attempt such a vigil seemed tantamount to a death sentence. Sometime early in the eighteenth century, the Russians began to risk what the Dutch and English dared not.

From numerous eighteenth-century voyages that were never recorded in Russia, later European chroniclers culled the myths and superstitions that the Pomori hunters carried with them as their spiritual freight. On first arriving at a well-known coastal cliff (probably on Edgeøya) that resembled a man in profile, the Russian sailors would kill a male reindeer and throw it off the precipice. The rationale for this act had to do with a resident demon the Russians called the "Spitsbergen dog." According to an old Russian tale that sounds like something out of the Brothers Grimm, a Norse prince had long ago come to Svalbard to live in quiet seclusion. With him he brought one hundred reindeer and a beautiful fifteen-year-old maiden to be his lover and eventual bride. Covetous of the maiden, the Spitsbergen dog transformed himself into a polar bear and carried her off when she came down to the shore to gather mussels.

The inconsolable prince consulted his books of magic and divined that his lover was confined inside a mountain on the south coast, where a cliff shaped like a man in profile plunged into the sea. He wandered searching until he came to a cleft in the rocks, inside which he thought he glimpsed his beloved. As he neared her, however, she fled, leaping agilely from ledge to ledge along the coast. At last she stopped on a promontory. The prince rushed forward to embrace her, only to realize she was not a maiden, but a reindeer beating its antlers against the rocks. The prince looked up at the summit of the cliff and recognized the profile of a man. In the next instant, a falling stone struck him on the head and killed him.

The Pomori's ritual deed of sacrifice on reaching that forlorn shore was at once a propitiation of the Spitsbergen dog and an expression of gratitude to the prince for bringing reindeer to Svalbard. According to yet another old Russian tale, some other Norse prince long ago sent colonists and reindeer in his ships to Svalbard, with the hope of settling that Arctic land. But during the winter the men constantly fell asleep, succumbing thus to scurvy. Only eight escaped, fleeing back to Norway, where they convinced the prince that the country was uninhabitable; but they left behind the reindeer that have flourished there ever since.

The Russian sailors were firmly convinced that the sleepiness that so afflicted them during the long, dark winter nights was the harbinger of scurvy. To ward off the fatal disease, they tried to stay awake nineteen hours out of each twenty-four. Inside their huts, they spent endless hours tying knots in ropes, untying them, then tying them again—"an occupation," Rudmose Brown dryly notes, "sufficiently monotonous one might think to put anyone to sleep."

From a very obscure mid-nineteenth-century source, one Charitonow, probably a Russian living in Germany and writing in German, Conway gleaned many vivid details about the Pomori overwinterers of the preceding century. The men were indeed for the most part heavy drinkers, while at the same time they were devout Christians. At the launching of an expedition from a port such as Archangel'sk, says Charitonow, a typical sailor would borrow 60 rubles in advance from his captain—one third of his pay for the whole voyage. The fellow then "drinks and enjoys himself until he has only two kopecks left. Once more sober, he goes to the church, confesses, takes the Communion, and then starts at last, after offering up a short prayer for his journey."

It was standard practice for the overwinterers to bring with them from Russia the materials with which to build a hut on the Svalbard shore. These were typically log cabins, notched tight at the corners, with small windows and a flat roof on top of which were placed heavy stones to keep it from blowing off in a gale. There were also peepholes built into the door and walls for spying polar bears. A notched stick often served as a calendar.

The *lodjas* and *kotches* in which the Pomori sailed to Svalbard were, according to Charitonow, "miserable boat[s]." "When one beholds these wretched shallops," writes the chronicler in 1851 (at which time the design of the vessels had changed little since the sixteenth century), "one trembles for the hunters." Trappers sometimes found whole crews frozen to death, drifting pilotless in boats near the shore. Charitonow asked a veteran of the Svalbard hunt, "What is done with them?" The man answered, "The bodies are thrown into the sea, and the shallop is repaired." Such macabre discoveries failed to daunt the sailors; as the veteran boasted to Charitonow, "It would take very different waves to make the Spitsbergeners fear the ocean."

On land, the Pomori used dogs to help in the reindeer hunt, and to set off howls of alarm when a polar bear wandered near. The Russians believed that a bear would never cross a track left by a man trudging in snowshoes.

The Pomori also hunted polar bears with dogs and muskets, even in open water from their boats, though this latter practice was perilous in the extreme. "After the first bullet wound," writes Charitonow, "the bear makes straight for the shallop, and woe to the hunters if they do not get away quickly. Putting his paws on the edge of the boat, the bear turns it over, and then this gentleman of the polar sea knows very well how to be ready for the trappers."

The Pomori tended to be excellent marksmen, though one authority swears they fired from the hip rather than from the shoulder. On arriving back in Russia, they usually gave a good portion of their salary to the parish church. The rest they spent on drink. "Brandy," lamented Charitonow, "and brandy alone is their ruin."

For all the hardships they endured on Svalbard, the Russian sailors could wax lyrical about the hunt that drew them to the high Arctic. In the words of one old Pomori song:

When Lent arrived
The sounds came to us
Of walruses screaming and making noise,
Calling us to get ready. . . .
We are not afraid of the walrus,
And are not ashamed of shooting them:
We shot them with guns,
We pierced them with lances
And stabbed them with bayonets
And tied them up.

The same ballad sings the Pomori's ambivalence on heading home:

We said good-bye to Grumant:
Good-bye, father Grumant!
You are terrifying, father Grumant,
All surrounded by mountains up high,
All covered with ice.
It is dangerous for us to live upon you.

An overwintering in the eighteenth century, or for that matter in the nineteenth, was no piece of cake even for the hardiest Russian trappers. Charitonow gives a vivid picture of the squalor of the huts: "Reindeer and other fat stewing on the fire diffuses an intolerable smell; hides hang in the [rafters] to dry, and the whole floor is covered with reindeer skins. Added to this in the dark winter time, an oil-lamp, fed with fish blubber, burns day and night."

The death toll of overwinterers during the eighteenth century cannot be calculated today, but it must have been high. The proliferation of dark legends about scurvy testifies to that fact. For that matter, the sheer ubiquity of old graves still visible on many a Svalbard shore—each tomb an oblong heap of stones, with no remaining trace of cross or headstone—bespeaks the rampant mortality of the winter hunt.

Yet the Pomori greeted this gamble with fate with an extraordinary insouciance. Pondering the overwinterers, Conway marvels, "One year eighteen men were sent forth. Twelve of them died and only six returned home after terrible experiences, yet every one of these six was ready to go back the first time he had a chance."

The Dutch and English had focused their attentions on the west coast of Spitsbergen, where the seas stayed ice-free most of the year and the whales were once so numerous. The Russians pioneered the far more treacherous shores of Edgeøya, for a single reason. Then and now, on that island on the southeast corner of the archipelago, one finds the vast majority of all of Svalbard's polar bears, whose pelts were prized by the hunters far beyond those of reindeer or even white fox. Edgeøya hosts, in fact, one of the two or three densest populations of polar bears anywhere in the world.

Before 1743, Khrisanf Inkov, Le Roy's narrative tells us, had himself wintered over more than once on the west coast of Spitsbergen. It was one thing, of course, to come to Edgeøya, as the other Mezen men had some time before 1743, build a hut out of timbers carried from Russia, lay in a supply of provisions, and make it through a single winter. It was quite another thing to be cast away with only two days' worth of gear and food and the clothing on their backs, as Aleksei and Khrisanf Inkov, Stepan Sharapov, and Fedor Verigin found themselves in May 1743. The challenge these four men faced, as they burrowed into their refurbished hut that first winter, huddled around their clay lamp, was in all likelihood a more harrowing one than human beings had ever before confronted on Svalbard.

4: The Stroke of a Pen

Having procured, with their makeshift bow and arrows, an ample supply of reindeer meat; having fashioned a clay lamp in which they could keep a small, smoky flame burning perpetually; and having chinked up and refurbished their hut, the four Russian sailors settled in for the winter of 1743–44. On October 26, for the first time, the sun failed to rise above the horizon. (The date given by Le Roy is Old Style, according to the Julian calendar then in use in Russia; it corresponds to November 6 in our modern Gregorian calendar.)

Inside the hut, the Pomori warmed themselves around driftwood fires laid in the big earthen stove their fellow Mezeners had constructed when they had first built the dwelling. But such a stove was useless for cooking meat (it was, according to Le Roy, "more like an oven, and consequently not well adapted for boiling any thing"), so the sailors had to accustom themselves to eating their reindeer raw. The lack of salt, says the chronicler, sorely aggrieved them.

The men might have built a separate fire outside the hut, on which to roast their venison, but they judged that "wood . . . was too precious a commodity to be wasted in keeping up two fires." Bodily warmth was more important than cooked meat. Eventually the sailors hit upon the expedient of hanging the meat from the rafters of the hut, where the smoke from the stove half cured it. In summer, they took the smoked meat and hung it outside the hut to dry it further. Their drying rack was made of pieces of wood attached "at the height of the roof of their cabin, beyond the reach of the polar bears." (This seems to confirm the otherwise puzzling assertion that the hut stood as tall as eighteen feet.)

There was, of course, no shortage of drinking water. During the warmer months, the men dipped their kettle in any of several "small rivulets that fell from the rocks." In winter, they filled the vessel with snow to melt atop their earthen stove.

Inevitably, the smell of the meat hung up to dry attracted polar bears. At some point—perhaps as early as the autumn of 1743—a bear drawn to the hut by the odor of reindeer flesh charged the sailors. Seizing their homemade lances, the men engaged in another protracted battle, at last slaying the great beast. During the full span of their stay on Svalbard, the sailors killed ten bears in all, every one of which (except, of course, the first) attacked them. A number of bears even made their way inside the vestibule of the hut, which must not have had a door that could be firmly closed. Of these, some could be driven away with cries and loud noises; others had to be stabbed with the lances until they died. "These animals being prodigiously strong," writes Le Roy, "defended themselves with astonishing vigour and fury." Remarkably enough, it seems that in none of those ten epic battles were any of the sailors seriously injured, for if one of them had been, Le Roy surely would have mentioned it.

The threat of the bears, however, instilled in the Pomori a state of perpetual watchfulness and anxiety. Le Roy says that the men "never dared leave [the hut] alone, no matter for what reason, nor without arming themselves with their lances, to safeguard themselves from the fury of these ferocious beasts, of whom they lived in constant fear of being devoured."

For reasons that Le Roy does not specify, the sailors were never able to kill a single walrus or seal. This is curious, for the waters off Edgeøya abound today (as they did in the eighteenth century) with these sea mammals. Without a boat, a seal or walrus in the water is uncatchable; but when they loll on the sea ice, seals at least make easy targets (hunters in other countries have routinely clubbed them to death). Le Roy states that the Inkovs told him that "they had frequently found on the beach some teeth, and even whole jaws of the seals, but never an entire skeleton of them."

For Le Roy, the moral of the sailors' story, which he draws four or five separate times, is that necessity is the mother of invention. In an odd way, this pat recipe contributes to Le Roy's condescension toward the sailors: it is not their extraordinary gift for invention that ensures their survival so much as sheer necessity producing the solutions, almost like a machine.

Nowhere is the sailors' ingenuity more evident than in crafting their clothes out of bear, reindeer, and fox hides. Unable to tan the hides conventionally, they soaked the skins for days in water, until the hair could be pulled out, then dried the skins and worked melted reindeer fat into them until they became soft and supple. For fur outergarments and bedding, they soaked the hides for only one day and left the hair attached. To sew their clothes, they made crude needles out of driftwood nails, working eyelets into them with the point of their knife (which must have grown blunter by the month). Bear and reindeer sinew served for thread. "Though there was neither taylor nor shoemaker amongst them," writes Le Roy in a rare moment of forthright praise, "yet they contrived to cut out their leather and furs well enough for their purpose."

For more than six years, the sailors' diet consisted only of bear, reindeer, fox, and water. With the disastrous Dutch overwinterings of 1633 and 1634 on record, with the experience of other Russians who had tried to spend the winter in the Arctic known to the Pomori by hearsay and by personal testimony, the four sailors understood that the greatest danger they faced through the long dark months was scurvy. It would not be until 1928 that vitamin C was isolated and thereby demonstrated to be an essential dietary element, the deficiency of which causes the deadly malady. In the absence of what we would call today sound medical knowledge, the Pomori in Svalbard had their own tried-and-true prophylactics for scurvy. Among the four sailors, it was Khrisanf Inkov, with his previous winter experience in west Spitsbergen, who counseled his comrades on the matter.

Khrisanf, writes Le Roy, "advised his unfortunate companions to swallow raw and frozen meat, broken into small bits; to drink the blood of raindeer warm, as it flowed from their veins immediately after killing them; to use as much exercise as possible; and last, to eat scurvy-grass (*Cochlearia*) which grows on the island, though not in great plenty." The scurvy grass, Khrisanf further insisted, had to be eaten raw.

One of the lamentable shortcomings of Le Roy's account is that it offers virtually no portrait of the four sailors as individual men, no hints of their different characters and temperaments. Around the threat of scurvy, however, the single vivid exception to that general stricture emerges. One of the four, Fedor Verigin, was, according to his comrades, "very heavy and very lazy." In addition, the man was "averse to drinking the reindeer blood, and unwilling to leave the hut when he could possibly avoid it." To his comrades, it thus came as no surprise that "soon after their arrival on the island," Verigin fell ill with scurvy. It was not long before the man was confined to his bed inside the hut. Even in these straits, Verigin could not bring himself to abide by Khrisanf Inkov's recipe for health; instead, he "always bore witness to an invincible repugnance for reindeer blood."

So, while the "lazy" member of the party fell into his spiral of helplessness, the other three enjoyed what sounds like perfect health. Le Roy offers an amusing if improbable vignette of that wilderness well-being: "In effect, since they frequently went on the hunt for reindeer and foxes, they exercised themselves so well that Iwan Himkof [Khrisanf Inkov], the youngest of the party, acquired such an agility that he could outrun the fastest horse—a feat to which I have been an eyewitness."

Thus the men endured a first winter on Edgeøya. In February, the sun peeped above the horizon for the first time in more than three months. On May 2, Old Style (May 13 in today's calendar), says Le Roy, for the first time the sun failed to set, wheeling through all the points of the compass, at midnight dipping near the horizon in the north but not quite touching it. Perhaps that same month, the sea ice broke up. With that dramatic event, as the floes cracked and groaned and were driven by the wind away from shore, the sailors' hopes were reborn. Le Roy never mentions such a vigil, but in the light of the experience of other sailors marooned in the Arctic (Edward Pellham's crew of eight in 1631 comes to mind), in all likelihood the four Mezen men climbed every day to the highest point of land within easy reach of their hut, then scanned the horizon to the east, the south, and the west, praying to the God in whom they devoutly believed to send them a glimpse of a sharp, square object gliding across the glistening water—the sail of a passing *lodja* or a *kotch* that might spell their deliverance.

By December 2000, I had decided that I had no choice but to pursue the evanescent tale of the four sailors as far as I could reasonably trace it. From the very start, I had set my hopes on the three possible lines of fresh inquiry that had leapt off the page upon first reading Le Roy. There were the notes of Klingstedt, the Auditor of the Admiralty in Arkhangel'sk, who had interviewed the sailors immediately upon their return to Russia—notes that Le Roy had borrowed to prepare his own narrative, and that I hoped he had returned to Klingstedt's (or someone else's) safekeeping. Le Roy had also alluded to a "manuscript" in Klingstedt's hand. In my fondest dreams, I imagined that both might still exist—the verbatim notes of the initial interview, and a manuscript of Klingstedt's that he had withheld from publication after reading Le Roy's *Narrative*.

There were the "artifacts"—the tools and weapons the men had manufactured on their island during their interminable exile, which they had brought home with them and presented as gifts to Count Shuvalov. These, I knew, included the miraculous bow with its bear-tendon bowstring; some of the deft arrows that had slain reindeer to the toll of 250; the pair of polar-bear-killing lances made of driftwood, rawhide, and flattened nails; perhaps the clay lamp that had saved the men from fatal darkness; and the suits of clothing and boots the sailors had fashioned out of reindeer and bear hides. If the august members of the Imperial Academy of Sciences had marveled over these prodigies of indigenous workmanship, might not some foresighted archivist have preserved them for posterity?

And there was that "X" the sailors had confidently marked with "the stroke of a pen" on Le Roy's copy of van Keulen's map, to indicate the place on Edgeøya where they had lingered for six years and three months. Even if that map were irretrievably lost, might there not be other scholarly gambits by which to deduce the location of the hut?

I realized that to pursue my search properly, I had to commit myself to another, far more thorough trip to Russia (with an interpreter in tow), and that somehow, I had to make my way to the southern coast of Edgeøya and figure out a way to search there for vestiges of the Pomori's passage. Though the prospect was daunting, it was at the same time exhilarating. I exchanged e-mails with Christian de Marliave, the French polar expert who had got me started on this whole business by tipping me off (through Michel Guérin) to Albanov's *In the Land of White Death.* Christian had once briefly visited the west coast of Edgeøya. He made it clear that there was but a single brief window during the year when one could count on reaching Edgeøya by boat—at the end of August and the beginning of September, when the sea ice posed no threat.

That bit of information determined my schedule. I would go to Russia in July 2001, then, armed with what I learned there, proceed directly to Svalbard toward the end of August. That left me more than six months to do my homework out of Cambridge, via long hours in the stacks at Harvard, via faxes Julia Bekman Chadaga could fire off to worthies in her native land, via Internet search and phone calls to experts who knew more about, say, polar bears, or scurvy, or eighteenth-century navigation, than I could hope to assimilate in half a year.

But where to begin? In gloomy moments, I had to confess that each of my three threads of inquiry—the shadowy Klingstedt, the fugitive artifacts, the vanished "X" on the map—amounted to a small needle in a large haystack.

The two Russian scholars who had most carefully studied the sailors' odyssey were V. U. Vize (the geographer aboard the ship that had rescued Albanov in 1914) and M. I. Belov. Each had published an annotated edition of the Russian translation of Le Roy, Vize in 1933, Belov in 1975.

It was interesting to see that Vize and Belov disagreed as to where the Mezeners' hut might be found. If I were to visit Edgeøya myself to search for the scene of the crime, every clue I could squeeze beforehand out of the scholarly commentary would prove invaluable.

How did I know, for that matter, that the sailors' ordeal had taken place on Edgeøya at all, as opposed to some other part of Svalbard? The answer was more complicated than it might seem at first blush. In the opening pages of his *Narrative,* Le Roy plainly states that

the destination toward which the *kotch* carrying the fourteen Pomori was headed in May 1743 was "to the west of Spitsbergen, the usual place of rendezvous for the Dutch ships, and those of other nations annually employed in the whale-fishery." The gale that blew the *kotch* off course carried it to the "eastward of those islands," until, "after some days," the boat was trapped in the ice some two miles off another shore.

The island near which the boat now perilously listed in the ice, Le Roy tells us, was known to the Russians as Maloy Broun ("Maloy" meaning "little"), as distinguished from Bolschoy Broun, or Great Broun. Later in the narrative, when Le Roy questions the Inkovs as to the nature of Maloy Broun, they state that the island "has many mountains and steep rocks of a stupendous height, which are constantly covered with snow and ice." This is an excellent characterization of Edgeøya as seen from the south, with its sea cliffs rising sheer a thousand feet out of the water, with higher summits, nearly twice that altitude, peering over those cliffs, and long, smooth glacial tongues that emanate from the extensive icecaps licking down broad valleys to within a few hundred yards of the sea. It is *not* an apt description of the island of Spitsbergen proper.

Moreover, as a glance at the map indicates (facing page 1), Le Roy's account of the gale-blown course of the Pomori's boat cannot be matched with any other fetching-up place than Edgeøya. However, as M. I. Belov, the 1975 annotator, was the first to point out, the name Maloy Broun "does not exist in Russian

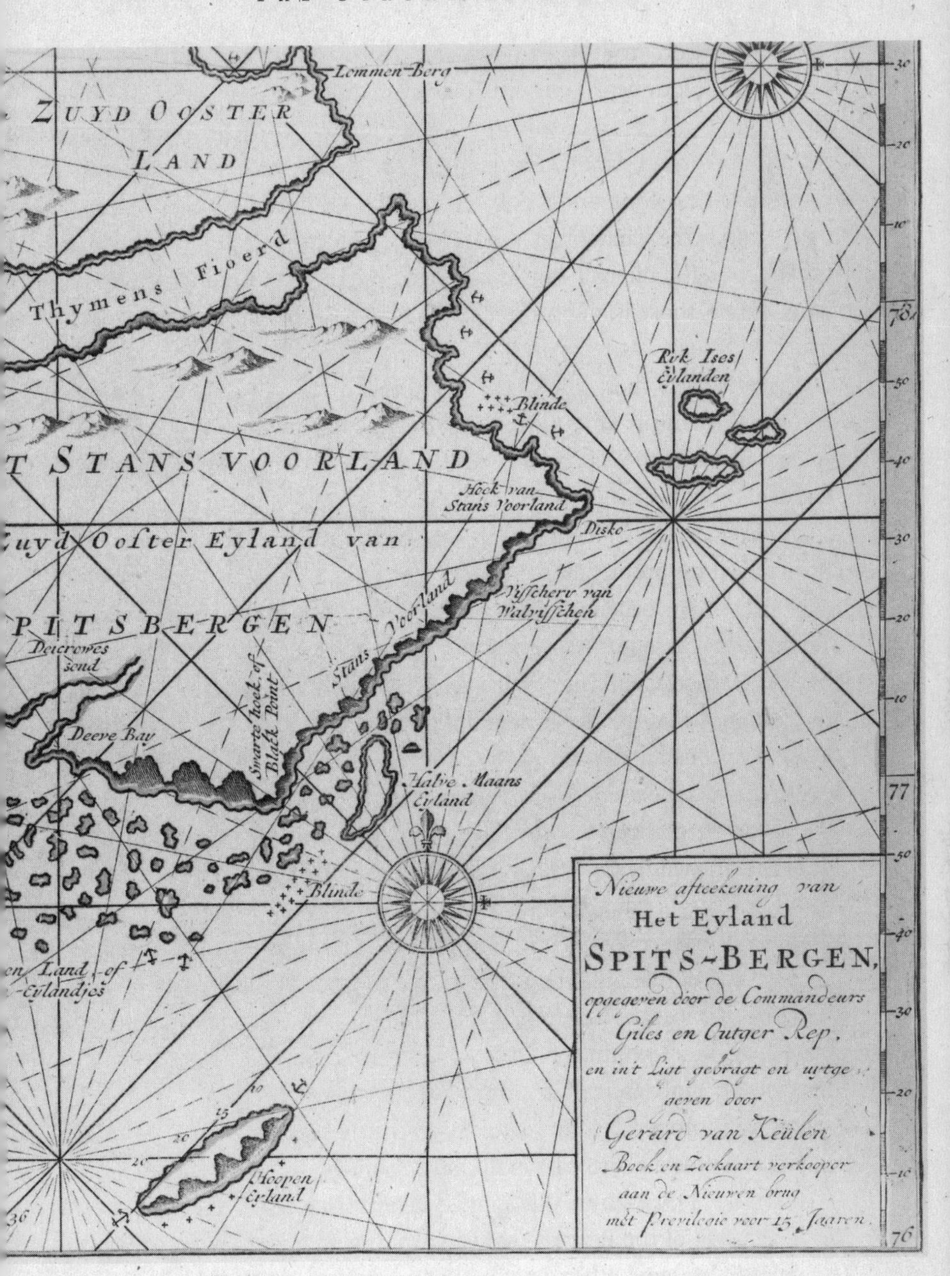

Detail from the same edition of Gerard van Keulen's map on which one of the Inkovs marked the castaways' hut. (Harvard Map Collection)

documents of the 16th through the 18th centuries." Scanning the records of Arkhangel'sk customs officials, Belov discovered that a common folk name for Svalbard in use during the period was "Grunt"—slang, apparently, for "Grunlandia" or "Grumant." Belov cannily concludes that Le Roy mistook "Grunt" for "Broun." The Inkovs must have called the island of their exile Maloy Grunt.

This bungling of nomenclature raised for the first time what would prove to be a critical question. How well did Le Roy speak and understand Russian?

Pierre Le Roy had first been called to Russia in 1731, to become tutor to the sons of Count Biron. By the time he interviewed the Inkovs in January 1750, he had thus resided in the country for more than eighteen years. Until this moment, I had assumed that Le Roy must therefore have been fluent in Russian. Now I had my doubts, which a little reflection only reinforced.

It was understandable, of course, that Le Roy had written his two versions of the sailors' narrative in French and German, the languages he had learned in his cradle. It was presumably his expertise in those two tongues that had led to his initial invitation to Russia. Ever since Peter the Great had embraced western Europe after 1697, reversing for good Russia's immemorial isolation from the civilizations around it, there had been a passionate vogue, especially within courtly and academic realms, for everything French, German, Dutch, and English. Catherine the Great, assuming the throne in 1762, would make French the fashionable language of the imperial court. Russian was demoted, as far as the nobility was concerned, to a peasant language.

What this implied to me was that it might have been entirely possible for Le Roy to have spent eighteen years in St. Petersburg without picking up more than a smattering of Russian. And even if he could speak a passable salon Russian, no doubt the northern accent of the Pomori from far-off Mezen would have sounded strange in his ears.

For the first time, I realized that, as he interviewed the Inkovs in January 1750, Le Roy must have used an interpreter. I could picture the academician, his hand cupped to his ear, straining to unscramble the sound of "Maloy Grunt," and writing down "Maloy Broun." In the same way, he would mistake "Inkov" for "Himkof," even "Khrisanf" for "Iwan."

Given the linguistic barriers between Le Roy and the two sailors, who were no doubt awed and overwhelmed by their first visit to the great capital, the confusions and outright errors of the *Narrative* seemed understandable. For six months I had read Le Roy in a state of tantalized exasperation, attributing his ambiguities to arrogance; now I began to cut the scholar a little slack.

To return to the question of where the sailors spent their exile: there is no doubt that Aleksei and Khrisanf Inkov knew exactly where they were. They had surely never before seen van Keulen's map—expensive Dutch documents of that sort did not circulate in the provincial ports of the Russian north. But they had their own map in their heads, and could correlate it easily with this chart that Le Roy now laid before them. Without hesitation, one of the two (probably Aleksei, the pilot) took up a pen and made a stroke on the van Keulen map to indicate the location of the hut.

It had been Vernezobre, the director of the blubber trade in Arkhangel'sk, who had first, by letter, called Le Roy's attention to the sailors' remarkable story. In another letter, written on November 15, 1750—thus eleven months after Le Roy had interviewed the Inkovs—Vernezobre added a mesmerizing postscript. Le Roy quotes the letter at some length:

> "The captain of a galliot [i.e., a *kotch* or *lodja*], called the Nicholas and Andrew, belonging to Count PETER IWANOWITSCH SCHUWALOW, wintered in *Maloy Brown*, in the year 1749. As he arrived there soon after the departure of our sailors, he found the hut in which they lived, knowing it to be the same by a wooden cross, which the mate ALEXIS HIMKOF had erected before the door, as a memorial of his having taken possession of the country, which, from his own name, he called *Alexeyewskoy Ostrow*, that is, *Alexis' Island*."

These two sentences raise a host of perplexing questions. The *Nicholas and Andrew* was not the ship that rescued the sailors, for that vessel returned to Arkhangel'sk in September 1749, whereas the former, according to Vernezobre, stayed on Edgeøya through the winter of 1749–50. Yet the *Nicholas and Andrew* evidently arrived at the hut with full knowledge of the survival drama that had played itself out there, for the crew recognized the place by the cross raised by Aleksei Inkov.

The Mezen men had waited for more than six years before the first passing ship had chanced to come in view. Now, it seems, in a span of not more than a few weeks between August 15 and the end of September 1749 (after which time the sea would have frozen once more), two Russian boats had separately found their way to that forlorn shore. The *Nicholas and Andrew* cannot, it would seem, have been part of a single flotilla with the boat that rescued the Pomori, or else she would have shared in the discovery. Instead, the two boats must have crossed paths somewhere off the coast of Edgeøya, where the crew of the *Nicholas* learned the piquant details of the Mezen men's ordeal.

Vernezobre's letter is the only source for the information that Aleksei Inkov erected a cross before the hut and that he claimed the island in his name. In the same letter, the Arkhangel'sk official added yet another fascinating twist: "Some *Samojedes,* having heard of the adventure of these sailors, and questioned them very circumstantially concerning the country, lately sent me a message, expressing their desire to make a settlement upon this island, provided a free passage were granted to them, their wives, children, and their raindeer."

The Samoyeds were a native group, ethnically and culturally distinct from the Russians, who had inhabited the Arctic coast long before the Pomori. They were above all reindeer pastoralists, who spoke a Uralic tongue that would not be converted into a written language until 1930. According to Vernezobre's missive, these natives were so fascinated by the Mezen men's story that they overcame linguistic and ethnic barriers sufficiently to "question them very circumstantially" about Edgeøya. No doubt the Samoyeds in the Arkhangel'sk and Mezen area knew, by 1750, that Pomori regularly sailed to Svalbard and sometimes wintered over; but it seems to have been the successful six-year endurance of the refugees that piqued the nomadic herders' fancy. If Pomori could survive in such a place, these natives seem to have implied to Vernezobre, we Samoyeds might flourish there with our families and reindeer: just get us there by boat, and we'll handle the rest.

This petition, which apparently went unanswered, casts an intriguing sidelight on the assertion of the Scandinavian archaeologists Christiansson and Simonsen that "if man has not followed the reindeer to Franz Josef Land and Svalbard it would be the only place in the world this has not happened." If indeed prehistoric reindeer herders had inhabited Svalbard at one time, it was so long ago that no echo of that colonization lingered in the oral tradition of Arctic Russia. Yet the Samoyed eagerness to pull up stakes and move to Edgeøya, after hearing about the place from the Mezen men, testifies to the intense appeal to native herders, as late as the mid-eighteenth century, of a land where reindeer roamed free, no matter how cold and barren that land might prove.

So, for some time after 1750, knowledge of the precise location of the Mezen men's hut seems to have been preserved. By the early nineteenth century, however, it was lost. V. U. Vize, writing in 1933, was at pains to figure out where the long exile had transpired. It was in his footnote to Le Roy's Russian text that I first came across the all-important Keilhau.

"The Russian camp on the southwest part of [Edgeøya]," wrote Vize, "described by Keilhau . . . is located in latitude 77 ½ degrees, and it was approximately in this latitude, as we shall see from Himkov's account, that the four sailors lived." Ergo, Vize seemed at first to say, the camp visited by Keilhau was the very site where the Pomori had spent their six years. But no: according to Vize, Keilhau ended up voting against that encampment, suggesting instead that the Mezen men had spent their exile on Halfmoon Island.

I perused my modern map of Svalbard. Halfmoon Island, or Halvmåneøya, to give it its proper Norwegian name, is the crescent-shaped isle, barely four miles long by one broad, lying off the southeast coast of Edgeøya, just east of Negerpynten, the "black cape" that forms one of the two southward-pointing prongs of Edgeøya. All well and good—but who the hell was Keilhau?

I went back to Widener Library, where I succeeded in finding a slim volume, published in Christiana, Norway, in 1831, titled *Reise i Öst- og Vest-Finmarken samt til Beeren-Eiland og Spitsbergen i Aarene 1827 og 1828,* by one B. M. Keilhau. Though I read no Norwegian, the language, thanks to its affinity with German, was not so opaque to me as unfathomable Russian. Clearly Keilhau's title had something to do with a Journey to East and West Finmark (northern Scandinavia) as well as Bear Island and Spitsbergen in the years 1827 and 1828. Inside the end-cover, I found a tantalizing woodcut illustration showing some half dozen contiguous wooden huts, a trio of tall upright posts topped with triangular frames. A polar bear ambled across the foreground, just yards from where the land shelved into the sea, while in the background loomed a broad, stratified mountain. The caption read, "Russisk Etablissement paa Öst-Spitsbergen"—which even I could render, without a dictionary, as "Russian Settlement on East Spitsbergen [i.e., Edgeøya]." Keilhau's own map recorded a dot labeled "Russisk Etablissement," very near Hvalpynten, at the southwest corner of Edgeøya.

As I eagerly pawed through the book, however, I recognized that I needed a Norwegian translator. (Keilhau has never been published in English, or, as far as I could ascertain, in any language other than Norwegian.) At Harvard, the secretary of the German Department (which included the Scandinavian languages), referred me to Tove Hellerud, a native Norwegian living in the suburb of Winchester, just north of Cambridge, who did occasional work as a translator.

After a pleasant chat by phone, I photocopied the Spitsbergen parts from Keilhau and mailed them to Hellerud. As I impatiently awaited her renderings, I read in Rudmose Brown's *Spitsbergen* that Keilhau was a professor of geology and "the first Scandinavian explorer of scientific training to visit Spitsbergen."

In the middle of January, I received a carefully handwritten translation from Hellerud in the mail. I tore through its pages, seeking the booty of enlightenment. On September 9, 1827, Keilhau's ship had approached Edgeøya, which he knew under the Norwegian name of Stans Forland.

> When day dawned we were approximately one mile from the southwestern part of Stans Forland, where there was supposed to be a Russian settlement. On some flat islands nearby we could already spot two crosses. . . .
>
> The next day we found the Russian settlement, which was situated at the entrance to Wibelands Water [today, Storfjorden, the huge bay that separates Edgeøya from Spitsbergen proper]. The boat was secured in a deep inlet close to the houses, where there was a superb harbor for small vessels. The settlement, which is one of the largest ones on Spitsbergen, and supposedly was built to house 40–50 men, was now deserted.

This was the settlement pictured in Keilhau's woodcut. The geologist prowled among the ruins. The houses were all built of "good logs," he recorded; the largest was thirty-three feet long by twenty-two wide, with a height of about ten feet. (These dimensions fail completely to match those given by Le Roy for the Mezeners' hut.) Inside, Keilhau discovered bunk beds, windows that had once held glass panes, "a large, beautiful baking oven made of brick," and a cabinet with a date inscribed in chalk (in Russian): "23 July 1825." The sad debris of habitation lay everywhere: wooden spoons and plates, stone lamps, playing cards and a checkerboard, a last for a child's shoe, plus quite a number of examples of a "rather unique contraption" made of a wooden stick attached to a clawlike appendage, "which seems to have served as a backscratcher"—against the lice that afflicted overwinterers in the Arctic.

Obviously this substantial colony postdated the Mezeners' six-year ordeal; in view of the chalked date, it had apparently been abandoned only within the last two years before Keilhau's visit. But it remained entirely possible that it stood atop the ruins of the Pomori's refuge from 1743 to 1749, particularly if knowledge of that site had stimulated subsequent Russian explorations of Edgeøya.

Keilhau knew Le Roy's narrative, of which he gives a thorough résumé. He seems, indeed, to have been the first explorer after the crew of the *Nicholas and Andrew* in 1749—or at least the first to leave any record—who deliberately sought out the by now lost site of the six-year vigil. Yet Keilhau concluded that the "Russisk Etablissement" was not the place where the Inkovs, Sharapov, and Verigin had undergone their tribulation.

In a single, maddeningly reticent sentence that would bedevil me through the following year, Keilhau delivered his verdict: "The settlement which we visited near the inlet to Wibelands Water lies exactly on 77½° latitude, according to the maps, but Himkov and his party's residence seems to have been on the eastern side of Stans Forland, and, judging from several circumstances in the story, I am in no way . . . inclined to believe that this large island itself is Alexiewskoi Ostrow, but that it may rather be understood to be the English map's Halfmoon Island."

Nowhere does Keilhau explain the reasoning that led him to this conclusion—an all the more beguiling one, in view of the fact that the explorer did not himself visit Halfmoon Island. More than a century later, in his footnote to Le Roy's Russian text, Vize repeated Keilhau's conclusion, only to disagree with it. Vize's demurral rested on a single discrepancy. The hut "described by Keilhau," says Vize, was perched on the very shore of the ocean. (This comment itself is perplexing, for Keilhau never claimed to have found the Mezeners' hut. He *did* describe, in copious detail, as summarized above, the huts of the Russian settlement near Hvalpynten. Might it be, I began to wonder, that in the scholarly chaos of the Soviet 1930s, Vize had never been able to lay his hands on a copy of Keilhau, so that he had to rely on secondhand accounts of what the Norwegian wrote? Or that, if he did have a copy of Keilhau in his grasp, he could not competently read the Norwegian?)

In any event, Vize believed that Keilhau had placed the Mezeners' hut close to the shore. But Le Roy clearly states, says Vize, that the four sailors actually had to hike "almost a quarter of a mile from shore" to find the hut.

What Le Roy actually wrote is itself slightly ambiguous. The English version of the *Narrative* claims that the four sailors hiked a mile and a half inland before finding the hut. (This, however, is a mistranslation from the German original, which gives the distance as *"eine Viertelmeile,"* a quarter of a [German] mile, which is equivalent to one English mile.) Le Roy's earlier French text places the hut *"un quart de lieue"* from the shore—"a quarter of a league." The *lieue,* or league, was one of those irksome distances whose length varied over the ages. In the eighteenth century, it meant either a common land league, or 2.76 miles, or a nautical league, 3.45 miles. In either case, the hut would seem to have been between seven tenths and nine tenths of a mile inland—a bit less than the German text suggests.

Whether one subscribes to the French or the German measurement, both serve to strengthen Vize's objection: the hut lay inland, not on the shore. But Vize is objecting to an assertion that, as I had discovered, Keilhau never made. Nonetheless, for reasons he himself does not specify, Vize decides that the hut must either have lain somewhere on the mainland of Edgeøya or "on one of the small islands located nearby."

Forty-two years after Vize, M. I. Belov took up the knotty question of the location of the hut. Discussing the copy of the van Keulen map marked with the stroke of the pen by one of the Inkovs, Belov gloomily concluded, "Probably it did not survive even in the archive of Le Roy, whose location is itself unknown to us."

Nonetheless Belov rejects Edgeøya proper as the site of the six-year vigil—though his single-sentence verdict remains as maddeningly unexplained as Keilhau's: "Naturally, an island of such large proportions (72,702 square kilometers) could not be the one on which the Polar Robinsons overwintered." Belov, who seems to relish poking holes in the work of his esteemed predecessor, Vize, goes on to say:

> Dozens of scholars have attempted to locate the small island discussed in the narrative. It seems to me that the greatest success was had by the Norwegian geologist B. M. Keilhau, who discovered in 1827 a hut belonging to the Pomori on Halfmoon Island, located to the south of Edgeøya. Over the entrance, an inscription reads, "This is an Old Believer hut." One of the crosses next to the hut reads: "22 April 1731."

This provocative passage nonplussed me with two surprises. The first was Belov's blithe assumption that the site of the Mezeners' ordeal had to be a "small island," not Edgeøya itself. Le Roy's own text seemed to state exactly the contrary, firmly placing the site on "Maloy Broun," which the academician then identified with the East Spitsbergen of van Keulen's map, an island that "forms a kind of pentagone: its length from east to west, is about one hundred and twenty, and its breadth, from north to south, about one hundred and fifteen English miles." (Once again, the English version mistranslates the dimensions given in the German original, which specifies twenty-three by twenty-two German miles, or about ninety-five English miles long by ninety broad.) This is unmistakably a description of Edgeøya, which indeed is roughly pentagonal (more so in van Keulen's map than in reality), though Le Roy overstates its dimensions, which are actually about fifty miles east to west by seventy miles north to south. Le Roy went on to question the Inkovs about the character of their island, whereupon they asserted (as quoted above) that it "has many mountains and steep rocks of a stupendous height, which are constantly covered with snow and ice." This description simply cannot apply to Halfmoon Island, whose greatest elevation is scarcely 150 feet above sea level, nor to any of the other of the Tusenøyane (Thousand Islands—the number is wildly exaggerated) that range off the south coast of Edgeøya.

Even more baffling was Belov's allusion to the cross with the 1731 date and the inscription above the door, "This is an Old Believer hut." I was wildly eager to believe in these scraps of corroboration, for they promised to explain everything. The hut built by the earlier Mezeners, which Aleksei Inkov was confident he could find in a day's hike on shore, might well have been built in 1731, only twelve years before the Pomori's *kotch* was trapped in the ice. The Old Believers were a sect of ultraconservative Christians who never accepted the reforms of the Russian Orthodox Church promulgated by the Patriarch Nikon in 1652. By the eighteenth century, the Old Believers were outcasts and hermits, and there were many of them in the Mezen area.

Yet where in God's name had Belov got his information? I went back to Keilhau. No, it was clear, the Norwegian had never come near Halfmoon Island, much less spied a hut there. Nor was there anywhere in Keilhau mention of a 1731 date carved on a cross or a building with "This is an Old Believer hut" inscribed above the door.

It took me weeks to solve the mystery, and then, I did so almost by accident. The bibliography in Sir Martin Conway's invaluable *No Man's Land* revealed that there was a second, independent account of Keilhau's journey, written by one Barto von Löwenigh, a German burgomaster who was also, in the quaint nineteenth-century phrase, an "amateur" of polar exploration. Traveling in northern Norway in 1826, Löwenigh had bumped into Keilhau and wangled his way aboard the Norwegian's ship.

I found Löwenigh's *Reise nach Spitsbergen* (1830) not in Widener, but in the library of Harvard's Museum of Comparative Zoology, embedded in one of those ponderous Teutonic miscellanies called *Petermanns Mitheilungen.* Although I can't read German very well, I had no trouble finding the page on which the burgomaster recorded the telltale inscription. Löwenigh was even helpful enough to copy the motto in Germanized Russian: "*Sija isba starawerska*" ("This is an Old Believer hut"). The only trouble was, the hut in question was not on Halfmoon

Island, but stood among the ruins of the big Russian colony near Hvalpynten—the "Russisk Etablissement" of Keilhau's woodcut.

So Belov, like Vize before him, had gotten his Keilhau badly garbled. Once more, I was inclined to attribute the man's errors to a Russian paucity of primary sources, not to sloppy scholarship: perhaps Belov too had read only a secondhand summary of Keilhau. This had not, however, kept him from jumping to the most summary of conclusions.

One more possible approach to the question of where the hut lay occurred to me early on. The Inkovs had told Le Roy the dates each year on which the sun first failed to rise in the autumn, and on which in late spring for the first time it never dipped beneath the horizon. Either date ought to give an accurate indication of latitude. As my modern map told me, the latitude of Keilhau's "Russisk Etablissement" was about 77° 32'N; the latitude of Halfmoon Island, 77° 17'N. If I could get a sharp fix from the dates the sailors reported, I could see where that line of latitude intersected the south coast of Edgeøya.

As the son of an astronomer, I understood the theory behind this computation, but I didn't know how to look it up. I got in touch with a friend of the family, Tom Bogdan, an astronomer who worked at the research center my father had founded in Boulder, Colorado. Eager to help, Bogdan gave me the address of a U.S. Naval Observatory Web site that displayed the requisite tables online.

As devout Russian Christians, the Pomori kept their calendar not by days of the month but by the saints' days. Thus they told Le Roy that the sun first failed to rise on the festival of St. Demetrius; it was the academician who converted this to October 26. Likewise the date of the "transit," when the sun first failed to set, which occurred on the feast day of St. Athanasius, or May 2.

I found another Web site that converted the Old Style Julian calendar to the modern Gregorian. In the mid-eighteenth century, the discrepancy was eleven days (it would reach fourteen by the beginning of the twentieth century, when at last Russia converted to the Gregorian calendar). Thus by the "true" solar reckoning, the key dates were November 6 and May 13, respectively.

Full of hope, I plugged these dates into the Naval Observatory almanac. The results were a disaster. The date of the sun's first nonappearance gave a latitude of 80° N, or about the level of the very northernmost parts of Svalbard. The date for the transit gave an absurd 71° N, near North Cape in Norway. I pleaded with Bogdan to check my calculations. He got the same answers.

Something was drastically wrong. Perhaps the sailors had lost all track of the true dates—but there was one very good reason, also reported by Le Roy, to know this was not so. More likely the haughty academician, cupping his ear to catch the Pomori's strange words, squinting at their interpreter, simply misunderstood once more what they were trying to say.

Maddening, frustrating, tantalizing, exasperating, and ultimately as elusive as fox fire . . . This search for clues as to where my heroes had spent their exile would prove to be the template for a year and a half of research.

But what did I expect? The truth about the past was always slipping through our fingers. A few years ago, I wrote a book about Kit Carson. The legendary scout and Indian fighter remains today an American hero; in his later years, Carson dictated an autobiographical memoir; research by American scholars into the Old West has been voluminous and assiduous; Carson lies a full century closer to my own day than the Russian sailors do; and I read English a lot better than I do Russian or Norwegian. Yet I found it almost impossible to learn (as had previous biographers) just where the plucky mountain man had spent the pivotal years of 1839–41, and what he had done during them. No wonder it was hard to find the Pomori's lost hut.

Contemplating an upcoming trip to Svalbard, I decided that what I would have to do was to walk every foot of the south coast of Edgeøya, searching for clues among the various beaches and cliffs. I got out my map. With a string, I measured the coastline between Keilhau's "Russisk Etablissement" just north of Hvalpynten and the last bare patches of shore on Stones Forland [Stans Forland] before the huge icecap called the Edgeøyjøkulen sprawls into the sea, preventing habitation along the rest of the east coast of the island. Even without all the little wiggles a real coastline affords, the string gave me 130 miles to explore. Two weeks, ten miles a day? In the back of my mind, I knew I was being naive, but it was only on finally reaching the desolate island that I would recognize that such a search was impossible.

Suddenly, out of the blue, came a revelation promising a new lead into my quest. Christian de Marliave e-mailed me the text of an article that had appeared the previous April in a Russian magazine called *Mir Severa* (*The Northern World*). The article was by one Viktor Derzhavin, a name unknown to me. Christian had thoughtfully arranged to have the piece translated into French.

Derzhavin's article about the Mezen sailors seemed to be a mere popular rehash of previous research. He repeated Belov's canard that Keilhau had found a hut on Halfmoon Island that "according to numerous indications can be identified as the dwelling that served as the sole shelter for the brave sailors."

The last paragraph, however, electrified me:

> Several years ago, an archaeological expedition from Moscow carried out a research mission in this region of the archipelago, but stopped a few kilometers short of this island, on account of a tight work schedule, and so missed the opportunity to investigate this out-of-the-way place. Thus scientific study of the legendary Pomori dwelling still lies ahead.

Christian had even enclosed a fax number for Derzhavin in Moscow (supplied by the magazine). At once I enlisted Julia to fire off one of her exquisitely phrased faxes to the author, but she balked. It was simply too gauche to address a dignitary in Russia without knowing his or her patronymic, to which, despite her finding the original article in Widener, *Mir Severa* gave no clue. It was not until February 10 that Julia solved this problem (I forget how), and sent a fax that opened "Esteemed Viktor Leonidovich!" We never received a reply.

Meanwhile, I called up Victor Boyarsky at the Arctic and Antarctic Museum in St. Petersburg. He barely knew Derzhavin's name. When I asked who, in his opinion, might have led the Moscow expedition Derzhavin alluded to, Victor confidently named Peter Boyarsky (no relation), the deputy director of the Heritage Institute in Moscow. "Esteemed Petr Vladimirovich!" hailed Julia tirelessly, and this time we got an answer—in English, no less. "Unfortunately," Boyarsky wrote, "your fax went through poorly and I could not make out your question regarding Viktor Derzhavin's article." Boyarsky went on to say that in the summer of 2001 he would be leading an expedition to Novaya Zemlya to look for Barents's sunken ship from 1596–97—a fascinating endeavor, no doubt, but not what I was after.

The identity of the archaeological expedition that had stopped short of Halfmoon Island remained a mystery for months. Meanwhile, I was trying to figure out just what it would take to get myself to Edgeøya in August. My first inklings were not encouraging. In the *Lonely Planet* guidebook to the Arctic, under the heading "Independent Expeditions in Svalbard," I read, "Virtually everything in Svalbard is controlled by the office of the governor, the Sysselmann[en], and independent travellers are not only discouraged, but they face a host of regulations aimed at protecting this fragile environment from the ravages of mass tourism." Forget about it, was the gist of *LP*'s advice; instead sign up for "an organised tour," which meant a cruise ship that poked around the islands, trundling its passengers on land for tightly leashed two-hour toddles in areas where the environment was not quite so fragile.

All of Edgeøya, I knew, was a nature reserve, a refuge for polar bears, which teem on that island as they do nowhere else in Svalbard. Nonetheless, I faxed the Sysselmannen office in Longyearbyen, and for good measure the Norsk Polarinstitutt in Tromsø. No answer from either of these important institutions. Was Norwegian bureaucracy as impenetrable as Russian?

From Cambridge, then, I was getting almost nowhere in terms of trying to locate the Pomori's hut. Yet Keilhau's conviction that Halfmoon Island was the place to look had lodged in my mind.

Likewise, I had little hope of making headway locating the "artifacts" from my desk in Cambridge, though Julia's faxes to Arkhangel'sk trying to raise Dr. Filippov, director of the Area Archive, amounted to a blind stab in that direction. As Ljudmila Feneva, of the Maritime Museum, had told me the previous October, if the stuff had survived anywhere in Arkhangel'sk, it would most likely be in that archive.

At last, in the dark days of January, Julia succeeded in getting through to the archive by telephone. It turned out that Dr. Filippov no longer worked there. Whoever Julia talked to said that they had indeed received her fax and had answered by return fax, which of course we had not received. Yes, they would be willing to search their archive for the Mezeners' tools and weapons, but only after I paid a search fee in advance. "Can't really blame them!" Julia e-mailed me, voicing solidarity with the impoverished savants of her native land. "Why should they work for free?"

I had my misgivings, but urged Julia to ask how much they wanted. It took three months to get a reply. "They said they were ready to look for the materials as soon as they received an advance of 70 dollars," Julia e-mailed me. "70 dollars . . . it's kind of funny and sad at the same time. Anyway, it's probably worth it." Julia sent back an okay to the archive's terms—whereupon, for the next three months, we heard not a peep. Having wangled a promise of $70, I wondered, were the archivists figuring out how to extort more money from the rich American? I resigned myself to waiting till I got to Russia to make a serious hunt for the artifacts.

There remained Klingstedt. No matter how I spelled his name, the Harvard library computer catalogue spat out nothing. All that I knew about the man was that he had been Auditor of the Arkhangel'sk Admiralty. I didn't even know his first name.

Then Julia pulled a rabbit out of the interlibrary loan hat. From some other university in the U.S., she fetched a tome called *Historische Nachricht von den Samojeden und den Lapplandern*, published in Riga in 1769. Though the author's name appeared nowhere in the book, some scholar had deduced it to be Timotheus Merzahn von Klingstedt. Clearly, it was the same person who had interviewed the sailors on their return to Arkhangel'sk in 1749.

The *Historical Report on the Samoyeds and Lapps* was printed in old-fashioned Gothic script, that ornate font, carved with a mini-chisel, in which a capital G looks like a baroque door knocker, a capital W like a soggy piece of French toast. Fortunately, back in junior high school, when my buddy Mike and I had dabbled at learning German under the tutelage of another friend's mother, she had insisted on inflicting Gothic texts upon us. "Someday you will have to read books printed like this," I recall her scolding, "and then you will be grateful to me."

Avidly I skimmed Klingstedt's treatise. Promising place names leapt out at me—Novaja Zemla, Archangel, Mesen, even Spitsbergen (the last in a phrase that looked like "those who have overwintered on Spitsbergen"). But when I was done, I had detected not a single reference to my sailors. Later I asked a friend fluent in German to peruse the monograph. He agreed: it was all about Lapps and Samoyeds. But at least now I knew Klingstedt's first name.

From the start, I had been trying to find out as much as I could about Le Roy himself, but the pickings were slim. Had he not chanced to interview the Inkovs, his whole career, which must have seemed a distinguished one to the man himself (and to his champions, such as Count Shuvalov), would have slipped completely through the cracks of history.

Belov supplied a few details, including the date of his arrival in Russia (1731); his posts as tutor to the sons of Count Biron, then later to the sons and nephew of Count Shuvalov; and his appointment to and subsequent dismissal from the Imperial Academy of Sciences. From a scrap of information in Belov—that Le Roy had been born in 1699 in the town of Vezel, duchy of Cleve, I launched another mini-search. Vezel proved to be modern-day Wesel, a small town thirty-five miles north of Düsseldorf in northwest Germany, only a few miles from the Dutch border.

A series of long-distance feelers eventually put me in e-mail correspondence with a Wesel native with the wonderful name of Dieter Füngerlings, who wrote excellent English. Füngerlings reported that there was not even a birth certificate on file in Wesel for Pierre Louis Le Roy. This was not surprising, however, for it was obvious to Füngerlings that Le Roy's birth in the town was a footnote to a mass emigration of Huguenots from France, fleeing the intolerance that the revocation of the Edict of Nantes in 1685 had wrought. "The registration of the birth of the Huguenot refugees in Wesel started in 1708," wrote Füngerlings. From the director of the local archive, my intercessor had gleaned an interesting context for Le Roy's appearance on the scene:

> Prussia, at this time a minor, not very important state in Europe was happy to get some but not all of these refugees. So they opened a kind of recruiting offices in the western parts of the Prussian state. The duchy of Cleve was the most westerly part of Prussia and so

> nearest to France. A lot of these refugees came to the recruiting offices to get the permission to enter Prussia and after getting this permission were directed to other parts of Prussia. . . . So it is very likely that Pierre Louis Le Roy (and his mother of course) were in Wesel at the time of birth purely by chance and not very long!

In Wesel, in fact, there were no documents of any kind about Le Roy. "It did not mean," reassured Füngerlings, "that he was not here in Wesel, but we have no written document."

Meanwhile, Julia had found another lead. In a history of the Russian Academy of Sciences written by one Pekarskii, the conscientious inquirer into Le Roy's life story was directed to the *Gazette Littéraire de Berlin* for July 25, 1774—only nineteen days after the professor's death. The piece was evidently an obituary. I knew that Le Roy had left Russia late in life and returned to western Europe—but exactly where, no one seemed to know.

Julia went after the *Gazette* via interlibrary loan. A number of American universities had patchy holdings of the obscure journal: Yale was strong on eighteenth-century issues, but unfortunately lacked those from 1774. We eventually learned that not a single copy of the crucial issue seemed to exist in the United States or France. In the end, it would take me a full year to find the July 25 number, and at last to perceive a shadowy vignette of Le Roy's life and hopes and deeds.

In March, I found myself in Paris for a few days. It seemed an opportunity to go after the French roots of various parts of my story. I went to the Bibliothèque Nationale, a high-tech paragon of what a great national library ought to be. Almost at once, I found a copy of the French original of Klingstedt's report on the Lapps and Samoyeds, published in Copenhagen in 1766. Even in French, Klingstedt uttered not a word about my sailors.

Yet an editor's preface commending the man to his readers made me want to weep over lost treasure. Klingstedt, who had spent "a very long time in Archangel," was "a man of spirit," the editor claimed, "employed for quite some time in this country [Russia], first in the military, at present in civil affairs. He combines all the qualities that make up a fine observer: an intense curiosity about the productions of nature, a thorough vigilance, and a great fund of wisdom." Oh, what Klingstedt might tell me about the Pomori he had interviewed in 1749!

A single paragraph in the man's discussion of Samoyed customs bore tangentially upon my pursuit. "As for the flesh of the reindeer," Klingstedt wrote, "they always eat it raw: for them it is a delicacy to drink the animal's blood warm, and they believe that this drink serves as a prophylactic against scurvy." Had Khrisanf Inkov learned his antiscorbutic recipes from the Samoyeds around Mezen?

On my way out of Russia the previous October, passing through Paris, I had ducked into a quaint little warren on the rue de Turbigo called the Bibliothèque de la Généalogie. Camped out at the crowded desks were graybeards and matrons feverishly tracing down their ancestors from the fourteenth century. I had only a few hours left before my flight to Boston. Rather than pursue any leads here, I succumbed to the librarian's tip that I dash over to another archive on the rue Saints Pères (eight stations on three different Metro lines away), to penetrate the Société de l'Histoire de Protestantisme Français. When I got to the latter establishment, it was closed. It seemed to be open, in fact, only for a few hours in the afternoons of Monday, Wednesday, and Friday.

Now, in March, I had time to wait for the French Protestant Society to open. There I hit minor paydirt. Under Klingstedt, I found a patriarch named Jonas, born in the town of Klingstadt (Sweden) in 1626, married in 1661, died in Stockholm in 1691. None of his eight children was named Timotheus, but, given the dates, one of the five sons was most likely the Arkhangel'sk auditor's father.

To my disappointment, the name Pierre Louis Le Roy fetched up no data among the Protestant records. Bleary-eyed from squinting at faded, typewritten ledgers (nothing computerized in this archival outback), I sensed the mad genealogist's inevitable mixture of triumph and despair. Out of the faceless mass of history's outcasts, I had caught frozen glimpses of *my* Klingstedt, *my* Le Roy. Yet they remained faceless as ever. Here loomed a gloomy premonition: what could I ever hope to accomplish that might bring into three-dimensional focus the faces I really cared about—those of Aleksei, Khrisanf, Stepan, Fedor?

That evening I had dinner with Christian de Marliave. He was eager to hear about everything I had learned since we had last seen each other in October. It was a chance for me to unwind, in the bistro just around the corner from Christian's apartment, over *gigot d'agneau* and a mellow Julienas. I vented my frustrations, and in the next breath, my hopes. "I mean," I said, "can you really believe that anybody would have just chucked out those wonderful things—the driftwood lances, the bow and arrows, the reindeer skin boots? All that stuff has got to be in an archive somewhere."

Christian took a drag on his cigarette and chuckled ruefully. He had spent the previous summer on an archaeological expedition to Siberia, looking for mammoth carcasses embedded in the tundra. "I must tell you a funny story, but a sad one," he began. "In 1908, a man whose name I forget gives to the National History Museum here in Paris the mummified parts of a great mammoth that was found in Siberia. It is the only mammoth in a museum outside of Russia. The man hopes to win the Légion d'Honneur by this thing."

Christian's smile broadened as he took another puff. "Fifty years later, they reinstall the mammoth. But in the meantime, they have lost three of the four feet. It is now a one-foot mammoth." He grimaced. "If they can lose three mammoth feet in only fifty years—my God, they are this big"—he raised his right hand level with his head—"then in 250 years—"

"I know, I know," I interrupted, my head in my hands. "Don't tell me."

"And the man never wins the Légion d'Honneur."

5: Dry Search

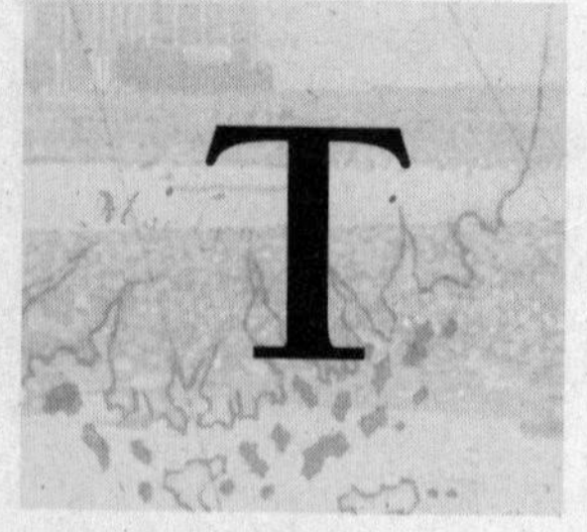

The most disappointing feature of Le Roy's *Narrative* is the scarcity of detail he lavishes on the sailors' existence after the first winter. Of the seventy-six pages the academician devotes to the story, he uses up forty-two getting the Pomori installed in their hut, with their lances, bow and arrows, lamp, and fur clothing. Rather than question the Inkovs closely about the unthinkable psychological ordeal they had undergone through the subsequent years, he hands them a kind of brief questionnaire as to the geographical, biological, and meteorological phenomena of their place of exile.

The reader is left to imagine the full horror of each summer the Mezeners passed without spotting a distant sail and the true genius of their adaptation to one of the most barren places in the world. Whether Le Roy made copious notes about such matters but failed to convert them into narrative, or was simply too incurious to ask the sailors about such matters, we can only speculate. It took him sixteen years after interviewing the Inkovs, we must remember, before he finally published their story.

The unfailing condescension that Le Roy exhibits toward "our unfortunate sailors" may help account for the man's short attention span. A phrase in the extended title of his *Narrative* gives a telltale hint as to his academic priorities: "Together with some Observations on the Productions of that Island, &c." It is as if the quasi-scientific notes about Svalbard that the Inkovs might yield up are more important than their own experience.

The few tidbits Le Roy drops about the psychology of the sailors' exile are compelling. In one of the most interesting paragraphs in the *Narrative,* he tells us,

> Excepting the uneasiness which generally accompanies an involuntary solitude, these people, having thus by their ingenuity so far overcome their wants, might have had reason to be contented with what Providence had done for them in their distressful situation. But that melancholy reflection, to which each of these forlorn persons could not help giving way, that perhaps he might survive his companions, and then perish for want of subsistence, or become a prey to the wild beasts, incessantly disturbed their minds. The mate, ALEXIS HIMKOV, more particularly suffered, who having left a wife and three children behind, sorely repined at his being separated from them: they were, as he told me, constantly in his mind, and the thought of never more seeing them made him very unhappy.

In the very next breath, however, Le Roy wrenches himself back to more practical concerns: "—But I will now give some account of that island, and relate what the sailors told me about it."

There follows the business with van Keulen's map, and the tantalizing glimpse of one of the Inkovs marking it with the stroke of a pen. But Le Roy must now deliver a little lecture in geography. An academic in his very bones, he proceeds to describe Edgeøya not from the Inkovs' testimony, but from his own perusal of the chart. Even worse, he interrupts himself to discuss a conjecture of the day, pertaining not to Svalbard but to Novaya Zemlya, that what looked like a true island was "not a part of our continent" but only "an assemblage of ice, which had gradually accumulated." Some explorer, digging into the ground on the latter island, had evidently discovered what we now call permafrost, giving rise to the suspicion (surely not on his own part, but rather on that of deskbound theorists such as Le Roy back in Russia) that Novaya Zemlya was nothing but a huge ice floe on which dust and soil blown from the mainland of Asia had congealed to create the illusion of land.

Sagaciously, Le Roy rejects this canard vis-à-vis Svalbard: "Thus much I will venture to affirm, that the island of East-Spitsbergen has not been formed by the ice, but that it is certainly real land; and the account given me of it by these sailors, puts this matter beyond all doubt." (*Gee, thanks, Pierre,* I jeered in my head when I first read this absurd passage, *nice of you to credit the Inkovs' "many mountains and steep rocks of a stupendous height" with being real!*)

The sailors' account of the island's weather, as recorded by Le Roy, contains a very puzzling statement. For seven weeks each year, they averred, from mid-November to early January, "it generally rains hard and continually . . . and all that time the cold is very moderate." This claim is completely at odds with modern meteorological observations on Svalbard. In Longyearbyen today, the median December temperature is 5° F, with a range from a high of 37° to a low of minus 31°. The precipitation, on the other hand (virtually all of it in the form of snow), is lighter in December than in any other month, the number of cloudless days greater than any other month. Variations no doubt exist between Longyearbyen, situated in a westward-facing fjord on Spitsbergen proper, and Edgeøya (where no one has ever kept long-term climate records), but not of a scale that could explain the perpetual rains through a mild December that Le Roy says the sailors reported.

From January on, the Inkovs' testimony about weather makes more sense. After the rainy season, the men indicated, "it becomes intolerably severe, especially when the wind is south. . . . The snow fell on this island in such great quantities during the winter, 'that it wholly covered their hut, and left them no way of getting out of it, but through a hole they had made in the upper part of the roof of their anti-chamber [*sic*]." The southeastern part of Svalbard today has the archipelago's worst weather. One modern source indicates that, at the higher altitudes on Edgeøya, annual snowfalls of as much as twenty feet are not uncommon.

Only once during their six years on the island, the sailors told Le Roy, did they hear thunder. During the winter, the appalling darkness was tempered by the moon, whose orbit across the sky follows a course independent from that of the sun, and by frequent displays of the aurora borealis. Because they thought it so important to observe the saints' days, the sailors went to great pains to keep a calendar. Le Roy says that, as good Christians, "who otherwise very strictly attended to the ceremonies of their religion," they were greatly disturbed at not being able to eat fish (and thus abstain from meat) on Fridays.

One of the most extraordinary accomplishments of the Pomori was their calendar-keeping. On the day they were rescued—August 15, 1743 (Old Style)—they reckoned it to be August 13. Over the course of nearly 2,300 days, they had lost only two (or, if they failed to add a day each for the leap years of 1744 and 1748, at most four). Le Roy was rightly astonished at this feat, for he knew the men had no chronometer, not even a sundial. During the three winter months of perpetual darkness, on a clear night the revolution of the constellations provides an accurate indicator of twenty-four hours' passage. When storms or clouds obscure the moon and stars, however, there is no way to gauge the passage of time except by what we now call one's "internal clock"—proved in many an experiment to be notoriously unreliable in humans.

Le Roy pressed Aleksei Inkov on this question, so much so that the man answered him "with some warmth." As this is the only passage in Le Roy's *Narrative* in which we hear either of the sailors speak, it is worth quoting in full. "What a fine pilot, Sir, would you think me to be," chided Inkov, "if I knew not how to take the altitude of the sun when he is before my eyes, or not to regulate myself by the course of the stars on the sun's not appearing, and by that means to determine the period of twenty-four hours? I had for this purpose made a staff, like that which I had left behind in our vessel, which I employed for making my observations." Le Roy takes Inkov to mean a Jacob's staff, a kind of primitive sextant. The pilot's spirited response still leaves unanswered the question of how he calculated time when the sun and stars were not visible.

It is a great pity that Aleksei Inkov did not see fit to leave his own account of his matchless ordeal. The question arises as to whether the four sailors were illiterate, as indeed most Pomori were. At one point Le Roy calls them "these illiterate sailors"—but this derogation in the English text turns out to be a loose translation of the German *"einfältige Bauern"*—"simple peasants." Indeed, the corresponding phrase in the French text is *"simples paysans."*

Le Roy squanders another long paragraph on an observation that today seems as absurd as his idea that Novaya Zemlya might be an ice floe. During their stay on Edgeøya, the four sailors were never afflicted with lice, unlike so many other mariners who had spent weeks in unsanitary quarters below decks on their ships. With his encyclopedic knowledge, the professor points out, "It is a pretty general observation, that sailors, who otherwise are very subject to vermin, and who, it is said, for that reason wear shirts of blue linen, get quite free from them on passing the equator; but no sooner do they repass the line on their return, than those vermin swarm among them as before." In the Pomori's case, concludes Le Roy, passing the Arctic Circle must have had the same lice-banishing effect as passing the equator. (What blue linen shirts have to do with discouraging "vermin" remains obscure.)

Two stray details concerning Le Roy's description of "Maloy Broun" would trouble me for months, until my own visit to Edgeøya gave me a possible insight. In the same paragraph as the Inkovs' account of "many mountains and steep rocks of a stupendous height," the sailors seem to inform Le Roy that the island "has no river, but a great number of small rivulets, which rise amongst the rocks and mountains." A glance at my modern map of Svalbard made it look as though quite major torrents drain the sprawling icecaps—streams such as the branching, unnamed river that flows down the valley called Dyrdalen toward a bay at the inward crook of Edgeøya's southern coast.

Also in the same paragraph, Le Roy remarks that the sailors found the clay that they succeeded in molding into a lamp "about the middle of the island"; and that, "The shores of the island are covered with sand and gravel, of which last a little is also found towards its center." The true center of Edgeøya looked on my map to be covered with icecap, and it would have required a bold jaunt of some forty miles, across rivers, thousand-foot-high ridges, and glaciers, to reach it.

In any event, the passage of the five years the sailors lingered in their Arctic exile after the pivotal first summer, autumn, and winter is telescoped in the *Narrative* into an undifferentiated, business-as-usual blur. Only the slow decline of Fedor Verigin demarcates those years. Fat and lazy, Verigin, so his comrades insisted, was stricken with scurvy "soon after their arrival on the island." Relentlessly unwilling to drink warm reindeer blood, the poor man took to his bed inside the hut. His affliction "afterwards became so bad, that he passed almost six years under the greatest sufferings: in the latter part of that time, he became so weak that he could no longer sit erect, nor even raise his hand to his mouth; so that his humane companions were obliged to feed and tend him, like a new-born infant, to the hour of his death."

After this passage, Verigin's plight goes unmentioned until near the end of the *Narrative*. The sailor's demise once more stirs Le Roy to the pitch of a rare psychological insight:

> When our four mariners had passed nearly six years in this dismal place, FEODOR WEREGIN, whose illness we had occasion to mention above, and who all along had been in a languid condition, died, after having in the latter part of his life suffered most excruciating pains. Though they were thus freed from the trouble of attending him, and the grief of being witnesses to his misery, without being able to afford him any relief, yet his death affected them not a little. They saw their number lessened, and every one wished to be the first that should follow him. As he died in winter, they dug a grave in the snow as deep as they could, in which they laid the corpse, and then covered it to the best of their power, that the white bears might not get at it.

Having narrated Verigin's death, there remains little for Le Roy to chronicle but his three comrades' miraculous rescue. On August 15, 1749, as the professor rather blandly states, "they unexpectedly got sight of a Russian ship." The Inkovs and Sharapov immediately ran to the top of "the hills nearest their habitation" and lighted fires. Then they ran back to the beach, where they frantically waved a flag made of a reindeer hide attached to a pole. They succeeded in capturing the crew's attention. As Le Roy almost comically puts it, "The people on board seeing these signals, concluded that there were men on the island who implored their assistance, and therefore came to an anchor near the shore."

Though Le Roy tells us neither the name of the ship nor the identity of its captain, he does remark that the crew were Old Believers. Like the Mezen sailors more than six years earlier, they had sailed out of

Archangel'sk. According to the chronicler, the ship had originally planned to winter over in Novaya Zemlya, but for some reason, at the behest of Vernezobre (the same director of the blubber trade who would soon alert Le Roy to the sailors' outlandish story), the crew bent their course instead for west Spitsbergen, still intending to winter over. A gale much like the one that had doomed the earlier ship blew the Old Believers' craft similarly off course, till it came to the southern shore of Edgeøya and the crew caught sight of the stranded men running along the beach.

The Inkovs and Sharapov made a deal with the captain to pay him 80 rubles for their rescue and to work as hands aboard the ship. It might at first blush seem uncharitable on the captain's part to have accepted payment and labor as the price of rescue. Reading between the lines, however, one realizes that the Old Believers abandoned their plan of overwintering in order to deliver the refugees back to Russia as soon as possible. Perhaps the Inkovs and Sharapov pleaded so eloquently against having to endure another winter on Svalbard that the captain took pity on them and acceded to their wishes.

Le Roy itemizes the goods the three sailors brought on board the rescue ship, which he calls "all their riches":

> which consisted in fifty pud, or two thousand pound weight of raindeer fat; in many hides of these animals, and skins of the blue and white foxes, together with those of the ten white bears they had killed. They took care not to forget their bow and arrows, their spears, their knife and axe, which were almost worn out, their awls, and their needles which they kept carefully in a bone-box, very ingeniously made with their knife only; and, in short, every thing they were possessed of.

Forty-four days later, the ship coasted into the harbor at Arkhangel'sk. Aleksei and Khrisanf Inkov and Stepan Sharapov stepped onto their beloved native land after an absence of seventy-six months, to a reception whose mingled joy and incredulity we can only imagine, since Le Roy does not bother to give us any account of it. "All three on their arrival were strong and healthy," he murmurs, before drifting into a perfunctory conclusion to his *Narrative.*

• • •

By the beginning of 2001, I needed to recruit a Russian translator-cum-research-assistant to replace Julia, for her work on my project was threatening to derail her Ph.D. dissertation. I also needed to figure out how to get myself to Edgeøya and explore its coast once I arrived there. I sensed that I could not pull off this job by myself. In my twenties and thirties I had organized quite a few mountaineering expeditions to Alaska, but I knew nothing about boats or coastal travel in the Arctic, and the bureaucracy of wangling permission from the Sysselmannen (the governorship of Svalbard) was beginning to look Byzantine. I needed an insider.

I used the Internet to find out which American-based adventure travel companies offered group tours of Svalbard. These were cruises, most of them aboard Russian research vessels converted to tourism after the collapse of the Soviet Union, that circled the archipelago in two weeks or so, lacing the passive journey with brief, well-supervised walks on shore to visit research stations or watch birds.

One of the travel companies recommended a fellow named Mats Forsberg, a Swede living in Tromsø, on the northern coast of Norway, who had run cruise ship shore excursions for a number of years. I e-mailed Mats and got a prompt answer. Like most Scandinavians, the fellow, as I would soon learn over the phone, spoke excellent English, though his command of the written language was a bit eccentric.

Mats told me that, indeed, I would never gain permission from the Sysselmannen without the aid of an "experienced guide" like himself. Though his schedule for the summer of 2001 was already getting crowded, he would be happy to organize and lead my trip—for an appropriate fee. But first, Mats e-mailed, "I need to have more info about who you are David, before the governor's people start to call me and ask a lot of questions, which they will."

Mats elaborated on the problems of gaining access to Edgeøya: "There are today a lot of expeditions asking for permission going into restricted areas. A lot, and today more and more of this expeditions are refused to go there. The reason is that they simply are presenting a too bad reason for going in there. There are so many unserious people trying to get permissions today."

Mats knew about the four Pomori shipwrecked on Edgeøya in 1743, but only as a vague story that had passed, I would soon learn, into the folklore of Svalbard. He had never read or heard of Le Roy. Mats's chief source for the tale was Sir Martin Conway's résumé of it in *No Man's Land,* and Conway, though otherwise a scrupulous historian, had got a lot of the details wrong.

Mats managed to get the Sysselmannen to send me the application forms for my independent expedition. These documents were intimidating in their own right. "You should stress historical, film, your background writing about this issue, and so on," Mats coached me. "If there is any historical scientific matter involved in this, just use it for what it is worth." I duly typed up a précis of my plans, laying on hard the historical and scientific significance of my venture—no mere romantic lark, this. Dropping the application in the mailbox, I crossed my fingers.

Mats concurred with Christian de Marliave that, on account of sea ice, the only good time for the trip was at the end of August and beginning of September. There were helicopters available for hire in Longyearbyen, at obscene rates, but Mats told me that the Sysselmannen would never approve access to Edgeøya by air. We would have to get there by boat. His plan was that we would meet in Tromsø in late August, fly to Longyearbyen, and round up our supplies in the capital city. Meanwhile he would work on buying us passage on one of the cruise ships for the several days it took to get near Edgeøya. There the ship would abandon us with our gear, food, and a single Zodiac—a sturdy rubber raft powered by outboard motor, de rigueur in the Arctic and Antarctic for ship-to-shore excursions. We would use the Zodiac to poke along Edgeøya's southern coast. After two weeks or so, another ship would pick us up.

It sounded a little risky to me to depend on cruise ships, whose primary agenda was to give their passengers as many snapshots of calving glaciers and spouting whales as possible, for our delivery and retrieval. It would not be possible to carry a radio that could raise Longyearbyen—the only device we might use would be a handheld walkie-talkie that could communicate with another radio on the right frequency across a gap of no more than six or eight miles. In case of emergency, we would have only a locator device, like the crash beacons installed in small private planes. If, for instance, we flipped the Zodiac and found ourselves floating in the Barents Sea in our survival suits, Mats would activate the beacon. A distress signal would, in theory, arc through space to the nearest satellite, which would relay the call to a monitoring post in Paris. The French would decode the signal and let the Sysselmannen know some folks were in trouble off Edgeøya. The government would launch a helicopter to look for us—weather permitting. If the search didn't take too long, we might just be plucked out of the sea by cable and winch shortly before we succumbed to hypothermia.

Thus as my trip to Edgeøya began to take on the prospect of reality, it also loomed as a bit daunting. I had, moreover, been thinking about polar bears. I had seen only one polar bear in my life—a locally famous inhabitant of the Denver Zoo when I was a kid. Blind and toothless, maddened by captivity and heat, for hour after hour, day upon day, he strode the same three steps forward, the same three steps back, in a rut he had worn in the concrete floor of his allotted cage—imprinting on my youthful mind an indelible image of the atrocity of incarceration.

I had seen quite a few black and grizzly bears in Alaska, especially in the Brooks Range. Thrice I had bears walk through my camp in the night. From an initial wariness that dictated carrying along a hefty rifle, I graduated to a state of Buddhist acceptance of even the most imposing specimens of *Ursus horribilis,* arming myself with nothing more potent than mothballs to sprinkle about camp when I was off climbing. Once a bear attacked a food depot I had left on a mountain pass, but fled without gobbling up the goodies after he bit into a can of pressurized butane.

Polar bears, however, were both bigger and more aggressive than grizzlies. I started studying up on these great mammals. A French guidebook to Svalbard that I picked up in Paris had a chapter called "Les Ours Blancs." Under the subhead "Accidents," I read some disquieting memoranda:

- September 6, 1987, two Germans were attacked on the isle of Edgeøya. One was scalped, the other had his arms and legs badly bitten. The bear that attacked them was killed the next year and stuffed. Ever since, he graces the foyer of the hospital in Longyearbyen.

- The best known case was that of an Austrian camper attacked July 18, 1977, in the Bay of Madeleine. He was killed with one blow.

- In the space of six years, from 1987 to 1992, twenty-six bears were killed, of which fifteen were in self-defense (seven by tourists, six by scientists, two by residents). Two important facts: twelve of the fifteen cases of self-defense took place near tents or cabins and seven of the bears were youngsters.

- [Testimony of one Eric Giuglaris]: "March 26, 1993. I returned to the Fredheim cabin. . . . At 5:00 A.M. I was awakened by the explosion of a pane of glass—and I mean explosion! The bear, stuck by his great size in the window casing, held himself a meter and a half away from me, his head in the center of the window. . . . I was still in my sleeping bag, my gun on the floor, without knowing what to do. The bear remained stiff, with a sly look, as he silently watched me. A few seconds later, I slipped out of my bunk, being careful not to touch him. I grabbed my gun, cocked it, and put it so close to his head that it rested on his fur. I fired off two shots just over his head without scaring him in the slightest. He remained in the window. After a few moments, he pulled back. I seized my flare gun and shot two charges in his direction. He fixed me with a disdainful look, then wandered off, obviously out of boredom rather than fear."

Along with polar bears and Zodiac catastrophes, I had another source of misgiving as I contemplated my trip to Edgeøya. Mats seemed a likable fellow over the phone and via e-mail, but I didn't know him at all. A three-week expedition with a stranger, governed by such a rigorous agenda as my search for traces of the Mezen sailors, promised all kinds of fiascos in the realms of cabin fever and logistics. I decided to invite two friends, not only for the leavening of their companionship, but for the expertise they might bring to my quest.

Michel Guérin, my French publisher, was a natural choice. It was he, after all, who had set this whole business in motion at the party in his Chamonix office in 1997, with his passing remark about Albanov's

In the Land of White Death. During the months I had now been pursuing the Pomori, Michel had been an eager spectator. Over the course of the five years we had been friends, we had gone on a few hikes together, and spent many an evening in the bistro discussing life and literature. At my urging, Michel had made his first two trips to North America, attending the Banff Mountain Film Festival and exploring Manhattan. On both occasions, I had served as his interpreter, for despite the fact that he voraciously read British and American books, his utterances in English sprang from an idiom so baroque not even Kingsley Amis could have mimicked it. (Michel had the classic intellectual's handicap of being unable to say anything simply.)

In his youth, the man had been a superb alpinist. Now, at forty-eight, he still climbed creditably and skied like a demon (his idea of a pleasant afternoon outing was to take the *téléphérique* up to the Aiguille du Midi and bomb down the Vallée Blanche and the Mer de Glace in time for an aperitif at his favorite café, l'M).

On Svalbard, I knew, Michel would be an invaluable resource, for I had never met a person so well read in the literature of exploration. He had, what was more, a gift for original thought that, as I had often seen, stood received wisdom on its head and shook it apart like a sea lion shredding a penguin. Though he had no ambition to be a writer himself, he coined pithy aperçus on the spot like no one I had ever been around.

Michel was a family man, devoted to his clever wife, Marie-Christine, and his adorable adopted children (they happened to be Russian), Alec and Katya. Yet as I had seen in Banff and New York, Michel had no qualms about prying himself free from Chamonix for a jaunt that tickled his fancy. And Svalbard was such a jaunt: Michel hesitated not a second in accepting my invitation. He greeted the prospect of the trip's various dangers—Zodiac flips, polar bears, and the like—with a cheery fatalism that would prove a welcome foil to my own fussy anxiety. He was, however, worried about the cost of the expedition. As he e-mailed me in the months before the journey, "I would prefer not to starve my kids before being eaten by the polar bears."

The other pal I wanted along was Vaughn Hadenfeldt, a mountaineer and wilderness guide, who runs Far Out Expeditions out of his home in Bluff, Utah. Vaughn had become my close friend after 1994, when I had met him while I worked on a book about the Anasazi, those prehistoric geniuses of the Southwest who had built such cynosures as Keet Seel, Cliff Palace, and Pueblo Bonito. Though guiding clients to Anasazi ruins and rock art was what Vaughn did for a living, on his off days he liked nothing better than to set off with a game partner on a high-speed lope into some canyon he had not yet explored. Though his knees were shot from too many years of carrying hundred-pound loads, he could still hike slickrock faster than anyone I had ever been out with.

Probing the Southwest with Vaughn was in one sense, however, a mortifying experience. I thought I had developed a good eye for artifacts in the dirt, for petroglyphs etched on boulders, but time and again I would step across the corner of a chert arrowhead poking out of the soil, only to have Vaughn gloat, "Did you happen to notice this little projectile point?" Or he would stand there, silent for fifteen minutes, as I admired a panel of white and red handprints painted on a sandstone wall, then, as I hoisted my pack to go, murmur, "Check out that stuff on the upper level."

Vaughn hid his fiercely competitive nature beneath the taciturn persona of a laid-back desert rat. An equally competitive type, I savored some of my happiest moments in the Southwest when I managed to find something Vaughn had overlooked—best of all, one blazing August day, when I stumbled upon an underground kiva with an intact ladder that Vaughn must have come within a long stone's throw of discovering himself.

Fifty years old, Vaughn was not only the finest wilderness guide I had ever met, but he had a better eye—for artifact, petroglyph, animal track, or route—than anyone I had ever gone hiking with. On Svalbard, he would be my eye, spotting the Arctic equivalent of those arrowheads I strode past oblivious. In addition, I could count on him for another inestimable talent. A lifelong hunter (though he had stopped going after deer and elk in the last decade), Vaughn was handy with guns—the kind of guy you wanted standing next to you when a polar bear came lumbering toward you.

Vaughn, too, accepted my invitation without a moment's pause, even though the trip would cut into his fall guiding season. For him, however, Svalbard promised a challenge of a wholly different sort from those that I worried about. Vaughn had almost never traveled outside the U.S. He had never been to Europe. We arranged to meet in Paris, though I knew that big cities thoroughly flummoxed him. It was not by chance that he lived in a town with a population of three hundred.

By his own admission, Vaughn was incompetent in foreign languages. Even though his wife, Marcia, spoke good French, in Paris he would prove as helpless as the greenest city slicker he was accustomed to shepherding through Grand Gulch. That August, when Vaughn ventured out on his own from our Left Bank hotel to a nearby café for a beer, I thought seriously of pinning a note in French to his sleeve, like the missive a mother might attach to her absentminded child on his way to kindergarten.

I let Mats know about the enlargement of our party. He was all in favor of a team of four, as long as I told the Frenchman, Michel, that the price of inclusion was "some bottles of excellent konjak."

At the end of February, I got a packet in the mail from the Sysselmannen. I tore it open. "The Governor has no major comments to your plans for research on the island," I read. It took me several minutes to realize that, in some reticent Norse fashion, this deadpan formula meant that I had gained permission for my Svalbard adventure. There were several kinds of red tape, including the demand that I buy rescue insurance to the tune of 125,000 kroner of coverage (about $14,000—the insurance itself costing only some $550). But to my delight, the coast was clear. And speaking of coasts—sometime in the coming August, Mats, Michel, Vaughn, and I would pull our Zodiac onto a forlorn shore of Edgeøya and begin looking for the needle in the haystack that the Inkovs and Sharapov had hidden there 252 years ago.

Meanwhile, in Cambridge, I confronted the dolorous task of replacing Julia. Early on, she had introduced me to Hugh Olmsted, a Slavic specialist in Research Services at Widener Library, whose expertise she had made use of in the past.

As I sat in Olmsted's office cubicle and delivered a résumé of the sailors' extraordinary exploit, I saw his eyebrows rise almost imperceptibly. When I finished, the first thing he said was, "How do you know this is a true story?"

Convinced at last of the authenticity of the saga, Olmsted suggested a number of lines of inquiry that Julia and I tackled in the following weeks. Now, early in 2001, I went back to the librarian's cubicle to see if he could recommend someone to pinch-hit for Julia and accompany me to Russia. To my initial surprise, he named only a single candidate: his wife, Masha.

Masha, it turned out, had been born in St. Petersburg. She had years of library and archival research in Russia under her belt (as did Hugh himself). She was on the verge of quitting a tedious part-time job at Harvard, and so would have lots of free time and might welcome a new source of income. Best of all, Hugh and Masha were already planning to spend much of the summer in St. Petersburg.

The three of us had lunch at Casablanca. Masha turned out to be a plump, gentle-faced, soft-spoken woman of thirty-five. Her English, though not flawless, was so good I realized that she would make an ideal translator. By the time we were sipping our espresso, we had made a deal. I would pay Masha an hourly rate (upped by 20 percent when she and Hugh collaborated on a research problem) for all the work she accomplished between now and July. I would buy her plane ticket (though not Hugh's) to Russia, and pay for all travel and lodging the three of us undertook in that country.

Sixty-two years old, slightly balding, with a gray, well-trimmed beard and wire-rim glasses, Hugh looked like the quintessential librarian. Growing up in Minnesota, he had recognized early on that he had a gift for languages. He had become, indeed, that truly rare thing—a genuine polyglot. Now he could read and speak French, German, Dutch, Spanish, Italian, Norwegian, Swedish, and Russian fluently. In graduate school he had also learned Bulgarian and Serbo-Croatian. He had, furthermore, studied Chinese, Sanskrit, Greek, Latin, and Old Church Slavonic.

Hugh's spoken Russian was so perfect that other Russians assumed he was a native. As I soon witnessed, he could also do a hilarious imitation of a Russian trying to speak English.

Hugh and Masha had met on one of his research trips to St. Petersburg and fallen in love. They were married in 1995, each for the second time, and lived for a year in St. Petersburg before moving to Boston.

By the time we parted outside the Casablanca, I was feeling sanguine about my quest. The only trouble was that it was going to cost me a pretty penny. Mats had forwarded me a proposed budget for our Edgeøya jaunt. The total came to some $22,000, not including Vaughn's, Michel's, and my plane tickets. I winced at the sum, but as I went over the itemized costs line by line, I couldn't find much to quibble with. By now, I was committed to what would prove to be by several orders of magnitude the most expensive journey I had ever undertaken.

Masha and I made an appointment for about a week later, when she would hand me her first research results. On the morning of our meeting, however, Hugh called. Masha was in bed with pneumonia. The nasty bug lingered for weeks, leaving her confined to the house. It would be more than a month before Masha had recovered sufficiently to turn her attention to "my" sailors.

Meanwhile I puttered on in the library. Instead of pursuing a dubious quest for a primary source other than Le Roy, I focused on narratives of other visitors to Svalbard in the century after the Pomori's rescue in 1749. Russian hunters had avidly pursued walrus, fox, bear, and whale during that century, and had performed more overwinterings than the sailors of all other countries combined. Yet, just as Rudmose Brown had grumbled, accounts of those journeys could not be found in Russian annals. The clearest images of that century of Pomori toil lay reflected in the mirrors held up to it by German, Norwegian, and British passersby.

One such traveler was Barto von Löwenigh, the German dilettante who had talked his away aboard Keilhau's expedition in 1826–27. Hugh translated for me some juicy chunks of Löwenigh's commentary. Several times, as Keilhau's ship drifted along the southern coast of Edgeøya, the men spotted Russian ruins, usually fronted with promise crosses erected to pledge good works to God in exchange for the sailors' deliverance. At the sprawling ruin just north of Hvalpynten on the southwest corner of Edgeøya—Keilhau's "Russisk Etablissement," of which his own book included a woodcut—Löwenigh identified (as Keilhau did not) the dwelling with the inscription "This is an Old Believer hut," and the April 22, 1731, date on the nearby cross.

Next to that century-old building stood two recent "bath-houses," as Löwenigh described them:

> The structures are new, but so light I scarcely know if they'll survive this winter. The flat roofs consist of beams with a certain amount of earth thrown upon them, where even now perfectly fresh grass is growing. These Italian roofs are not suitable for Spitsbergen, and can satisfy only a hardened Russian.
>
> The Russians also have the habit of each time taking the windows back home with them. And so on all sides a mass of water comes pouring in, which freezes on the floors. At the moment ice a meter thick lies in the rooms.

Despite finding Russian ruins strewn with gear along the south coast of Edgeøya, as well as on some of the Tusenøyane (Thousand Islands), that summer Keilhau and Löwenigh encountered no Pomori in the field. The German, however, had had a long talk with the Russian consul in Hammerfest, Norway. On Svalbard, like a self-taught archaeologist, Löwenigh further deduced the character of these hardy sailors from the debris they left behind. By 1827, the Russians were not only setting fox traps on every other ridgeline or hummock, but had devised bear traps. "The polar bears," writes Löwenigh, "frequently thrust their delightful snouts in through the windows. The doors have apertures in them, through which one shoots the bears." (One wishes the chronicler had supplied a sketch of these contraptions.)

Löwenigh was full of admiration for these absent Pomori. "The Russians are the real masters of Spitsbergen," he opines. "Since the end of the seventeenth century the Dutch have let slip this northern outpost from their sight, and the Norwegians have been visiting it for only a few years." In his enthusiasm, the German, whose prose inclines to the romantic, rises to a pitch of empathic witness:

> The Russian [hunter] . . . is scarcely ever without success. His ships are so stoutly built that they defy the pounding from the ice, and a truly incredible self-sufficiency permits provisions to be scarcely taken into consideration. He is strengthened in this by his religious sentiment. As soon as he has erected his cross he believes himself to

> be in the special protection of the divinity, and scorns the raging ice sea. With similar adroitness he pursues his walrus- and dolphin-capture [?], his seal-taking, his fox- and polar-bear-hunt, and by the way gathers the priceless eiderdown without concerning himself as to whether he himself will ever rest in it.

Testimonies such as Löwenigh's make it clear that, though in one sense it was an isolated, anomalous event, the survival for more than six years of the men from Mezen was embedded in a long, rich tradition of skillful Russian overwintering on Svalbard. The German's generous encomium to the Pomori serves as a welcome antidote to such condescensions as Jeannette Mirsky's picture of "huge bearded men" with "thick, clumsy fingers," of "large cumbersome boats manned by Russian peasants who were ignorant of compass, clock, sounding-line, and the simplest kind of nautical observation."

Curiously, for all his interest in the Russians, Löwenigh never mentions the Mezen sailors on Edgeøya from 1743 to 1749. Keilhau, in contrast, gives a fairly long summary of their survival epic.

In the ghostly recesses of microfilm at Harvard, I came upon an old book that took quite a different tack on the Russian experience on Svalbard in the eighteenth century. In 1775, an Englishman named Daines Barrington published a treatise titled *The Possibility of Approaching the North Pole Asserted.* Barrington was not a traveler to Svalbard himself, but a kind of geographical theorist, one of the first to take a serious interest in the quest to reach 90° N. He agitated so persuasively before the Royal Society that the Crown sent two ships north in 1773. (A mate on board one of the vessels was the fourteen-year-old Horatio Nelson.) Theirs was the first full-fledged attempt ever to reach the North Pole, though Henry Hudson in 1607 had proposed to reach China by sailing straight across the Arctic Ocean. The ships reached 80° 36'N off the northwest coast of Svalbard—half a degree farther north than Barents had sailed in 1596—before ice forced them south again.

It was not Barrington's treatise itself that interested me so much as an appendix added to its 1818 edition, the one I found on microfilm. Here a Colonel Mark Beaufoy, also a member of the Royal Society, floated a wild scheme as an alternative to Barrington's plan to sail to the Pole. If ice perpetually blocked navigation north of the 80th parallel, why not take advantage of that fact? More specifically, as Beaufoy urged, why not travel to the North Pole in winter, setting out from Svalbard with sledges drawn by reindeer?

And who knew more about Svalbard than the doughty Pomori? Somehow, Beaufoy transmitted a series of detailed questions to certain authorities in Archangel'sk. These were translated into Russian, answered by the sailors themselves, and sent back to Beaufoy, who had the responses translated into English. The savant's "Queries Respecting the Probability of Reaching, from the Island of Spitsbergen, the North Pole, by Means of Rein-deer, during the Winter: and Answered by Persons who Wintered There" presents a fascinating and occasionally amusing Pomori Q&A, distilling much of the Russian wisdom vis-à-vis Svalbard at the beginning of the nineteenth century.

The Pomori sketched out for Beaufoy the course of their usual journeys to the archipelago. If it was to be a summer's hunt only, they sailed from Russia at the beginning of June and returned in September; if a deliberate overwintering, they left in July and came home the following August or September (thus benefiting from much of two summers' hunt as well as that of the winter).

How bad were the snowstorms, Beaufoy naively asked. "The storms of snow are very frequent, continuing for two, three, and four days, and sometimes for as many weeks," the anonymous veterans replied. Just as the Inkovs had told Le Roy, these sailors reported that it was not uncommon for winter drifts to cover a hut, so that the men had to enter and exit through a hole in the roof.

To ward off scurvy, the Pomori swore by vigorous exercise (just as Khrisanf Inkov counseled his mates), which they got mainly by shoveling snow off the roof and away from the walls of their huts. They also ate as much as they could of "a particular sallad or herb, which grows there on stones"—no doubt *Cochlearia,* the scurvy grass the Mezen men relied on.

Like the other Mezeners who had built the hut that became the castaways' refuge in 1743, the early-nineteenth-century Russian sailors brought with them boards and bricks to build a winter hut, constructed "in the same manner as the peasants' houses here [in Russia]." The huts were as large as twenty by twenty-five feet. (Unfortunately, the informants failed to indicate how tall their prefab dwellings loomed.) Food for the winter was "rye flour (of which they make bread), salt beef, salt cod, and salted halibut, butter, oat and barley meal, curdled milk, peas, honey, linseed oil." (As I read this list, I thought how much the Inkovs, Sharapov, and Verigin would have given for a stash of provisions like that!) The overwinterers did not depend solely on their Russian clothes to fight the cold, but routinely crafted ponchos and boots out of reindeer hide.

Besides water, their chief beverage was a weak beer made of rye. "Spiritous liquors are entirely excluded and forbidden by their employers," averred Beaufoy's informants, "as the Russians, when they had it, drank so immoderately that work was often neglected entirely."

One can imagine the Pomori in Arkhangel'sk rolling their eyes as they listened to the questions in which Beaufoy began to vaunt his preposterous scheme of sledging to the North Pole in winter. They themselves traveled "on snow skaits" (probably snowshoes) in winter, dragging small hand sledges behind them. "Horses or rein-deer would be of no use to them," insisted the veterans, "nor have they any." This was not the answer Beaufoy wanted to hear. "Does any danger arise either in crossing the land or the ice, from the drifting of the snow?" he queried. The Pomori scolded back: "They do not journey in winter, as beforementioned, except to islands at trifling distances."

In a further query, Beaufoy pops the question: "Does it appear possible to cross the ice in winter to the North Pole? If it does not, what are the obstacles?" The informants must have regarded the Englishman as a perfect fool, but they responded patiently, "The likelihood of a passage to the North Pole does not seem probable to the fishermen, as they have not had an opportunity to attempt it; and, from their observations, think all passage impossible, as the mountains of ice appear monstrously large and lofty. Some of the ice is continually drifting about; so that in many places water is discerned." (An excellent description of the Arctic pack, this.)

One must remember that Beaufoy had written out all his questions before hearing any of the Arkhangel'sk men's answers. In the next query, he bores on: "If the passage should be deemed practicable, in what manner should it be attempted?" To which, patient as ever: "As the fishermen think all passage impracticable, it is not in their power to give any answer to this demand." Now Beaufoy goes off the deep end, proposing the building of six-man huts to be conveyed on sledges and planted every two hundred, four hundred, or six hundred miles. The Pomori gently scotch his harebrained hopes. Finally Beaufoy asks for volunteers to accompany an English expedition to the Pole. The Russians politely decline. No doubt to them, the very object of the expedition seemed unfathomably abstract, compared to the amassing of a fortune in bear and fox skins or whale and walrus blubber.

Needless to say, no such attempt on the North Pole as Beaufoy envisioned was ever launched. The accidental by-product of Beaufoy's mad plan, however, was the questionnaire published in 1818, which gives as good an insight into Svalbard overwintering as any Russian document that has come to light. And the brunt of the Pomori's detailed answers is to make the reader recognize just what a rigorous and dangerous business that overwintering was.

In two critical senses, on the other hand, Beaufoy's questionnaire cannot touch the mystery of the Mezen men's survival from 1743 to 1749. None of the Pomori who answered the Englishman's queries ever spent more than a single winter in a row on Svalbard. And every one of them went there planning to overwinter, equipped with a prefabricated hut and provisions to last a year. None of them found himself, as the Inkovs, Sharapov, and Verigin did in May 1743, suddenly marooned with barely two days' gear and food and the clothes on their backs to confront the Arctic wilderness.

SO it went for me through the winter and spring of 2001. An English mariner named S. Bacstrom had made a whaling journey to Svalbard in 1780. Near the ruins of Smeerenburg, the once grand Blubber Town of the Dutch, Bacstrom's crew visited a hut occupied by Russians. "The common men," writes the mariner, "made a strange appearance; they looked very much like some Jews in Rag-fair or Rosemary-lane: they wore long beards, fur caps on their heads, brown sheep-skin [no doubt reindeer skin] jackets with the wool outside, boots, and long knives at their sides by way of hangers." Despite the Archangel'sk men's insistence that their employers forbade strong drink, Bacstrom's men were regaled with rye bread, reindeer tongues, and brandy. The Englishmen traded a keg of gunpowder and "half a dozen good table knives and forks" for six white fox skins and various cuts of venison. "We drank the Empress of Russia's and King George's health," relates Bacstrom.

The mariner gives a detailed description of the Russian hut. In many respects, it dovetails with Le Roy's account of the Mezeners' hut on Edgeøya, down to the huge brick stove and the small windows; the smoke from the stove could be directed into the back room, where it served to cure the hanging meat. Yet, says Bacstrom, the hut was built "so low that I touched the ceiling with my fur cap." At sixty feet by thirty-four, the spacious building had three times the floor area of the hut described to Le Roy by the Inkovs.

For twelve hours the visit continued. The men were able to converse through the Russian team's surgeon, who happened to be German, for Bacstrom spoke that man's language. The ship that had deposited the twenty-one Russians had left them in July to winter over: the next summer's vessel would pick up these "colonists" with their hunting spoils and drop off a new crew. The Russian captain, who had wintered over once before, made it sound like a piece of cake, claiming that even in December, thanks to the moon and the aurora borealis, "it seldom or never is so dark that you cannot see before you," and that winters in St. Petersburg were actually harsher than here in northwest Spitsbergen.

The men expected to reap a bountiful harvest of whales, bear and fox skins, eiderdown, and "unicorns' tusks, which is an ivory that never turns yellow" (apparently narwhal horns). The mates received no salary, and only a thousandth share each of the year's bounty (Russian sources indicate a more realistic share of one hundredth of the expedition's take); yet if a man thereby earned 50 or 60 rubles, he could live on that for a whole year in Arkhangel'sk.

The famous whaler and naturalist William Scoresby visited Svalbard several times in the early nineteenth century. Scoresby narrates the unsettling discovery in 1771 by an English captain named Whitby, who had landed at King's Bay (near the present town of Ny-Ålesund in northwest Spitsbergen) to gather driftwood. Just the previous year, Russians had built a hut here, which Whitby's men came in sight of.

> They hollowed as they approached it; but no one appeared. The door being defended by a small open court, one of the party opened

> it; and, applying his eye to the hole for the latch, observed a man extended on the floor, as he thought, sleeping. Receiving no answer to their shouts, they at length opened the door, and found the man a corpse. His cheek, which was laid on the ground, was covered with a green concretion of mould; and his covering, besides his clothes, was only a Russian mat.

Whitby's men found a scattering of clothes and jackets in the hut, but no other Russians, dead or alive. They concluded that the last survivor, the man they had found on the floor, had buried all his mates before succumbing, like them, to scurvy. On the beach, the Englishmen found the Russian ship, fully equipped with oars and sail, ready to launch a voyage home its crew would never make.

These narratives from the century after the Mezen men's rescue in 1749 helped me to flesh out the picture of the heroic, tragic—and, for the most part, unrecorded—history of the Pomori on Svalbard. But what remained entirely frustrating was that none of these later adventurers, except for Keilhau, bothered to speculate just where the six-year survival feat recorded by Le Roy had taken place.

This struck me as curious, for Le Roy's *Narrative* was so popular a work by the 1770s that it was translated not only into English and Russian, but also into Dutch, Italian, and Swedish. The story evidently had a certain mythic resonance at the time, for it inspired other authors to turn the Pomori's ordeal into a homiletic parable. J. H. Campe, for instance, was an immensely successful German children's writer of the day, whose simplified version of Defoe's *Robinson Crusoe* went through many editions. At Widener, I found Campe's 1825 *Polar Scenes* (translated from the German), which concludes with a long chapter called "Surprising Adventures of Four Russian Sailors at the Island of Spitsbergen."

Campe cribs shamelessly from Le Roy, without acknowledging his source. He invents a few details just for dramatic effect: thus, killing their first polar bear with their lances, the sailors "plunged the sharp part down his open mouth." But the German uses each pivotal turn in the men's fate to apostrophize his readers, like a kindly but exacting schoolmaster. At the juncture when the sailors have fired their last musket ball, Campe pauses:

> Reflect for a moment, my young readers, what you would have thought of to satisfy the wants of nature, and defend yourselves from the attacks of bears, had you been in the situation of these unfortunate people! I will give you three days to think of it, and this was all our islanders had, for their last shot was fired, and they were now eating of the last rein-deer.

Le Roy himself had constantly drawn morals from the Pomori's deeds, particularly in the trite, recurring formula, "necessity is the mother of invention." Campe squeezes more tendentious lessons from the tale. It is not enough to say that Aleksei Inkov sorely missed his wife and children. According to Campe, "Oh, how often were his eyes bathed in tears, when those of his companions were closed in sweet repose!" Yet Aleksei swallowed his grief to perform his share of the chores. The moral:

> You see, then, my young friends, that such feelings as can be easily repressed when occasion requires it, must be good feelings; such do not debilitate the soul, but rather exalt it. . . . But if we suffer ourselves to be subdued by any feeling, however good or noble, so as to be incapable of fulfilling our duty, or so as to fall into slothfulness and complainings, we may be good people, but we are not men; we are poor weak women in men's clothing.

How, then, had this extraordinary story become so obscure by the late twentieth century? For, as Masha Olmsted would tell me that spring, as she began enlisting colleagues in St. Petersburg to lay the groundwork for our summer search, none of them—even those who were professional historians of literature—had ever heard the slightest whisper of the old tale.

At last Masha had recovered from her pneumonia. Using the Harvard libraries, she and Hugh set to work on a number of research tasks. Masha faxed a nudge to the Arkhangel'sk Area Archive, to whom, through Julia, I had agreed to pay $70 just to start them looking for Klingstedt's notes. Once more, no answer. Meanwhile both she and

Hugh read all kinds of background material in Russian to place the Pomori's story in context. Of course, they were charging me by the hour for all this toil; and by May, when they had racked up more than $4,000 worth of work with hardly a tangible result, I was beginning to fear that my obsession, like an out-of-control gambling addiction, could end up bankrupting me.

Suddenly Masha had a breakthrough. Back in February, Julia had sent a fax to Viktor Derzhavin, the Moscow archaeologist who had written the popular article about "my" sailors for the magazine *Mir Severa,* with its tantalizing allusion to a recent expedition that had run out of field time just before zeroing in on the Pomori's lost hut. This fax had never been answered. But somehow Masha had found a phone number for Derzhavin, and now, in early April, she gave him a call.

The archaeologist unraveled the mystery. The fax had arrived at Derzhavin's institute nearly illegible, with its greeting amputated. Derzhavin had assumed the fax was meant not for him, but for his boss, one Vadim Starkov—apparently a very important man. Starkov had not bothered to take the smudged missive seriously.

It was this very same man, however—Vadim Starkov—who had led the expedition a few years ago that had hoped to find the Mezeners' hut. Derzhavin gave Masha his superior's phone number.

Director of the Arctic Department of the Institute of Archaeology of the Russian Academy of Sciences, and indeed his country's leading northern archaeologist, Starkov would come to haunt my quest like a sibyl out of Greek myth—half prophet, half witch. Now, as Masha spoke to him long-distance for the first time, the man expressed astonishment that an American should have discovered the obscure story of the eighteenth-century sailors, much less intended to track down its fugitive verities.

On the surface, he exuded friendly encouragement. But almost at once, he asked, in a way that seemed to Masha more a demand than a true query, that I put off my search on Edgeøya for a year, until the summer of 2002. Starkov would be extremely busy this summer, he said, with archaeological expeditions to Yakutsk, the Ob River, and west Spitsbergen. In 2002, we could search for the hut together.

When Masha told him that a year's postponement was out of the question, Starkov became more peremptory. "The only time this summer I can go with this man to show him where the hut is is from August 5 to 10," he said. "He will go with me to Svalbard then." Patiently, she explained that I had already contracted with a Norwegian guide for an expedition at the end of August.

"Which Norwegian?" Starkov snapped. "I know them all." But the name Mats Forsberg meant nothing to him.

Masha hesitated, then asked the obvious question. "Do you know where the hut is?"

There was a long pause over the line from Moscow. "I know approximately where it is," said Starkov, measuring his words. "But there are a big number of variables where it might be. The area is really too big to look in." Then the man repeated his exhortation that we prosecute the search together, between the 5th and 10th of August. Masha explained that the state of the sea ice dictated my sailing to Edgeøya at the end of August.

"Nonsense," answered Starkov. "We can rent a helicopter. I do it all the time."

Viktor Derzhavin would later confide in Masha that, in his opinion, the search for the Mezen men's hut had lingered on Starkov's back burner for years, until Derzhavin's article in *Mir Severa* rekindled the flame. Then, when this American appeared out of the blue, fully intending to hunt down the scene of the crime, Starkov saw treasure slipping through his fingers. The Inkovs, Sharapov, and Verigin were not "my" sailors—they were Starkov's.

All at once, Starkov started talking to Masha about Klingstedt's manuscript. "You know, this manuscript has never been published."

"Do you know where it is?" Masha asked, holding her breath.

"You know," Starkov repeated, "this manuscript has never been published." And, after Masha assented, he actually uttered the statement a third time—his sibylline incantation dangled over the void of my ignorance.

Finally, the great man relented. "You should look in the Archive of the Institute of History within the Academy of Sciences in St. Petersburg," he said.

Masha was nonplussed. For all the research she had conducted in her native city, she had never heard of this archive.

About the artifacts—the tools and weapons the Pomori had brought back from Edgeøya and presented as gifts to Count Shuvalov—Starkov was more discouraging. "These things are absolutely, totally lost," he said to Masha. "Many people really looked and didn't find them."

"Who?"

"Vize and Belov," answered Starkov. The latter scholar, in fact, had been Starkov's good friend.

"You won't find these things in Archangel'sk," he went on. "I know it for sure. They aren't there. They are also not in the Arctic Museum in St. Petersburg. And they are not in the Kunstkamera." Then, sibylline to the hilt, he added, "But if you want to look, of course start in Archangel'sk. If those things were brought to St. Petersburg, they should only be in the Kunstkamera."

"Did Belov find Klingstedt's manuscript?" Masha sagely asked.

"No. I don't know. Who knows? Maybe he did find it," answered Starkov. Then, after a pause: "As well as the Archive of the Institute of History, you should also look in the Military Naval Archive."

Masha hung up thoroughly confused. We had agreed, however, to meet Starkov in Moscow on July 31 and August 1, the only days he would be home between his expedition to Yakutsk and another expedition on the island of Spitsbergen proper. He would be running a conference in Barentsburg on Svalbard starting August 26. He demanded, through Masha, that I attend, but she told him that by August 26 I would be in the field myself. There was no changing the dates Mats Forsberg had lined up with the cruise ship that would carry us to Edgeøya.

Starkov's tip about Klingstedt's manuscript, however, was the solidest new lead I had clutched in some nine months of probing. It left me wild with anticipation. When Masha learned, however, that the Archive of the Institute of History would be closed while we were in St. Petersburg, she came up with a good plan. We would hire a colleague of hers to perform the search before we arrived. Aleksei Kasparov was a young Ph.D. in archaeology and paleontology, so he was already an expert at archival research in St. Petersburg. He didn't have much free time before setting off on an expedition of his own to the Crimea, but for only $75 he agreed to undertake our search and send Masha detailed reports by e-mail.

Kasparov's dispatches began to arrive in June. I had thought that the tangles of bureaucracy that had hamstrung my own research efforts the previous October were exacerbated by my being a foreigner who spoke no Russian. Kasparov's misadventures disabused me of this notion.

June 16, 2001. Began the search for the manuscript. Worked in our Archive [of the Institute for History]. Our girls told me that the document wasn't there and couldn't be: our holdings are exclusively in archaeology, and nothing older than the nineteenth century. They told me that something like that should be looked for with the greatest chances of success in the Naval Archive. . . .

I proceeded there. In order to get access to the registers, I had to obtain a letter of referral/recommendation from my institute, written in a standard form. I'll get this letter on Monday.

June 19. Today the girls in the office printed up the letter of referral for the Naval Archive, in accord with the model format I gave them. But since now is the time when all the expeditions are being sent out, the office is tied up completely with business trip authorizations, extracts from official orders, and the like. And so it was well into the evening by the time I obtained my document. Now I have to get it signed by the director. The latter, however, is on vacation, so I am obliged to chase down one of the assistant directors. In any case, I'll get the problem solved no later than Wednesday. . . . Tomorrow [Tuesday] in the institute is nonworking [*neprisutstvennyi*, "nonpresence"] day.

In a wonderful book that I was reading, called *Among the Russians*, in which Colin Thubron narrates months of travel around the country in his own car during the last years of the Soviet Union, he writes of Russians in general, "Bureaucracy has multiplied precisely because they are so bad at it." I would take this mordant judgment as an epigraph for my quest.

June 23. Concerning the search for our incunabulum. Today I was in the Naval Archive. This was the first time in my life that I had worked there, and I was absolutely flabbergasted by the enormous extent of the materials. . . . I discovered the documents in the archive are, not surprisingly, systematized and accessible through military features. Name lists of officers, registers of ships, and such like. The only way our document could have wound up here would have been by chance, since it doesn't have the slightest hint of anything military about it. It has to be hunted for by what they call the "dry search" method, looking through folder after folder, document by document. I got somewhat discouraged, and let drop something to the effect that this wasn't the sort of task that you could expect to finish in a day. The archivist lady laughed and told me that people work in the archives for years, working their way through mountains of documents one at a time.

I dragged my bones to the systematic catalogue and told the guy on duty about my woes. The guy undertook to help me. The first thing he asked me was the name of the ship [on which the four Pomori had sailed from Archangel'sk in 1743]. That I didn't know. When he found out that we didn't have the ship's name, he got visibly upset.

Was there any chance, Kasparov asked Masha, that we could retrieve the ship's name, or the name of its captain? Alas, Le Roy had not seen fit to record those details.

June 23. With the State Historical Archive on the English Embankment the following story unfolded. I called the director's secretary and found out that nobody had been admitted there for some time, and that if some document were needed a request would have to be filled out and the professionals would find it themselves. But you have to pay money. The rates run from 600 to 1,200 rubles [$22 to $44], except you only have to pay if the document is actually found.

Finally, on June 28, in the Archive of the Academy of Sciences, Kasparov found some letters written by Klingstedt. The handwriting was extremely poor, the sentences almost illegible. So far as Kasparov could discern, the letters had to do with meteorological observations. Back in the Naval Archive, our tireless agent found "ten fat volumes called 'Descriptions of the Documents of the Archive of the Ministry of the

Navy.'" In these, Le Roy was not mentioned once, but Klingstedt a number of times. All the entries, however, had to do with Klingstedt's salary, promotions, awards, and the like.

Back at the State Historical Archive on the English Embankment, Kasparov showed up with money in hand to request a search.

> My order WAS NOT ACCEPTED! A polite consultant lady emerged to meet me, attentively studied my request, in which I set forth the entire polar odyssey on two pages, and told me that they didn't have anything of the sort and couldn't have. . . . She advised me to look in the Russian State Archive of Ancient Acts. The latter is, however, in Moscow, and inquiries must be addressed there by mail.

On his last day of searching, in yet another archive, the dogged Kasparov made his way through yet another catalogue of holdings. "Of all the figuring personages who make their way through our story," he wrote Masha, "the only one mentioned is Count Shuvalov. The word 'Spitsbergen' isn't even found in the index!"

Then at the Archive of the Academy of Sciences, Kasparov made a second attempt to read Klingstedt's letters, only to discover that "they are written by hand in cursive, and either in Latin or in Swedish! And so I looked at these letters with the same sort of vacant stare as the ram in the Russian proverb who is confronted by a new gate." In vain, Kasparov skimmed these indecipherable missives, searching for a word that looked like "Spitsbergen."

So, in the last analysis, our young scholar had discovered absolutely nothing. Surely no researcher, however, had ever more richly earned his $75 for trying.

I began to wonder about Vadim Starkov. Was the man sincerely convinced he knew where Klingstedt's manuscript was? Or had he flung out his prophecy simply to lead us down the wrong path?

Summer was upon us. I had no time left for further dithering among the research facilities of Cambridge. Whatever else I might learn about my fugitive Pomori would come on the ground in Russia and Svalbard. Despite all the setbacks and frustrations, despite the "dry search" that had stretched across my last nine months of obsessing about the old story, I was full of high hopes about what I might find in St. Petersburg,

Archangel'sk, Mezen, and Edgeøya. Hugh and Masha would head off to Russia in mid-July. I would follow a week later.

On the day of their departure, I was surprised to get a phone call from Masha. Her voice sounded both alarmed and sheepish. There was a din in the background.

"Where are you?" I asked.

"At the airport," she answered.

"What's the matter?"

"I've had an accident."

6: Take Me to Vadim

The day before flying to St. Petersburg, Masha had fallen on a swimming pool deck at her home and severely sprained her knee. Now it was swollen to half again its normal size, and she could barely put any weight on that leg.

She and Hugh came very close to calling off their trip altogether. And if they had, then I might as well have called off my year-long pursuit of the Pomori's lost story. It had taken them—trained scholars already familiar with Russian archives—five months just to get up to speed on the fugitive tale so that we might know where and how to begin looking for new material. In St. Petersburg, there would have been no way I could have found a bilingual aide and proceeded with my quest.

In the end, it was Masha's loyalty that compelled her to disobey her doctor's orders and undertake the grueling flight to Russia with her injured leg. As it was, she would be on crutches for almost two weeks, and just getting around St. Petersburg would prove an ordeal.

As for myself, I was beginning to wonder whether the whole project was jinxed. In the wake of Le Roy's confusions and lacunae, the bottomless bureaucratic abyss of Russian archives, Kasparov's game but futile stabs, Starkov's red herrings, Masha's pneumonia, and now her sprained knee, my "research" was beginning to resemble a wild-goose chase rather than the orderly scholarly inquiry I had hoped to generate.

On my first evening in St. Petersburg, Hugh and I sat at an outdoor café on Nevskiy Prospekt and people-watched. The previous October, it had been chilly here, with a raw drizzle oozing out of leaden skies. Now, toward the end of July, the famous White Nights were upon us. It was warm enough for shorts and T-shirt, and it didn't get semidark until close to midnight (at 60° N, St. Petersburg lies at roughly the same latitude as Anchorage). The beautiful women on the sidewalks were fetchingly underdressed, and the beer was cold.

The next morning we went to the Arctic and Antarctic Museum to drop in on my "old friends," Victor Boyarsky and Masha Gavrilo. Victor was in his usual ebullient mood, and despite making last-minute plans for a trip with clients to the North Pole (wearing his second hat as director of his own polar tour company), he laid aside his work to set up interviews and visits for me. Masha Olmsted told me later that, on reaching each colleague by telephone, Victor invariably opened, "Famous explorer Boyarsky here! Tomorrow I am going to the North Pole, but today I have a favor to ask of you. . . ." With a simple phone call, Victor accomplished what months of faxing from the U.S. had failed to do.

Later we had dinner with Masha Gavrilo at a quirky vegetarian restaurant called the Idiot Café, a theme eatery based on Dostoyevsky, who—so the menu claimed—had once opened a restaurant, which had quickly failed, on this very spot. In these congenial surroundings, Gavrilo, an expert on Arctic birds, delivered a fascinating soliloquy on the Pomori's survival tactics. "Why do they not catch birds?" she wondered out loud. Nowhere does Le Roy mention a single bird or egg as part of the sailors' fare. "Eider ducks prefer small islands, to avoid fox. If there is ice between island and mainland, so the fox can go across, ducks will skip breeding."

The sailors had, however, according to Le Roy, used bird feathers to fletch their arrows. "If you have feathers," Masha commented, "not necessarily do you find eggs. Feathers can blow on wind. On Edgeøya, with heavy ice, is much lower numbers of birds. But if you have cliffs, you should have eggs. Maybe it is more efficient to hunt reindeer than to look for single birds."

What kind of birds' feathers might the sailors have used for their arrows, I wondered. "Feathers come from molting birds," Masha answered. "Eiders molt at sea, so feathers wash up on shore. Also barnacle geese. Goose feathers make best arrows. Glaucous gulls, second. Is ducks also okay." For one of the first times in Russia, I thought, I've actually learned something.

We began making the rounds of libraries and archives. Victor Boyarsky had suggested we look in the Ethnographic Museum. A phone call ascertained that all its savants were out in the field on various expeditions. We decided to show up anyway, on the chance that someone might admit us. But when we got there, a sign on the door announced, in English, "The museum exposition is close with the technical reason. We serve only the ordered groups."

On the other hand, at the Russian Geographical Society, a friend of Victor's, one Maria Fedorovna, received us. Masha gave her a small jar of Vermont maple syrup, the kind of present that, I learned, often greased the bureaucratic wheels in Russia. The woman spoke no English, so Hugh explained the story of the Mezen sailors (which she had never heard before) and patiently translated her comments for me.

Maria Fedorovna mentioned that the Geographical Society was planning an exhibition for 2005 on relations between Russia and Norway. I nodded and smiled, as if I thought this was a good idea. She named a friend who worked in the Kunstkamera, an expert on the Pomori, who, unfortunately, was in Norway at the moment. She dug out a letter written by Count Shuvalov. She showed us old programs from past Geographical Society exhibitions. She consulted an address book in which she found the 1981 phone number for M. I. Belov, the scholar who had most assiduously studied the sailors' tale. (When we tried to phone, in hopes of locating Belov's widow, we found that the number was disconnected.)

It took me a while to realize that Maria Fedorovna was essentially acting out a polite charade. Because she was a friend of Victor's, she felt obligated to try to help these friends from America, but she had no clue where any materials might lie that could genuinely advance our search. Yet at the end of our meeting, she produced a manuscript that at least had a certain curiosity value. It was an 1801 census of Mezen. The total population of our sailors' hometown was then 1,601. These souls were broken down into some odd categories. There were 58 merchants with 48 wives. One thousand three hundred and twelve of the 1,601 residents were officially "middle class." There were 11 clergy. Mezen had zero peasants, zero noblemen, and zero foreigners, but, strangely enough, 66 criminals, of whom 4 were women. Maria Fedorovna ventured the guess that these ne'er-do-wells had been exiled to Mezen for misdeeds performed elsewhere.

These faceless statistics, I realized, no doubt included some of the descendants of Aleksei and Khrisanf Inkov and Stepan Sharapov. But they did not, by themselves, give me much of a feel for the town.

When they had moved to the States in 1997, Hugh and Masha had retained ownership of their small apartment on Prospekt Stachek, on the southwest side of St. Petersburg. In their absence, they lent it out to friends and colleagues, and the apartment served as a kind of office for a book-acquiring business that they ran. To save me money, they offered me a guest bedroom in the apartment as an alternative to a hotel. Though far from my favorite haunts on Nevskiy Prospekt, the homey apartment, cluttered with books like a grad student's garret, made a comfortable lair. The cramped kitchen was the center of the apartment's social life, for friends dropped in at all hours and coffee was nearly always percolating.

The first evening, when Hugh and I had headed home around midnight, instead of taking the subway, Hugh simply stuck out his first two fingers as he stood by the curb. A private car promptly stopped. Hugh negotiated a fee of 70 rubles (about $2.70) to take us on the fifteen-minute ride to the Olmsteds' apartment.

Somehow, the previous October I had failed to notice that this system of private vehicles spontaneously serving as taxis was in full sway across St. Petersburg (and, Hugh explained, in most other Russian cities of any size). Apparently, the drivers trusted the passengers and vice versa, even at midnight on Saturday.

"It's a great system," Hugh said to me in the car. "Everybody wins."

"Wow," I said. "Last fall I was paying cabbies $20 to take me half as far."

Hugh chuckled. "Yes, but it's maybe not to be attempted by the monolingual American."

That, of course, was the gauntlet I needed. In the late-July heat wave, St. Petersburg was teeming with revelers, and I was not willing to cut short my nightlife just because the subway stopped running at midnight. I studied my phrase book, then took the plunge late one evening. I stuck out my fingers; a car stopped. "Prospekt Stachek," I pronounced, "*sorak adeen*" (number 41). When the driver hesitated, I said, "*Sto rublay?*" (A hundred rubles.) That usually did the trick. It was de rigueur to sit in the passenger seat, not in the back. As we trundled along in late-night silence, I would ask, "*Vui gavareetye pa angleeskee?*" ("Do you speak English?") The answer was usually, "*Nyet*," followed by a fluent soliloquy in Russian. I found "*Ya nye paneemayoo*" ("I don't understand") a useful formula. As the car drew near Hugh and Masha's apartment, I would waggle a finger, indicating "*zdyes*" ("here"). And then, always, a friendly "*Spasibo*" ("Thank you") and "*Da sveedanya*" ("Good-bye") on parting.

Walking the St. Petersburg streets, as I sounded out the Cyrillic of billboards and street names, I was way ahead of my last October's fumbling phonics. I had a moment of illumination in the subway when I recognized, in a poster affixed to the wall of the train, "*krasniya pobeda*"—"glorious victory." A beaming woman stared back at me from the poster. With my dictionary, I rendered the rest of the words. It turned out I was looking at a shampoo ad. The glorious victory was over dandruff.

Bad though my accent was, the drivers seemed to comprehend what I was saying. No matter what the hour, I never got a ride that made me nervous. Hugh was grudgingly impressed at my pluck, though as a congenital penny-pincher, he insisted that 100 rubles ($3.30) was way too much for a ride across St. Petersburg.

The whole question of whether a certain practice in a foreign country is hazardous or not—like accepting a ride from a stranger at 2:00 A.M.—is a deep and unanswerable one. On the whole, I tend to be cavalier in other lands. Hugh and Masha inclined toward the cautious, and seemed to think my late-night escapades were a bit foolhardy.

Back on the scholarly hunt, we finally ascertained the whereabouts of Belov's widow. She was, unfortunately, at her dacha in the country, unreachable by telephone. High summer, it turned out, was the favorite time for city dwellers to retreat to their dachas.

We did, however, win an audience with one Elena Soboleva at the

Kunstkamera, the venerable museum that, as many people had told us, would have been the only extant institution in 1750 that might have received the Pomori's "artifacts." An imperious woman in her fifties, Soboleva seated us at a big desk and proceeded to rattle off a long and tedious history of the museum, half in English, half in Russian. Gradually I realized that the recitation of nineteenth-century reorganizations of various collections was a kind of smoke screen, to cover the unlikelihood of finding any particular object from the eighteenth century.

"We have research departments by regional areas," Soboleva droned on in Russian. "We don't have good indexing of sources. The new departments lost track of what came from where. We have Shuvalov holdings in several regional areas. Perhaps you should look in the Russian Geographical Society."

"We did, just the other day," said Masha, suppressing a sigh.

Impatient, I turned to Hugh and began to itemize the Mezen men's gifts to Shuvalov—the lances, the lamp, the bone box, the bow and arrows, and so on. I expected him to render my list in Russian, but Soboleva interrupted me in English. "Our museum comprises two million objects!" she exclaimed.

I took in her purport. "Are you saying it's hopeless?"

"Of course!" But unwilling to end on that dismal note, she nattered on in English, "Everything is in storage. By region. Southern storage, they say they have nothing. Slavic is closed already. To get anything, you must have a special permission. A letter, maybe, from Museum of Arctic and Antarctic."

We staggered out of the Kunstkamera to nurse our wounds with beers at a sidewalk café. The weather was holding glorious. Students from the nearby University of St. Petersburg strolled by, it seemed to me, without a care in the world.

Later, we perused a printed catalogue of the Kunstkamera holdings. The scattershot listings underscored Soboleva's "hopeless" verdict:

> *European Department*: Hunting accessories: belts, powder kegs, powder measures, bags for buckshot, flint and steel, skis, birchbark covering for hunters' shelters. Russians: Archangel'sk region: call nos. 1063-607, 609; 1101-118-119; 6723-264-265a.

I was grateful to Hugh and Masha for their hospitality. Unfortunately, with it came a kind of parental fussiness, especially on Hugh's part, even though he was only a few years older than I. When I sneaked into the apartment after midnight, turning my key as quietly as possible in the lock, I was plunged back into some adolescent drama in which Mom and Dad agonized over my illicit prowlings.

"Everything go all right last night?" Hugh would ask at breakfast.

"Fine," I answered, like a sullen teenager.

This weird tension reached a peak over my day with Polina Viira. A pretty, twenty-five-year-old redhead of Estonian extraction, Polina and I met in a cybercafé on the Griboedov Canal. Hearing me speak English to the proprietor, she asked me (in English) what I was doing in St. Petersburg. It turned out Polina made her living as a tour guide for foreigners; she also lined up potential Russian brides for Germans, Brits, and Americans. Her English was good, though not fluent. I asked if she could guide me on a day's excursion to Novgorod.

When I announced my plan to Hugh and Masha, they were horrified. I didn't understand how dangerous Russia could be, they said. Sometimes thugs pretending to be guides took foreigners out in the country, robbed them, murdered them, and dumped their bodies in the forest. I could not imagine the sweet-faced Polina as a murderer, so I brushed off their qualms.

In the end, against my wishes, Hugh and Masha insisted on showing up at the café where I was to meet Polina the next morning, so they could check her out. It was Sunday, and my godparents were willing to skip church to ensure my safety.

The meeting was awkward in the extreme. We all pretended just to be grabbing a morning coffee and pastry together, but Polina knew, she later told me, exactly why Hugh and Masha were there. In Russian, Hugh grilled Polina, rather cruelly, I thought, on the history of Novgorod. Finally he silently nodded his approval to me.

It was a three-hour drive south to Novgorod. A lawyer friend of Polina's, who spoke no English, did the driving. When we stopped at a gas station to use the bathroom, I briefly conjured up a scenario in which this gentle pair might rob me and leave me, if not dead in the forest, at least penniless and monolingual on the roadside. I patted my hip pocket to reassure myself that my billfold was where it should be.

Of course nothing happened, except that I enjoyed my happiest day yet in Russia. Novgorod, which means "New Town," is often, in fact, called the oldest city in Russia, having supposedly been founded in A.D. 862. Despite having been attacked and ravaged many times over the centuries—most recently by the Nazis in World War II, not because the place had any strategic significance, but simply to rub salt in the Russians' sense of their heritage—the walled town on a small hill beside the Volkhov River shelters a stunning collection of old churches and monuments, ramshackle but evocative of the Middle Ages.

Novgorod was important to me because it was the town from which virtually all the Pomori had migrated north across trackless wilderness toward the Arctic Ocean, beginning in the thirteenth century. In particular, the Inkov clan had come from here: the name had once been almost as common in Novgorod as Smith or Jones in the United States. During our four hours of strolling through the fortified town, I gained a vivid medieval impression of the place as the last stronghold of civilization, with the unknown north beckoning just beyond the city wall. I saw the Inkovs and their like as the Russian equivalents of our Daniel Boones and Kit Carsons, pushing the timid American frontier to explore the Great West that stretched limitless beyond their stockades.

But it was also a relief to escape, if only for a day, the vague atmosphere of parental disapproval that seemed to waft about the Olmsteds' apartment. For the first time, perhaps, as Polina and I sipped Moldavian wine over lunch in a former women's prison converted to an upscale restaurant, I began to unwind, and thus to realize just how much stress this wild-goose chase had loaded onto my shoulders.

My reaction to the Olmsted ménage was, of course, uncalled for. During these days together in St. Petersburg, Hugh and Masha were laying completely aside their own work in the book-acquiring business. My search had gotten under their skin as well.

Hugh, in particular, was finding new angles in Russian sources by which to cross-examine Le Roy's narrative. Some of these had to do with the aftermath of the three survivors' return to Russia, a subject on which Le Roy himself was deplorably succinct. Yet the few scraps the academician dropped were juicy ones.

Once back in Russia, Le Roy wrote, the Inkovs and Sharapov "were strong and healthy; but having lived so long without bread, they could not reconcile themselves to the use of it, and complained that it filled them with wind. Nor could they bear any spiritous liquors, and therefore drank nothing but water."

One of the finest anecdotes in Le Roy illustrates the skepticism with which his colleagues at the Academy of Sciences initially greeted the Pomori's tale. Having received the gifts the sailors proferred to Count Shuvalov, Le Roy passed these objects around among his confrères, to elicit their professional opinions.

> One day, when I showed the bone needle-case above-mentioned to some of those gentlemen, and told them the sailors had, according to their account, made it with their knife, they answered me that it could not be; that it was impossible they could have given it so regular a form with a knife, that the box had undoubtedly been turned in a lathe, and that the men had deceived me in pretending it to be their work. . . . I defended them, and during our dispute Mr. HOMANN, a very skilful ivory-turner, casually entered the room. We presently agreed to abide by his decision; and turning to him, I gave to the question a quite different turn, that Mr. HOMANN might not be thought to have decided in my favour only out of civility. "Be so kind," said I, "to determine a small difference between these gentlemen and me: I say that this box is turned, and they maintain the contrary." Mr. HOMANN, having carefully examined it, answered, "The Gentlemen are in the right; this box was never made by a turner; it is a bone which has been scraped to this form."

In a quirky book by one M. Stavnitser, called *Russians in Spitsbergen*, I found brief though important further proof of the veracity of the sailors' tale. It was a summary of the account of the rescue by the captain who had picked up the three refugees on Edgeøya, offered as testimony some years later before a government commission. According to the captain, the men on the ship saw a column of smoke. Next to the bonfire stood a long pole with a deer skin hanging from it, and the crew saw three figures running along the shore. These details jibe with Le Roy's account from the Mezen men's point of view, though Le Roy has them waving the reindeer skin flag, not simply displaying it atop a pole.

The name of the captain of the rescue ship was even known. He was Amos Kornilov, and he was an Old Believer. In a copious miscellany called *Lomonosov and the Arctic,* by V. A. Perevalov, Hugh found further details about Kornilov, who turned out to be a close friend of the great poet and scientist. In 1764, Kornilov was one of a number of veteran Arctic captains summoned to St. Petersburg to testify before the marine commission about the nature of Svalbard and Novaya Zemlya. By then he was an old man, with ten Spitsbergen voyages under his belt; he had overwintered there twice.

Some of Kornilov's remarks about those journeys glance surprisingly off the Mezen men's experience from 1743 to 1749. According to the Old Believer, birds—"wild geese, seagulls resembling ducks, and others"—formed a substantial part of his parties' winter diet on Svalbard. The sun disappeared for good on October 10 (Old Style), and first stayed all day above the horizon around March 30. (These dates are quite at odds with the corresponding dates reported by Le Roy, namely October 26 and May 2. Of course, we do not know at what latitude Kornilov overwintered.) From November 4 through January 15 (Old Style), there was, according to the captain, "only darkness."

Kornilov's testimony also suggests a reason that, despite all the Russian voyages to Svalbard in the first half of the eighteenth century, the Mezen men had to wait six years to see a passing ship. In five different years scattered across the two and a half decades after 1720, Kornilov reported, the pack ice dealt terrible blows to the hunters' boats.

> In every one of those years, some seven to eight ships perished, from which less than a tenth of the people survived. Among these, some saved their lives by making their way to Norway in small boats; and four people [i.e., the Inkovs, Sharapov, and Verigin] lived six years on Spitsbergen without bread and without clothes, satisfying themselves with only reindeer meat; and they wore clothing of reindeer skins.
>
> And during those six years nobody managed to make it to Spitsbergen to hunt on account of the danger of the ice.

The mass summoning of Arctic veterans to the capital in 1764 was to lay the groundwork for a new attempt—the first by Russians—to discover the Northeast Passage. The scheme, like that of Barents in 1596, was to use Svalbard as a gateway to the hypothesized open sea beyond. As a result, in 1765 and again in 1766, Captain V. I. Chichagov carried his country's hopes on the most ambitious Russian voyages of exploration since Vitus Bering's in 1741. Both expeditions were utter failures, as Chichagov wandered helplessly among the shifting floes off the northwest coast of Svalbard. He was lucky not to get frozen in.

This new Arctic thrust was the brainchild of Catherine the Great, who had taken the throne in 1762. According to an 1821 historian, the tsarina was inspired by the story of the Mezen sailors:

> The most wise Catherine, who had occupied herself with study during her entire eighteen years of residence in Russia [before ascending to the throne], took a desire to glorify Her name with geographic discoveries. By chance there came to this Great Sovereign's attention a modest book under the title "Adventures of Four Sailors on the Island Spitsbergen." Their grim existence on that sterile land touched the sensitive heart of the Monarch.

From that inspiration sprang the Chichagov expeditions.

Browsing through this source, Hugh made an even more striking discovery. Among the captains summoned to St. Petersburg in 1764 was Khrisanf Inkov! If he was thirty years old at the time of his 1749 rescue, as Le Roy says, Khrisanf would now have been forty-five. The historian had evidently recorded his name without the slightest inkling that he was one and the same man with Le Roy's castaway "Iwan Himkof."

Hugh also carefully translated the whole of Belov's preface to the 1975 Russian edition of Le Roy. It was Belov who had discovered the true names of the sailors in a census record from 1762. There he had also learned more about the sailors' lives before and after their ordeal. Aleksei Inkov had been born in the year 1700 (this dovetails closely with Le Roy's report that the pilot was fifty years old when he interviewed him in January 1750). "The above-described Aleksei has a wife,

Marfa, 34 years old," writes Belov. This statement is quite confusing. Was Marfa thirty-four years old when Aleksei married her, before his 1743 shipwreck? Or was Marfa a second wife, thirty-four years old in 1762?

Further complicating the business is the census's list of five children by Marfa and Aleksei: two sons, aged four and two weeks, and three daughters, ages twenty, nineteen, and three. Le Roy, one recalls, claimed that Aleksei dearly missed his wife and three children while on Edgeøya. If the ages given by the census are correct, and refer to the year 1762, only the two oldest daughters could have been born before Aleksei was stranded on Svalbard.

Khrisanf Inkov, the 1762 census claims, was now forty-one years old (again, a rough corroboration of Le Roy's recording his age as thirty in 1750). He had a thirty-two-year-old wife, also named Marfa, and twin six-year-old boys. There is no contradiction here: Khrisanf evidently started his family sometime after returning to Mezen in 1749. On account of his ordeal, the records further note, he had been "released from sea-hunting by order of the magistrate until December 1, 1762."

Thanks to these records, we know not only the names of the Inkovs' wives and children, but of their fathers. "Aleksei and Khrisanf stemmed from a native line of Mezeners," writes Belov. "It is known that representatives of the Inkov family had more than once traveled to Spitsbergen and Novaya Zemlya." Indeed, "Aleksei and Khrisanf's great-grandfather" had gone to Novaya Zemlya in 1673 "and traded in walrus tallow in Arkhangel'sk."

Belov also found mention of Sharapov in the 1762 census, which identified his father's name, as well as the date of his death—1757. Two censuses conducted before the shipwreck, those of 1710 and 1722, gave Belov a few more details. In the latter record, Sharapov was said to be twenty-six years old. Sharapov was thus some four years older than his superior, the pilot Aleksei Inkov; at the time of his stranding on Edgeøya, the sailor would have been forty-seven, and he died at the age of sixty-one. In the 1710 census, Belov located Verigin's family, and deduced that Fedor must have been forty-six or forty-seven years old—also older than Aleksei—at the time of the shipwreck.

The picture Belov's dry statistics flesh out, then, is a somewhat surprising one. Among the four Pomori who performed one of the greatest survival feats in history, only one—Khrisanf Inkov, twenty-two at the time of his stranding—was a man in the prime of life. The other three, at ages forty-seven, forty-six or forty-seven, and forty-four, were already long in tooth; in terms of the life expectancy of the day, they were almost old men.

The 1762 census revealed a further benchmark of the Pomori's extraordinary survival feat. It was the fact that in the last previous census, taken in 1748 (which document Belov was unable to find), all four men were officially listed as having perished. That they could still be alive, five years after not having returned from their voyage to Svalbard, exceeded the credulity of even the toughest of Mezen observers.

The single most poignant detail about the subsequent lives of the three surviving sailors was the collaborative fruit of the research of Belov and several other scholars. It is the fact that Khrisanf subsequently perished of scurvy, with his two sons, trying to overwinter on Novaya Zemlya.

I found that revelation almost overwhelming. Why would anyone want to go back to the Arctic after having spent six almost hopeless years on Edgeøya, I wondered, much less deliberately overwinter again? (Yet history is full of sailors, soldiers, and explorers returning to the wildernesses that came close to killing them.) And what went wrong on Novaya Zemlya? How could a man who had had the pluck to survive six winters in Svalbard, with only two days' food and gear at the outset, not have the savvy to get through a single winter when, presumably, he was equipped with supplies calculated to last a year?

Belov also discovered the closest thing to a second primary source for the Mezeners' tale that any scholar had yet come across, one completely independent of Le Roy's account. In 1796, an engineer and economist named Fedor Kiselev had compiled a comprehensive *Atlas of the Arkhangel'sk Province,* with a particularly rich description of the fishing and trapping industry of the Pomori. Belov found this by now rare document in the Senate of the Central Historical Archive in St. Petersburg (yet another repository no one had bothered to mention to us). In Kiselev's atlas, Belov found two paragraphs that summarized the shipwrecked sailors' story, as it had been related to Kiselev by a hunter from Mezen.

What piqued my fancy, in this "Oral Testimony of a Hunter from Mezen," despite the brevity of the account, was not only its discrepancies with Le Roy, but the fact that it apparently represented the word-of-mouth tradition handed down over four and a half decades on the streets of Mezen, rather than a learned academician's one-time interview with the sailors.

Strangely enough, the names of the sailors given by Kiselev's informant are completely different from those recorded either by Le Roy or in the census records. The three survivors are given single names only: Kryska, Turpanov, and Kabanov. The key to the passage is that the hunter explicitly calls these appellations "nicknames." As Belov points out, it was common among "simple folk in old times" to have nicknames that bore little resemblance to their Christian names. Later, in Mezen, I would learn just how complicated the local practice of multiple nicknaming still is today.

Kryska, moreover, is clearly Khrisanf Inkov, for the hunter corroborates the sad denouement unearthed separately by several twentieth-century scholars: "After their return from St. Petersburg, they returned numerous times to Grumant and Novaya Zemlya, where about eighteen years ago Kryska, having traveled there with two of his sons, perished with all the hunters dispatched with him by the merchant Andrei Dudin, most probably from scurvy." Eighteen years prior to Kiselev's recording this story would give 1778 as the date of the tragedy. By then, Khrisanf would have been fifty-seven years old, his sons twenty-two. How much more heartbreaking, I thought, that the sons died with their father on what one surmises was their first expedition to the Arctic.

The hunter's testimony furnishes insight into the survivors' later lives that we find nowhere else. All three men, if the oral tradition can be trusted, went back to both Novaya Zemlya and Svalbard (Grumant) "numerous times."

According to the Mezen hunter's version, the doomed ship in 1743 was only one of a flotilla of eight, all driven before a gale and caught fast in the pack ice. The four sailors who volunteered to go on land did so to hunt reindeer and stock up on meat, not to look for an old hut. By the time they got back to the shore, all eight ships had vanished, never to be seen again. In this telling, the survivors made their bowstring from reindeer tendons. There is no mention of killing polar bears. Their arrowheads were made not of nails, but of sharpened bone. Le Roy's conceit that Khrisanf Inkov was so lithe he could outrun a horse is here made general: as Kiselev writes, "Their scanty diet, need for nourishment, and habit of ceaselessly working and moving about eventually made them so light that they were able to overtake reindeer at full speed, without the aid of skis, and stab them with their knives." No mention of a fat and lazy Verigin, though the hunter claims that the rescue vessel carried the body of the single sailor who had died back to Russia.

What to make of this all too brief alternative version of the story? A précis passed down by word-of-mouth over forty-seven years struck me, on the face of it, as less reliable than the firsthand interview of Le Roy, no matter how much the academician got wrong. On the other hand, several details in Kiselev's version seemed plausible. I myself had wondered why reindeer tendons should not serve just as well as polar bear for the making of a bowstring. Bone arrow tips sounded easier to fabricate than flattened nailheads, and promised to work better (hundreds of "primitive" cultures the world over have independently invented the bone arrowhead). And why, with the rescue ship at hand, would the Inkovs and Sharapov not have dug up the body of their lamented comrade, so they could take Verigin's remains back to the motherland for a proper burial?

Yet there seemed no way to choose between the conflicting versions, no further test of either's veracity. I came away from Kiselev's phantom oral testimony more perplexed than ever, with a heightened appreciation of the damnable ambiguity of truth.

The brunt of all these ancillary findings, however, was to give me a deep new respect for the Pomori. The castaways whose traces I sought were veterans embedded in a long tradition, stretching back into the seventeenth century and probably long before that, of sailors probing the Arctic in small boats. Theirs was a profoundly dangerous trade: on any given voyage, there was a substantial risk of perishing. And yet men like the Inkovs and Sharapov took all this for granted, so much so that after an ordeal unmatched before or since in the northern latitudes, they willingly went back to the Arctic again and again. It was what a Pomor hunter-sailor did.

• • •

Our days in St. Petersburg were dwindling: on August 6, we would fly to Archangel'sk. Before that, moreover, we planned to take the train to Moscow to pay obeisance to the soothsayer Vadim Starkov and, if we were lucky, to learn from him something concrete about where to look for the Mezeners' hut on Edgeøya.

Finally we won an audience with a certified authority in our subject, a scholar named Tatiana Aleksandrovna Bernstam, who was an expert on the Pomori. A woman in her late fifties, she struck an imposing figure, with her red hair pulled severely back, oversized violet-rimmed glasses through she which she coolly appraised us, a mouth pursed painfully around each judicious utterance. Yet, in the somber chamber of the Kunstkamera where we met, she proved a genial host, serving us coffee cake and Tchibo, a kind of instant coffee, poured into chipped porcelain cups with their handles broken off.

Unlike our other consultants, Bernstam was acquainted with the sailors' story. Before we could discuss it, however, we had to listen to a résumé of her academic career: the mentors who, perhaps out of envy, truncated her pioneering first book ("'She's too young to be so good,' they said; 'let's just publish half of it'"), the snobs who thought northern peasants and sailors were beneath serious study. Bernstam was passionate about the Pomori. "I wanted to write about them," she said through Hugh's translation, "because they are the most vivid ethnic group in Russia. They are always distinct from other Russians, because they went north. They would have gone even farther, but they were stopped by the ocean."

We had, moreover, to endure the latest installment of the endless Russian game of "Oh, you should talk to ———." "There is a lady in Archangel'sk," said Bernstam, "whom you should talk to. Her name is Ksenia Gemp. She is a local luminary. Perfect to ask about these things. She knows German. She knows all the old stories." Bernstam paused. "But she may not still be alive."

Oh, well, I thought, wearily jotting all this down, *that name itself—Ksenia Gemp—is worth the candle.*

Slowly I realized that Bernstam was not particularly interested in "my" castaways. But gradually she delivered tidbits from her vast store of knowledge that I found interesting. "The Pomori stopped going to Spitsbergen in the middle of the nineteenth century," she said, "because they turned to logging. Their towns became the logging factories for all of Russia. It was in the time of Tsar Nicholas the First."

Through Hugh, I retold Le Roy's story about the hand-carved bone box his fellow academicians had thought a fake. "Of course they made it with just a knife," said Bernstam. "These men were self-taught. They were Pomori."

As we left the séance, I felt the familiar exhaustion that seemed to be the price of each little stage in my fool's progress. So many appointments, so much cross-lingual dialogue, only to wring a few further droplets of understanding out of the stone of my old story. Yet I still hoped, as we got ready to take the train to Moscow to visit Vadim Starkov, that sooner or later those droplets would coalesce into a pond big enough to sail my quest across, finding the comprehension I sought on the far shore.

It was a midnight train that would take some eight hours to spirit us the four hundred miles from St. Petersburg to Moscow. We would no doubt arrive bleary and befuddled in time for breakfast with the great archaeologist. For Masha, still on crutches, the trip promised to be a trial. An hour before heading for the station, she called Starkov's number. Instead of the man himself, she got his wife, who sounded slightly hysterical.

Starkov's expedition was stuck in some place called Tiksi, on the Lena Delta in Arctic Siberia. Persistent fog had prevented the bush plane from picking the team up. The archaeologists were not even in radio contact with the pilot. Starkov's wife had been sitting beside the telephone, waiting for any kind of news.

We delayed our train ride by one day, then by another. Each time Masha called, Starkov's wife sounded more frantic, for she had hoped that the ringing telephone heralded a call from her husband, returned to civilization and only a routine flight away from home. But the fog, the pilot reported, was holding tight to the ground. The team was in no real danger, for they had plenty of food, but at this rate Starkov would have to go straight from Moscow to his Spitsbergen dig, which would already be delayed in starting.

Masha explained that we were almost out of time ourselves before flying to Archangel'sk. By the third day, it was clear we were not going to meet Starkov in Moscow. We canceled our train tickets.

"Tell the American not to worry," said the archaeologist's wife. "Never mind that he can't meet Vadim in Moscow. When he goes to Spitsbergen, he should just say, 'Take me to Vadim.' Anyone will take him to Vadim from anywhere in Spitsbergen."

7: The Widows Inkova

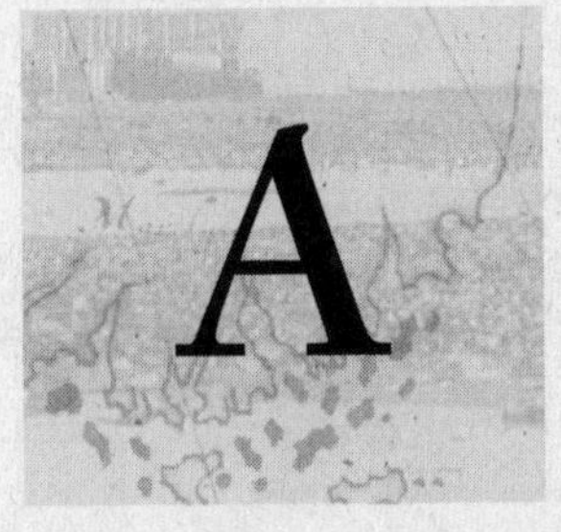

A rriving the previous October in Arkhangel'sk, where a few dead leaves clung to the trees and winter was in the air, I had seen the town as a gloomy sprawl, its outskirts blighted with oil rigs and decrepit factories. Now, at the height of summer, as Hugh, Masha, and I rode to the center in our citizen taxi, the old seaport took on charm. The sun was high in the sky, and even here, at 65° N, it was warm enough so that the residents were strolling about in short-sleeved shirts.

After checking into the Dvina, the cozy hotel where I had stayed the previous autumn, I walked down to the harbor, only three blocks away. As I stood there, gazing out at the big steel freighters that lay scattered about the generous waterway, watching the tide creep upstream, I had what can only be called, in that hackneyed literary conceit, an epiphany.

The most poignant single anecdote in Le Roy's *Narrative* concerns the moment when Kornilov's ship pulled in to Arkhangel'sk, on September 28, 1749, with the three survivors from Edgeøya aboard. Writes the chronicler,

> The moment of their arrival was almost disastrous for the pilot's wife, and for him in consequence. When the ship arrived, she hap-

> pened to be walking along the dock. Having recognized her husband, whom she tenderly loved, and whom she had so long wept over as dead, she lacked the patience to await his disembarking from the ship, but rashly rushing forward to embrace him, she fell into the sea, and narrowly escaped being drowned.

Now, in a surge of vicarious longing, I thought: *This is exactly where that happened.* I pictured Aleksei's wife afloat in the tide before my feet, and sailors leaping from the dock to save her.

Hugh, Masha, and I stopped in at the Maritime Museum, where ten months before I had admired the historical displays of Pomori craft. Now, with all the reading and research I had since undertaken in my brain, the exhibits pulsed with new significance. The previous October, I had scarcely noticed the small, doll-like models of Arctic sailors, based on data from 1711 and 1764; now these glass-encased figurines gave me my only glimpse of how the castaways might have been attired at the moment of their stranding. They would have had either buckled shoes or boots that reached to mid-calf, red-and-white-checked shirts, matching jackets and trousers, skull-fitting caps made of wool. A baggy woolen poncho, pulled over the head, might have supplemented their garb. Still, this was clearly no outfit in which to face the winter 10 degrees north of the Arctic Circle. And, as Le Roy reminded me, the men had gradually unraveled every stitch of their clothing to serve as wicks for their vital lamp, replacing each garment with one made of reindeer hide.

The beautifully detailed models of the Pomori's boats—the three-sailed *lodja* and the smaller two-sailed *kotch*—made the ancient designs articulate. With Masha translating the captions, I noted that the boats were capable of a top speed of six or seven miles an hour. In a straight line, it is 1,100 miles from Arkhangel'sk to Svalbard. Le Roy says that in May 1743, the ill-fated bark covered that distance in eight days. That makes an average of 5.7 miles an hour, sailing steadily night and day, so evidently the hunters were pushing their ship to its very limit.

I saw how the round bottoms of the boats prevented them from getting frozen into the pack ice. Peering at the huge, heavy rudders mounted aft, I imagined two strong men struggling to control them. The *lodja* could carry up to three hundred tons, so the notion of bringing one's prefab hut in pieces to Svalbard no longer seemed so unlikely. In another display were pieces of a seventeenth-century boat excavated on Novaya Zemlya by Peter Boyarsky—the same expert who had responded so helpfully to Julia's fax. Taut cords of juniper root still sewed together the planks that had made up the hull, and I saw how they allowed the boat to flex instead of breaking under the assault of ripping tides.

Lodjas date from the thirteenth century. The *kotch* is even older, and the display caption claimed that its design had changed almost not at all between the eleventh and the nineteenth centuries. Here were the "large cumbersome boats manned by Russian peasants" that Jeannette Mirsky had sneered at: quite evidently, they were superbly adapted to Arctic seas.

While we browsed, a thin, fit-looking, trim-bearded man of about forty, nattily dressed in a black suit and tie, was lecturing a tour group in Russian. When he was done, Masha introduced herself.

It was the first in a series of encounters in the Russian north that, after all my months of frustration, began to yield real dividends for my quest. The tour guide was a local fellow named Sergei Terent'ev, a self-taught historian of Pomori culture. Even better, he had been part of a team of avid sailors who, starting in the late 1980s, had thoroughly researched the *lodja* and the *kotch,* built an authentic replica of each, and sailed them on a number of voyages duplicating those of the Pomori in the eighteenth century. In 1990, Sergei himself had sailed on the replicated *kotch,* named the *Pomor,* from Arkhangel'sk all the way around Scandinavia and into the Gulf of Finland, disembarking at St. Petersburg. Other mariners, the year before, had sailed the *Pomor* from Arkhangel'sk to Svalbard and back to Norway. The voyage out had taken seven days—a span that neatly corroborated Le Roy's assertion of an eight-day journey from Russia to Svalbard.

Everyone who had sailed aboard the *Pomor* was deeply impressed with her performance in rough seas and high winds—as were their comrades aboard the *Grumant,* as they had named the reborn *lodja.* To comply with local regulations, each boat had occasionally accepted a tow in and out of a busy harbor, but otherwise her twentieth-century sailors had handled her with no technology that was not available to their predecessors two and a half centuries before.

When Terent'ev learned why we had come to Arkhangel'sk, he dropped everything to join us for lunch. Over blinis and *shashlik*, he poured out a flood of fascinating data. It turned out that at the very time the Pomori had set off for Svalbard at the beginning of the eighteenth century, their ancient way of seafaring was under serious threat. "The time of Peter the Great," said Sergei, "was a time of a great destructive force. Peter said to the Pomori, 'Stop doing things the old way. Do them the way the Dutch do.'"

Just a few days before, in St. Petersburg, I had paused on a stroll along the banks of the Neva to admire a bronze statue. It was, I deciphered, a gift from the Dutch in 1996. It depicted Peter the Great as a simple craftsman, axe in hand, calipers and hammer at his side, in the act of building his own little dory, somewhere in Holland.

At the time he acceded to the throne, in 1682, Peter was only ten years old. For the next fourteen years, until the death of his half-brother Ivan V (with whom Peter nominally shared the tsardom), a fierce struggle between competing factions left both youthful rulers in danger of losing their lives in a coup d'état. As a result, Peter grew up not in the palace in Moscow, but with his mother in a village called Preobrazhenskoye, outside the capital. In a nearby colony of foreigners, Peter first fell under the spell of western European ideas. The catalyst was a beat-up old English sailboat Peter found in a shed.

In 1697, now in full power at the age of twenty-seven, Peter led a conclave of 250 ambassadors to Holland, France, and Great Britain, to absorb Western ideas. This so-called Grand Embassy ended forever Russia's immemorial isolation from the countries to its west. Peter himself went undercover as a lowly sergeant, and spent four months as a carpenter in a shipyard of the Dutch East India Company. It was this apprenticeship that the statue on the Neva commemorated.

The very founding of St. Petersburg, in 1703, and the shifting of the capital there from Moscow, amounted to Peter's grandest gesture of embracing the West: perched at the mouth of the Gulf of Finland, the new city lay only two hundred miles from Helsinki. Russian history tends to view Peter's reforms as wholly for the good. Yet, as Sergei was now telling me, the tsar's love of all things Dutch had proved, at least as far as the Pomori were concerned, nearly disastrous. Fortunately, with Peter's death in 1725, the sailors from Arkhangel'sk and Mezen could go back to doing things the way they had since the eleventh century.

Using a detailed drawing the reconstructors had made, Sergei pointed out the features of the *kotch.* Six huge, thin-bladed, thick-handled oars supplemented the sails. "They use these for going in and out of port," our expert commented, "and when there is no wind. Sometimes two men on one oar. The oarlocks are made of seal leather." He pointed to the shallow hold. "They have a small stove and living quarters underneath. Storage in the middle." In the diagram, the sails looked so big they seemed to overwhelm the boat. "In a strong wind," said Sergei, "it takes three people to pull the sail up. Everything in the ship is made of wood. The ropes are of linen.

"The only bad thing," he went on, "is that it is very hard to turn a *kotch.* Two people to hold the rudder. Ropes from both sides tied to the rudder, to keep from wobbling. You leave some slack." I pictured the fourteen men in 1743, driven headlong to the northeast before the gale that had sprung up their ninth day out of Arkhangel'sk, helpless to deflect the boat's runaway course toward the sea ice.

It was a measure of how obscure the Mezen men's survival story had become even in northern Russia that, although Sergei knew of it through oral tradition, he had never read or heard of Le Roy. We placed the Russian edition before him on the restaurant table. "Fourteen men," he mused. "I think they are in a *kotch,* not a *lodja.*" Apparently ignorant of such distinctions, Le Roy calls the boat simply a "vessel" or a "ship."

In the very first sentence of the main body of his narrative, after six prefatory pages, Le Roy writes that the Pomori's ship "was destined for *Spitzbergen,* to be employed in the whale- or seal-fishery." Reading the Russian version of this sentence, Sergei promptly spoke up, "No. Russian whaling comes later. Fourteen men are too few to deal with a whale. Too hard to pull it ashore. And a *kotch* is too small for a whale. And they do not have to go to Spitsbergen for seal. They find seal in the White Sea.

"No. I think they were going to Spitsbergen to hunt walrus. The walrus tusks are small and very valuable. From the ivory, they make many things. Furniture decorations, gun handles, knife handles, inlays, dishes, plates. Little boxes. Icons. The ivory from mammoth is browner in color."

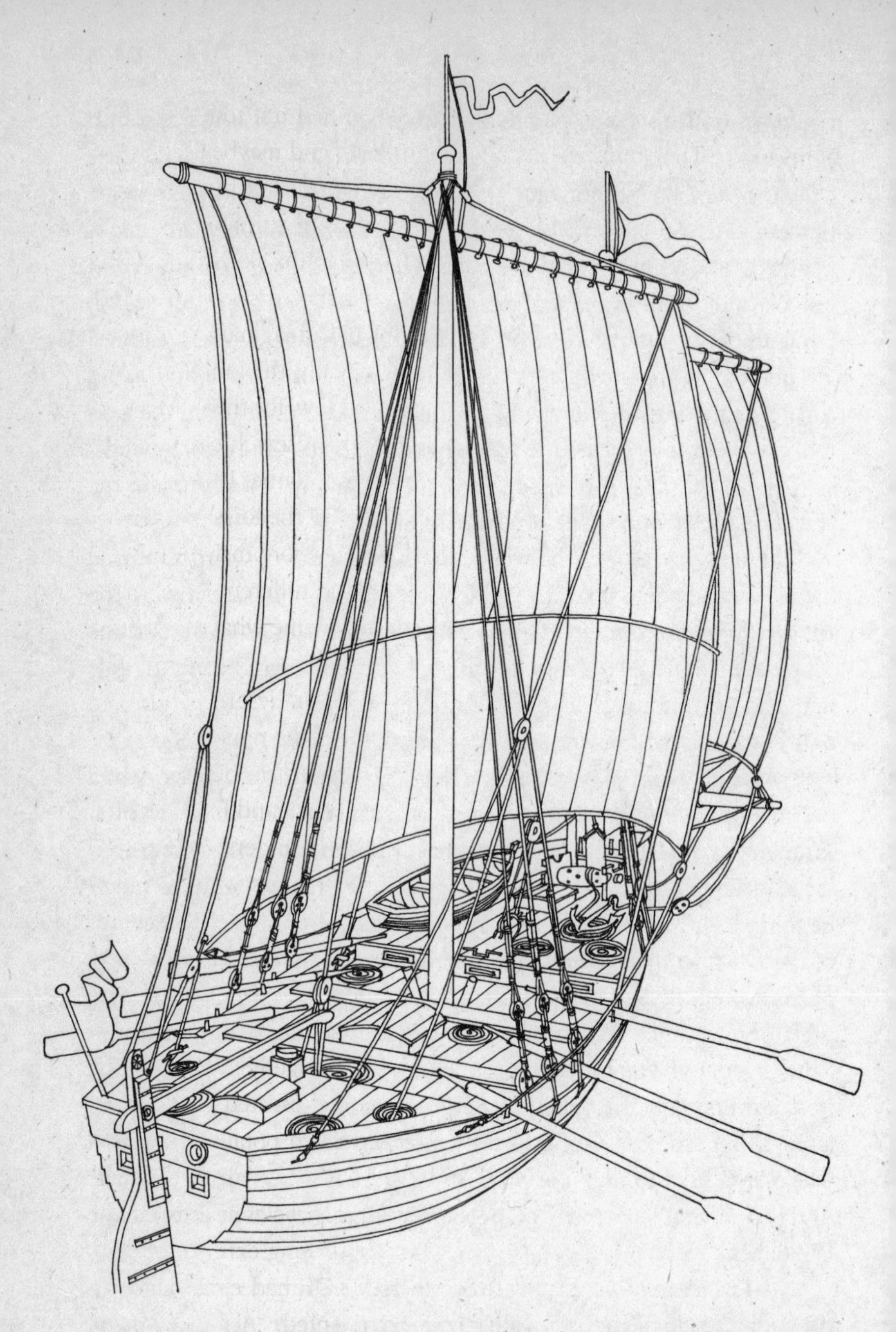

Design of an eighteenth-century Russian *kotch*, the type of ship in which the four castaways sailed to Svalbard in 1743, as reconstructed by the Polar Odyssey Club (Petrozavodsk) and the Scientific Institute of Culture (Moscow), 1990. (Courtesy of the Polar Odyssey Club, Petrozavodsk, and the Scientific Institute of Culture, Moscow)

Absorbed in skimming Le Roy's text, Sergei had not touched a bite of his food. "They hunt walrus," he reaffirmed, "and maybe fox. If they winter over, they kill reindeer for food. They hunt fox in the winter, because the white, thick coat is more valuable. In summer the fur is not white. If they overwinter, they get just enough fox skins and walrus tusks to fit in their *kotch.*"

For most of a year, I had been beating half-imaginary bushes in hopes of scaring up a new primary source—ideally, the long-lost manuscript and/or notes of the elusive Klingstedt. Now, for the first time, I had become the accidental beneficiary of a new research strategy, one that would prove fruitful in the upcoming weeks. Rather than plead on bended knee before the implacable bureaucracy of the Russian archives for a prowl through their holdings, I might gain more insight into the old story by simply asking a series of experts in different fields to go through Le Roy with a fine-tooth comb and show me what that combing yielded.

Sergei read on, pausing to frown over Le Roy's description of the hut. "I cannot believe the building was that high," he remarked. In the Russian text, the unit of measurement was the *sazhen,* but it worked out, just like the corresponding phrase in the French and English texts, to eighteen feet. "Perhaps this man Le Roy did not understand Russian units?" Sergei ventured. "Did he interview the sailors with an interpreter?"

"We don't know," answered Hugh. It was the same puzzle that had first occurred to me months before.

As he read about Aleksei Inkov's keeping of the saints' days through more than six years, Sergei's eyes grew bright. "Exactly," he said. "For instance, my grandmother would never say, 'We planted potatoes on the thirteenth of June.' She would say, 'We planted potatoes the third day after Pentecost.'"

Sergei came to the passage in which the ship *Nicholas and Andrew,* in 1749, had returned to the site of the Mezeners' long exile, finding "a wooden cross, which the mate ALEXIS HIMKOF had erected before the door." Looking up, our new friend commented, "A Pomor sees a storm, he prays to God, 'Please save me, and I'll build a cross to You.' It's a promise cross."

Finally Sergei put Le Roy aside, to deliver a soliloquy on the hardiness of the eighteenth-century Northerners he so admired. He used the present tense. "The Pomori," he averred, "live on fish, meat, fur, berries. But Pomoriya is so rich a region, they can do more than just survive. Potentially, they can be wealthy. In the rest of Russia, most people can barely get enough to feed their family. Here a man can leave his family to sail to Spitsbergen, spend the winter, confident he will survive, and return with more than he had. Here, this is normal.

"And the Pomori are always personally free. Here there is an old saying, 'God is high up, and Moscow is far away.' This means they do not rely on anyone else."

Sergei tapped the Russian edition of Le Roy with his knuckles. "These sailors grew up as Pomori. They were trained seafarers and hunters. Every day meant risk. Constant struggle, generation after generation. These were guys whose hearts did not fail in tough times. They knew how to deal with all kinds of adversity. They didn't give up."

That evening, from the Hotel Dvina, Masha called Vadim Starkov's wife in Moscow once more. There was still hope that the great archaeologist and I might rendezvous somewhere in Spitsbergen. "Vadim is still in Tiksi!" the woman declaimed in her slightly hysterical way. "They have a radio now, but they are stuck there. Eleven people all stuck! They're really very prominent scholars. Oh, I wish your American could meet these scholars—they are known all over the world. Zviagin—he is a specialist in making faces from the skulls."

Masha couldn't get a word in edgewise. "Tell your American not to worry," went on Starkov's wife. "He will be taken straight from Edgeøya to Vadim, and Vadim will tell him everything so well that he will become a Pomor himself!"

The next day, we had another stroke of good fortune. Our way paved by Victor Boyarsky's telephonic introduction from St. Petersburg, we arrived at the Arkhangel'sk Area Archive to a warm reception. The director, Nikolai Alexeevich Shumilov, and the head of the Department of Information, Tatiana Anatol'evna Sanakina, installed us in the archive's reading room and asked what they could do to help. The former was a slight, balding, almost mousy fellow; his deputy, a big, strong-faced woman. Both wore the scholar's mandatory wire-rim glasses, though while Shumilov gazed straight through his, Sanakina tended to peer over the upper rims of hers.

Masha Gavrilo and Victor Boyarsky in the Arctic and Antarctic Museum in St. Petersburg

Hugh and Masha Olmsted in Mezen—the author's research colleagues and interpreters in Russia

Promise cross in Mezen, dedicated to the Pomori

Elizaveta Aleksandrovna Inkova (left) and Nina Fedorovna Inkova—by marriage, the last two survivors in the Inkov line

The Zodiac and supplies, shore of Halfmoon Island

The team in front of Bjørneborg: left to right, Mats Forsberg, the author, Vaughn Hadenfeldt, Michel Guérin

A typical bear "trap" on Halfmoon Island, the ground littered with bones of slaughtered bears

Wading a tidal channel off Edgeøya in survival suits

Reindeer from twenty yards, Edgeøya

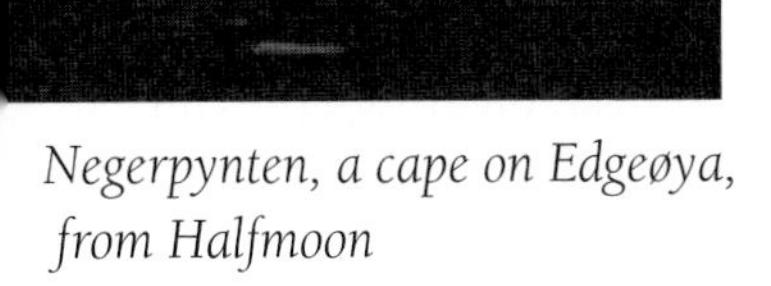

Negerpynten, a cape on Edgeøya, from Halfmoon

Whale skull carved with initials of early Norwegian hunters

Grave of unknown Norwegian hunter, "GTS," Halfmoon Island

Intact rudder from an eighteenth-century Russian kotch *or* lodja, *Halfmoon Island*

Vaughn with the lamp he fashioned from Edgeøya clay

Ruins of eighteenth-century hut on Halfmoon—possibly the same refuge used by the shipwrecked sailors from 1743–49

Fresh polar bear tracks in hard ground

The eighth polar bear,
seen from a respectful distance

Bjørneborg, with Edgeøya in the distance

Ten months after my futile attempts to phone the by then retired Dr. Filippov, the comedy of errors of our efforts to communicate back and forth was untangled. Back in January, Julia had finally got someone from the archive on the line. Three months later, some researcher in Arkhangel'sk had faxed a request for $70 in advance to begin a search. Julia had faxed back an okay, after which we heard nothing.

"We never received your answer," said Shumilov with a wan smile. (Julia had sent the fax three times.) "All our numbers have changed." This seemed a malady endemic to the Russian telephone system. "But we thought, you do not like our proposal of $70."

I hastened to assure Shumilov and Sanakina that a $70 research fee was the least of my problems. Goodwill wafted through the reading room like a heady perfume. Yet my first stab got nowhere: neither savant had ever heard of this man Klingstedt.

We started going through the index to the Arkhangel'sk Provincial Chancery records. It was not quite a "dry search," for the records were at least chronological. We began at May–June 1743 and worked forward. Hugh skimmed the old handwritten Cyrillic, hoping for a glimpse of some mention of a *kotch* headed off toward Svalbard. Instead, we perused such entries as "Directors of Senate on Exchange of Prisoners of War with Sweden," and "Official Decree of Dispatch of 500 Vats of Wine to . . ."

Most of the entries were as dry and official as that, although a few hinted at human drama: "Interrogation of People Caught and Accused of Various Crimes," "Discovery of Old Believers in Cells of Vyg Monastery." Alas, not a word about the departure of a star-crossed *kotch* in 1743, nor about the return of the three survivors six years later. Apparently mere walrus-hunting expeditions to the high Arctic were beneath the interest of the chancery.

Not a trace of Klingstedt. "Did Victor Boyarsky tell you," offered Shumilov, "that all the Admiralty records are now in St. Petersburg?" I shook my weary head. This was beginning to look like another round of the unwinnable Russian game, "Oh, you should talk to ———."

But then Sanakina delivered the archive's pièce de résistance. It was a simple cardboard folder enclosing an old, sixteen-page manuscript. Hugh read the title, translating for me: "Historical Description of the Sailing to Grumant (Spitsbergen) of the Four Mezen

Sailors Aleksei and Ivan Himkov (Inkov), Stepan Sharapov, and Feodor Virugin."

Aflame with hope, I blurted out, "Who wrote this?" and "When was it written?" The archivists shook their heads. No one knew.

The title itself seemed to indicate that the manuscript was derivative from Le Roy, for it copied his misspellings of the sailors' names. The parenthetic "Spitsbergen" and "Inkov," however, made us take a second glance. It was soon clear that this title page, in a different hand from that of the manuscript, was a modern addition—a kind of cover page, written by someone in the archive who was aware of Belov's corrections of Le Roy—to explain what the manuscript was about.

The Cyrillic handwriting in the main text looked to Hugh, who had pored over many such documents, to be nineteenth-century in style, though it might have been earlier. We photocopied this treasure and carried it back to the hotel to study. Masha took on the task of reading the difficult scrawl. It would require hours for her to render its phrases for me in English, but the labor was worth every minute.

The manuscript writer's own brief title, placed at the head of the first page and underlined, read "Sailors from Mezen and Their Amazing Life on Spitsbergen." As Masha struggled with the knotty text, I grew increasingly puzzled—and intrigued. It was clear that the writer knew Le Roy's narrative, and was even partly dependent on it, for chunks of passage read as almost verbatim echoes of the academician's text. Yet there were also numerous discrepancies, and several key details wholly absent in Le Roy. Were we dealing here, I wondered, with a true primary source, even if penned in the nineteenth century, based partly on Le Roy, but partly also on oral tradition around Arkhangel'sk? If so, this fragile manuscript would represent the only alternative primary source ever found, except for the laconic "Oral Testimony of a Hunter from Mezen" dug up by Belov.

The manuscript agreed with Le Roy that it had taken the sailors eight days to reach Svalbard's shores. Curiously, though he was not named, the "captain" of the vessel was also reported to be "the owner of the ship." Now the anonymous writer threw us a monkey wrench. The ship, he wrote, intended to reach the "eastern side of Spitsbergen, where ships usually go," but "the wind suddenly changed, and the ship was brought to the western shore, which was separated by a wide channel from a big island." These cardinal directions exactly reversed the ones given by Le Roy. I would ruminate over those phrases for a long time, trying to make them fit the map, before concluding that the writer had simply confused west with east. Certainly the usual place of resort of ships in the eighteenth century was the west coast of Spitsbergen.

Such a glitch was hardly conducive to confidence in the manuscript's accuracy. On the other hand, Le Roy had made his own basic mistakes—not only in the names of the sailors, but, if Sergei Terent'ev was right, in claiming the men were after whales and seals rather than walrus and fox.

Indeed, the very next sentence seemed to correct the writer's muddled geography, for he wrote of the runaway vessel, "This adventure upset everybody; and it was known from previous experience that on the eastern side there was much more ice than the western." An accurate depiction of the waters off Edgeøya.

The small boat was soon gripped fast in the sea ice. "When they saw the ship in such danger," claimed the writer, "everybody shouted, 'We're dead! We're dead!' "

This vivid incident, unmentioned in Le Roy, provoked in me a skeptical reflection. It was entirely possible that the manuscript we were now trying to read was a mere latter-day rehash of Le Roy, with touches added out of the chronicler's imagination to enhance the human drama. Was this fugitive document merely an unacknowledged rip-off of Le Roy, like the German children's writer J. H. Campe's 1825 *Polar Scenes,* with its preachy lessons drawn from the ordeal, its invented details such as the sailors thrusting their lances into the mouth of the polar bear they attacked?

I didn't think so. Most of the details in which the manuscript disagreed with Le Roy were more puzzling than vivid. There was no evidence anyone had tried to publish this account. I pictured instead a scribe in this lonely subarctic seaport, sitting down to put on paper all that was known of a strange tale that had begun to fade from human memory, calling not only on Le Roy, but on some other source, most likely local gossip and lore.

There followed a very important passage: "The land in front of them [the sailors on the ice-bound ship] was not Spitsbergen, but a small island, situated near the eastern shore of Spitsbergen. And it was called East Spitsbergen." Edgeøya was indeed often called East Spitsbergen; thus is it named (as well as by the appellation "Stans Voorland") in van Keulen's map, the very one on which one of the Inkovs made his "stroke of the pen." Yet no one would call Edgeøya a small island. I began to think hard about Keilhau's insistence that Halfmoon Island (which perfectly fits the above description) was the place to look for the castaways' hut.

Now the manuscript author followed Le Roy to the T, down to giving the four Mezen men the same wrong names (e.g., Alexis Himkof) as the academician had. The sailors remembered their fellow townsmen having previously built a hut somewhere nearby, and they went on shore to look for it. The list of what they carried with them is virtually identical to Le Roy's, except that the singular gun becomes "guns." The Russian words *ognivo* and *trut* translate literally into Le Roy's "steel and tinder." The ship was stuck four *versts* from shore, or about two and a half miles (Le Roy says "two English miles").

The anonymous writer's account of that perilous passage across the shifting ice is once again more vivid and more detailed than Le Roy's. The men "started on ice with canes. . . . Their way was on ice, which was not fastened together, and constantly heaving because of the waves. They had to jump from one piece of ice to another with great care, in order not to get between the ice. Otherwise, they would die.

"But they got safely to the island, where the land was bare, covered with snow, ice, and unapproachable rocks."

One sentence suffices to record the discovery of the hut. As Masha read the next line, however, I was nonplussed. The hut, she translated, "stood from the seashore four hours' drive."

I interrupted her: "That can't be right. Four hours' *drive?*"

Masha squinted at the manuscript. "That's what it says. *Ezdy,* 'drive.' The word means in a vehicle, not on foot."

"What? A carriage? This is bizarre."

The description of the hut perfectly matched Le Roy's, down to the dimensions, which are given in *sazhens.* The windows, however, were "holes that could be opened and closed when wanted, [which] serve instead of windows."

The following day, having returned to the shore to discover the ship gone, the men "stood motionless for a long time, as if struck by thunder, looking at each other with sad eyes.

"After that, they felt better, feeding themselves with hope that maybe the ship driven away by storm would return. But their hope was in vain—it didn't return, and even in Russia there was no news about it, so probably it vanished in the sea."

This passage pushed me to another reflection. The homeliness of the anonymous author's writing was no mere effect of Masha's impromptu translation: it was the true stamp of his prose. Reliant though the man was on Le Roy's account, there was no trace in his manuscript of the academician's rhetorical flourishes, nor had he the slick storytelling gift of a J. H. Campe. The writer sounded like a homegrown historian trying to get the tale down as plainly and truly as he could.

More puzzlements. Masha read, "They realized their situation. Situated on an uninhabited island, surrounded by harsh air."

"Harsh air?" I interjected.

"That's what it says."

"Not 'cold air'?"

"No. *Surovyi,* 'harsh.'" She read on, "They had no hope ever to leave this place."

The men set to work repairing the hut. "When they learned that the island is full of reindeer, these pilgrims during hunger hunted them and killed one deer and ate it for several days. . . . In a short time all the powder and bullets were finished, and they didn't have anything to kill reindeer with or defend themselves from attacks from polar bears."

The account of the men's fabrication of lances, then later, of a bow and arrows, echoed Le Roy's, though it was much truncated and the two deeds were confusingly entangled with each other. "They used water from the streams between rocks, but still they lacked a lot. Their main misfortune was the fact that the air was very unhealthy and harmful."

"Harsh air again," I commented. "I wonder what the guy means."

As in Le Roy, the sailors were forced to undercook their meat and to eat it "without spices." "It was boring," continued the anonymous writer, "to have the same meal every day, and they started to think about changing their life, and to change the ——— with." The key word, in its fine Cyrillic scrawl, was undecipherable.

After months of gritting my teeth through Le Roy's pomposities and learned digressions, I found myself liking this other chronicler's clunky, homespun sentences. The only question was how accurate the forgotten historian might be. Four hours' drive? Harsh air?

In the anonymous manuscript, all four sailors got scurvy the first winter, not simply Fedor Verigin. Only after the initial attack did "one of them" remember the preventive measures—exercise, scurvy grass, drinking reindeer blood warm, and, adds the writer, "not worrying about damp air and cold." "For the same purpose," the chronicler editorializes, "it's very good to eat frozen fish and meat, but on these shores they didn't see fish, and even if there were, what could they catch them with?" Sure enough, Verigin, "fat and lazy," could not bring himself to drink reindeer blood. "He lay in the hut with pleasure on his soft bed, while his comrades roamed the snow. . . . The first three sailors got well and became strong. . . . Feodor Verigin, who in the meantime was only resting, suffered from the illness, so that for several days he could not get up and move from his bed. And then he could not even raise his hand to his mouth. He was in the same state for six years and suffered since then, until death brought an end to his sufferings."

The gist of the paragraph was the same as Le Roy's. But the anonymous writer was no plagiarist: he seemed at pains to convey the same historical truth in his own language, however awkward.

The question of scurvy and its prophylactics had occupied me since my first reading of Le Roy. Back in Cambridge, I had consulted an expert hematologist, Dr. James D. Levine, an assistant professor at the Harvard Medical School who was on the staff of Beth Israel Deaconess Medical Center in Boston. He confirmed the fact that scurvy was caused by nothing more nor less than a deficiency of vitamin C. Of the preventives the Mezen men swore by, only scurvy grass, *Cochlearia,* would have been an effective medicine. I wondered how much vitamin C there might be in reindeer blood.

"There's not a lot of vitamin C in meat products," answered Dr. Levine. "And heat in general destroys vitamin C." I pointed out that the sailors had been unable to cook their venison. "Perhaps it's simply easier to drink the blood warm than chew it after it's coagulated," he offered. "On the other hand, it takes very small amounts of vitamin C to prevent scurvy."

I asked about exercise. "Exercise," answered the professor categorically, "maintaining good health—these have nothing to do with scurvy."

Yet throughout the centuries, explorers of all nations, not merely Russia, had sworn by exercise as an antiscorbutic. In a fascinating book by Kenneth J. Carpenter, *The History of Scurvy and Vitamin C*, I found a cogent explanation. After citing many passages in early explorers' works in which the deaths of comrades are attributed to "indolence" or to the refusal to exercise, Carpenter argues that the observers mistook the effect for the cause. One of the first symptoms of scurvy is extreme lassitude. The crewmate unwilling to work vigorously about the ship or camp most likely was already in the grips of the malady, rather than being congenitally lazy.

I also had my doubts that scurvy was the cause of Verigin's long illness. Most scurvy deaths on Arctic expeditions occurred within the first winter. It did not seem likely to me that Verigin could have languished through six years with a full-blown case of scurvy. Dr. Levine confirmed my doubts. "Scurvy develops within a couple of months," he said. "What were the sailor's symptoms?"

I read him Le Roy's two sketchy paragraphs, which mention "the greatest sufferings" and "most excruciating pains," as well as Verigin's inability to sit up unaided or raise his hand to his mouth. "Scurvy can cause pain," said Levine, "but it doesn't cause neurological deficits." I wondered aloud what the sailor's true illness might have been. "It could have been anything," answered the doctor. "Perhaps a neurological disorder from the lack of some other vitamin. I'm very skeptical he had scurvy. If he had, he would have died in the first year."

The anonymous writer of the Arkhangel'sk manuscript adds a piquant detail about Verigin's decline, which does not appear in Le Roy: "The three sailors left [healthy] moved from mountain to mountain with great difficulties, and luck followed them. Most of their underwear they used for bandages for their sick comrade." The account that follows of the sailors making their own clothes from bear and reindeer hides is close to Le Roy's.

As had the academician, the manuscript writer singles out the torment of Aleksei Inkov, on account of the wife and three children he had left behind in Russia. The homegrown historian, however, waxes more poignant than Le Roy: "Very often it happened that after a hard day's work, he returned into the hut for rest, but his heart was in Russia, in the circle of his beloved people. Often it happened that he cried tears when his comrades enjoyed sleep. But when he thought about his weakness, he tried to get away from his sad thoughts, and to start working with his former enthusiasm."

All too soon, the writer has the sailors being rescued. In his account, they are out scouting for driftwood one day, "looking to this side and to that side where their beloved Russia lay," when suddenly they see the faraway ship. As in Le Roy, they build a bonfire and frantically wave their reindeer-skin flag.

Unlike Le Roy, the manuscript author records the rescuers' incredulity: "People on the ship got astonished when they found three people clothed in skins and furs, and most of all they were surprised when these poor people started to talk Russian." The roster of booty carried aboard the rescue ship dovetails with Le Roy's, as does the offer of 80 rubles for passage home. The manuscript writer, however, claims that it took five more months to return to Arkhangel'sk, which cannot be true. "When they arrived, crowds of people gathered to look at them. . . . Finally, the islanders came to land wearing their Spitsbergen clothes."

With that mundane sentence, the phantom manuscript ends. Having scribbled down Masha's impromptu translation, I studied it for days. I became convinced that the document was in part a true primary source, reflecting some other font of information, probably oral, however indebted its writer was to Le Roy. Beyond that vague affirmation, however, I could not go. The manuscript was a classic example of an unprovenanced artifact, like a pothunted vessel seized in some government raid. By now, no one could say who had written the manuscript, or when, or even how the archive had come into its possession.

How much did this new account really add to Le Roy? Not much, I had to confess, though the odd touches and details that were not in the academician's account served in my mind to shade and deepen slightly the portrait of the sailors. The cryptic "four hours' drive" from shore to hut would plague me for months. Whatever the writer meant, it seemed to indicate a much greater distance than the mile or two thirds of a mile of Le Roy's German and French accounts. Even if the phrase meant simply "four hours' walk," one would expect a distance of at least six miles.

Perhaps the single most important phrase in the manuscript for my quest was the comment, "The land in front of them was not Spitsbergen, but a small island, situated near the eastern shore of Spitsbergen." Once on Svalbard myself, I would keep that clue in the front of my brain.

I had not found Klingstedt; but I had found a parallel account that was utterly obscure, interesting, and possibly of primary value. Le Roy's *Narrative*, however, remained the principal source for the forgotten story.

As we had gathered up our belongings, including the photocopy of the mysterious nineteenth-century manuscript, in preparation for leaving the Arkhangel'sk Archive, I had reached for my billfold. Tatiana Sanakina had given me a puzzled look. "To pay you the $70 for searching," I said, through Hugh. She blushed mightily, then murmured, "Oh, no, you don't need to pay us anything."

On August 8, Hugh, Masha, and I flew to Mezen. The battered Aeroflot prop plane climbed out of an Arkhangel'sk rainstorm and sailed northeast through sparser and sparser cumulus clouds. The trackless taiga far below gleamed a rich, wet green in the slanting sunlight, reminding me of the Arctic slope north of Alaska's Brooks Range. It is possible to drive to Mezen: trucks do so, but the journey takes more than a day, winding three or four times the 150 miles that separate the town from Arkhangel'sk by air, and the roads are so bad, it makes for a perilous expedition in even the best of weather. It is also possible to get to Mezen by boat, but with the vessel poking into every cove along the Zimniy Bereg to drop off and load up natives, the trip can last most of a week.

We landed in late afternoon on a metal runway, then taxied up to the dilapidated wooden warehouse that served as a terminal. A man named Vasily, a slim, dark-haired, handsome fellow wearing the uniform of the army he had once served, immediately offered to be our taxi driver. For 150 rubles (about $5.60) he would haul us and our baggage into town. We squeezed all our stuff into his dented Lada and hopped on board. The dirt road meandered among permafrost-induced ponds, at one point fording a small river.

During my weeks in Russia, I had found not a single person who had ever been to Mezen. Masha Gavrilo had raised a depressing specter. Under Stalin, many of the traditional northern towns, she said, had been purged, their inhabitants shipped off en masse to Siberia or other godforsaken purlieus, the old houses torn down to make room for belching factories. Masha had visited one or two of these hellish "new towns" and had almost wept at the desecration. It was possible that such a fate had befallen Mezen, she suggested, in which case no scrap of oral tradition would linger about the premises.

Thus I was deeply relieved, as we crept into the outskirts, to see that Mezen had been spared Stalin's improvements. Wooden sidewalks lined the potholed main drag. Beautiful old two-story houses, hand-carpentered out of wood, stood screened by copses of silver birch. Two horses and a multitude of dogs claimed the right-of-way.

We were the only guests in the only hotel in town. Calculating our bill, the woman behind the desk deftly flicked the beads of an abacus. (We would see these ancient calculators in use in every store in Mezen.) There was no hot water, and my room was the only one with a bath. No soap, no toilet paper, no toilet seat: and when I flushed it, for twenty seconds the toilet issued shrieking hisses over a ground bass of emetic gurgles.

We went out for a walk. It was a perfect summer day—about 60°F, the sun low in the northwest at 9:00 P.M., its rays reflecting off the Mezen River, which surged into the distance below the high bench on which the town had been built. Magenta fireweed blazed in the yards, and stands of tall green grass gave way at the end of the side streets to the green mounds of far-off haystacks.

Even the teenagers, strolling in gaggles of five and eight down the main street, affecting their hip swaggers, could not resist staring at us. Two old women sitting in a backyard called us over. "Take *our* picture," they commanded Masha, who was photographing a rainbow. "Who are you? What are you doing here?"

Masha explained. One of the women pointed at me and gasped: "He came from America!"

"Are you going to other places?" queried the other.

"No, just Mezen," said Masha.

"He came from America just to come to Mezen!"

We were the first Americans, the women claimed, ever to visit Mezen. Later I would learn that this was not quite true: twenty years before, an American professor of Russian history had come to take pictures of the buildings, and about a decade ago, an American woman of Norwegian ancestry had come looking for distant relatives, the progeny of a single survivor of a Norwegian shipwreck at the turn of the century, after the Mezen men had saved his life and offered him shelter. There had also been a French journalist, a Swiss TV crew, a Swedish writer. But the total number of western European and American visitors ever to come to Mezen might be counted on the fingers of both hands.

We meandered to the western edge of town, where we could gaze off the bench toward the river that was the reason for the town's existence. It was so warm, the birches and willows so lush with dark green leaves, that I was tempted to see Mezen as a temperate rural paradise; but cord after cord of firewood stacked tight to the walls of the wooden houses bespoke the severity of the winter here, only fifty miles south of the Arctic Circle. We found a pair of promise crosses erected on the edge of the town's high shelf, their triangular headpieces facing the river. One had a small brass plaque on it, whose legend Hugh translated: "To the Mezen Pomori who have conquered the northern seas, from their grateful descendants. August 2, 1997."

We had been told that there was a good small history museum in Mezen. Like virtually every other institution in Russia to which we had foolishly hoped to gain entry, it was closed for an indefinite duration. But Vasily, our driver, knew the director and phoned him up. The man was on vacation but at home—fortunately, Mezen was so rustic that there was no need of a dacha to escape the urban rat race. Pleased and surprised to have international visitors, the director agreed to open the museum and talk to us the next morning.

Vasily Ivanovich Drannikov, a thin, sharp-featured, professorial sort, sat us down in the museum's musty main room and gave us an extended lecture on local history. He wielded a wooden pointer, like the grade-school teachers of my youth, to guide us around northern Russia on a cluttered map he hung from a lectern. Having spotted at once a small display on the wall devoted to "my" castaways, I was wild with impatience to ask Drannikov about them, but there was no derailing the chronological trudge of the man's train of history.

First hunter-gatherers after the last Ice Age; Finno-Ugrek tribes around 5000 B.C.; Nenets or Samoyeds herding reindeer to the east; trade routes to the Siberian fortress of Mangazea by 1000 B.C.; émigrés fleeing north from Scythian invaders; at last, the first true Russians arriving around the ninth century A.D.—it was not uninteresting stuff, but Drannikov's presentation was so dry and pedantic, I tried to fast-forward his tape by interjecting leading questions. Alas, before Hugh could even get these anxious queries out of his mouth, Drannikov waved his pointer and resumed his discourse on, among other subjects, the etymology of the term Samoyed (it meant either "self-eater" or "one who eats by himself"—in either case, the classic putdown of "civilized" folk giving a name to the barbarians they encountered in the wilderness).

The oldest settlement here, near the mouth of the Mezen River, was the now nearly abandoned town of Lampozhnia, twelve miles upstream from present-day Mezen, founded in the thirteenth century. Its raison d'être was to serve as a trading post on the long trail from Novgorod to Mangazea; it was only later that its inhabitants began to dare the Arctic Ocean that spread before the river's mouth, some thirty miles downstream.

Lampozhnia's date seemed to contradict Belov's blithe contention that the Pomori had discovered Svalbard in the eleventh century. For once, my interruption reached Drannikov's ear. A thin smile seized his face, as for the first time he showed evidence of a sense of humor: "More often people consider the fifteenth century for discovery of Svalbard," he said. "But I would not argue with the late professor Belov. Of course, we're happy with what Belov says. So why argue?"

Drannikov droned on, quoting verbatim from a Samoyed petition to Ivan the Terrible in 1545, complaining about Russians stealing their land; then from a 1619 decree by Tsar Mikhail forbidding an ocean route to Siberia. Finally, an hour into our lecture, the director stood up and aimed his pointer at the panel celebrating the "Polar Robinsons" of 1743–49. A woodcut dramatized the men's rescue: reindeer-skin flag frantically waving as the distant ship draws near. The display reflected

Belov's discoveries, giving the sailors their right names. But it was soon clear that Drannikov, for all his local learning, knew nothing about the four Edgeøya castaways that we hadn't already absorbed.

"How well is this story known in Mezen today?" I managed to ask.

The answer surprised me. "The people know it now because the school groups come to my museum. Nobody knew the story from oral tradition. The museum reopened it. And then the newspapers wrote about it several times." Later I would realize that this blanket affirmation amounted to Drannikov's pat on his own back. The man was a control freak: what we were allowed to learn had to come only from his mouth, in the due course of recitations that sounded like a textbook talking out loud.

"Are there any direct descendants of the sailors here today?" I asked.

"No direct descendants. But there are two widows Inkova, women who were married to the last men named Inkov. I will introduce you to them later."

This was the most exciting news I had heard in Russia. "When?" I blurted out a bit peremptorily.

"Late this afternoon. After a short drive into the country, to show you a typical village as it would look in the eighteenth century."

At last we adjourned for lunch, in a gloomy, cavernous cafeteria, one of only two restaurants in town, where a hearty meal for the four of us cost only 84 rubles (about $3). Here, bereft of his pointer, Drannikov loosened up a bit to reveal some interesting facts about Mezen today. The town's population was about five thousand. (The 1797 census had given a figure of 1,522.) The oldest house still standing was built in 1800. All the local churches had been destroyed in the Russian Revolution; today, a single church received worshippers, its priest a retired doctor from St. Petersburg. Only one man in town, the local teacher, spoke any English (and that, as I would discover, pretty badly).

The local practice of bestowing nicknames on everyone, which might have accounted for the discrepancy between the sailors' names given by Kiselev in the 1796 "Oral Testimony of a Hunter from Mezen" and those discovered by Belov in the census records, was thriving in Mezen today. In fact, it was commonplace for a townsperson to have two different nicknames, a family handle (usually endearing), and a street name (often obscene: e.g., Kherovich, or "son of a prick").

There was no doubt that Inkov had once been one of the most common surnames in the region, nor that the family had bred generation after generation of Arctic sailors. There was an Inkov Fjord named after a heroic member of a Russian-Swedish expedition in 1903 that searched for the lost expedition of the German explorer Baron Toll. There was a Guba Inkova, or spit, on the Arctic coast, as well as a cape named for an Inkov far to the east. The brook that flowed through the center of Mezen, in fact, was the Ruchei Inkova—Inkov Creek.

The town's economy had declined since the collapse of the Soviet Union in 1991. "That is why you see more horses lately," said Drannikov. Indeed, I had noticed that horse droppings littered the dirt streets. The director launched on a paean to the local steeds: "A Mezen horse doesn't need much food. He eats moss and fish, and survives in winter by pawing through the snow to eat the grass. They tried Estonian horses here, and Hungarian horses, but off the roads they got stuck in the snow. A Mezen horse, it is smaller, it gets stuck in snow up to the chest, but it can jump out like a mouse."

The name Mezen, Drannikov pointed out, means "felicitous" or "successful" place. I had to concur. The ramshackle town, with its wooden sidewalks, its architectural gems of handcrafted wooden houses, was as beautiful a subarctic village as I had seen anywhere, easily the match for my favorite towns in Alaska, the Yukon, or Iceland. Since the moment we had arrived, a painful sense of longing had lodged in my heart, as I imagined the sailors stranded on frigid Edgeøya, dreaming of their hometown in high summer.

The "short drive" south to visit a traditional hamlet would turn out to last six and a half grueling hours. We would return to Mezen at 11:00 P.M., exhausted, having missed our rendezvous with the widows Inkova. And when I learned, through a stray remark overheard by Hugh, that the hamlet we drove to was Drannikov's birthplace, and realized that, not owning a car himself, Drannikov had manipulated us into using Vasily's taxi service to pay an overdue visit to his friends and relatives, I was silently furious.

Yet in the end, we would be able to reschedule our meeting with the widows for the next morning, on our last day in Mezen. And once I had calmed down, I had to admit that the journey south had been valuable in spite of Drannikov's hidden agenda.

That afternoon, fifty miles from Mezen, after two and a half hours of driving on a bad dirt road, we came to Pogorelets. The name means "the burned place," in allusion to an 1896 fire that destroyed the whole village. Yet so tradition-minded were the locals that the reconstructed houses and barns were, Drannikov indicated, probably closer to what Mezen looked like in the 1740s than Mezen itself, with its Soviet-style brick and cinder block buildings scattered among the handsome old wooden structures.

Among the dozen or so buildings that made up Pogorelets, I was surprised to see that even a simple farmer's homestead rose as a spacious, two-story edifice. "They kept the cows and horses inside the house in winter," explained Drannikov. "The sheep and goats were left in the street." On the outskirts of Arkhangel'sk a few days before, the three of us had visited the astonishing Karely Architectural Museum. Here, in the midst of forested hills, stood scores of old wooden buildings, which had been taken apart, transported to this site, and rebuilt board by board. Most were from the nineteenth century, a few from the eighteenth, and a good portion of them came from the Mezen area. At Karely, I had likewise been struck by the generous size of peasant homesteads, inevitably two stories tall, some with third-story attics. Most impressive of all were the towering churches, whose roofs were made of unpainted shingles exquisitely tailored to fit the Byzantine curves of domes and steeples.

All this architecture bore on that puzzling assertion in Le Roy that the Mezen men's hut on Edgeøya had stood eighteen feet tall. No need in Svalbard, of course, for a first floor to shelter cows and horses in winter, but perhaps the building tradition was so ingrained that a Mezener found it hard to halt construction at the first story.

For an hour we walked the fields and lanes of Pogorelets. A defunct windmill, itself two stories tall to catch a maximum of wind, stood guard in a mowed field over several high-heaped haystacks. A pretty white church, crowned by twin silver onion domes, dominated the southern outskirts of the village. Wooden fences zigzagged between fields, demarking ancient family boundaries. We sat on a bench overlooking the Mezen River, here a placid stream festooned with rowboats moored in coves.

Unfortunately, our idyllic stroll was marred by the relentless company of two local drunks. One of them seized our driver, Vasily, by the hand, shook it vigorously, and refused to let go. He reeked of alcohol. Vasily handled the man with a phlegmatic calm, even when the handclasp threatened to turn into a fight. Masha later recounted for me the dialogue between the two.

"Who are you?" the drunk had demanded.

"My name is Vasily."

"Where from?"

"Mezen."

"So what? I'm from here. I live here." The man slurred this pronouncement several times over, then, "So, it doesn't impress you? You got a problem with it?"

The other drunk latched on to Masha, whispering urgently in her ear, "Take my picture! Take my picture! Take my picture with you. Take my picture and fuck me!"

Our host in Pogorelets (and, I later divined, Drannikov's relative) was one Ivan Mikhailovich, a rugged, silver-haired farmer who looked much younger than his seventy years. A pair of crude tattoos adorned his muscular forearms—naked mermaid and heart pierced by sword. Ivan invited us into his house for tea. At Drannikov's urging, we had brought our own food. Though we tried to share our bread, bologna, cookies, and beer with Ivan and his wife, they insisted they had already eaten dinner. The tea was served in old porcelain cups, and Ivan's wife offered us homemade currant jam to spread on our bread.

Ivan was embarrassed about the drunks who had harassed us—"bastards," he called them. "There are more of them than there used to be," he sighed, prompting a comment from Vasily: "The less money, the more drunks."

Despite the perfect weather, the windows in the overheated kitchen were shut tight. I remembered a remark of C. S. Lewis's: "Those who work in the outdoors by day keep their windows closed at night." I let my gaze travel around the spic-and-span room. A good third of the kitchen space was occupied by a square clay oven, fully five feet tall. Suddenly Le Roy's description of the stove in the Mezeners' hut, which I had had trouble visualizing, stood realized before my eyes: "an earthen stove, constructed in the Russian manner; that is, a kind of oven without a chimney, which serves occasionally either for baking, for heating the room, or, as is customary amongst the Russian peasants, in very cold weather, for a place to sleep upon." I was delighted to hear Ivan, questioned by Hugh, declare that he and his wife slept atop their own oven on the bitterest winter nights.

Pouring our tea, the wife apologized to Masha for not offering us more. "I don't have a cow anymore," she said. "If I had a cow, I would serve you milk and cheese and butter."

Ivan took up the lament over hard times: "We used to have a cow, but she got old and we sold her. We have a bull that we will use for meat. Then probably get another bull.

"There's nowhere else for me to work. Up until Perestroika, there were a 150 head of cattle in Pogorelets. Then everything started to go to hell."

I asked Ivan if he knew the story of the sailors on Edgeøya. "I know something of this story," he began, but the officious Drannikov interrupted: "People do know the story now, because of my museum and the newspapers. The schoolchildren learn the story."

Ivan ignored his relative to expatiate on his personal linkage to the past: "We still know what life was like in the old Pomori days. And I know all of life here in Pogorelets, bit by bit, since 1931, when I was born. And before that, I know everything from my parents."

Before we left, we visited the cemetery, a scattering of headstones enclosed in a wrought iron fence, at the center of a clearing fringed by tall fir trees. Six or eight promise crosses, each carved with the obligatory prayer in Old Russian, proclaimed an immemorial debt to the Savior of the souls interred beneath the lush grass. Shining through the fir branches, casting light bursts on the Mezen River below our bench, the sun slid north, three or four degrees above the horizon. Nowhere that I had been in Russia—not even on the banks of the Fontanka on the finest of the White Nights in St. Petersburg—seemed as lovely as Pogorelets, cradled with lush meadows, its graveyard secluded in the forest.

Later I would sense that Drannikov was not particularly keen to arrange our rendezvous with the widows Inkova, for fear that two old women might upstage his carefully orchestrated chamber of commerce presentation of his hometown. Which, of course, was precisely what they did.

We greeted the two women early the next morning at a little coffee shop annexed to the town's main grocery store. It was another warm, beautiful day, but the widows Inkova had their heavy coats buttoned to the chin and bright-colored scarves tucked tight around their heads. Elizaveta Aleksandrovna Inkova, apparently in her late sixties or early seventies, had white hair, a firm mouth, and penetrating eyes. Her friend Nina Fedorovna Inkova was at least a decade younger; tall, with black hair and pink-framed glasses, she had a face that made me wonder whether there might be a trace of Samoyed in her lineage.

Elizaveta's husband, who had died in 1994, had been a carpenter; Nina's, deceased the same year, had operated a construction crane. We asked about their husbands' ancestry. "All Inkovs are from Novgorod," proclaimed Elizaveta. Nina added, "But now there are no men left in Mezen with the name Inkov." She smiled. "There are only us women and our creek." Both widows had been born in Mezen and had spent their whole lives here.

My first question, of course, was what they knew about the sailors from 1743 to 1749. "From childhood on," Nina insisted, "we knew this story. There is no doubt that our husbands are related to Aleksei and Khrisanf Inkov." So much, I thought, for Drannikov's smug claim that his museum had revived the forgotten tale.

It turned out that Nina had made an assiduous study of the old story, encompassing many years of local inquiry. She pulled out a handwritten chart that Hugh copied down. This fascinating document proved to be a family tree. Working backward from her husband, she had traced his ancestors to one Fedor, born in 1867. More remarkably, working from patronymics and local census records, she had hunted down Aleksei Inkov's great-grandfather, also named Fedor, who was recorded as having ventured out on an expedition to Novaya Zemlya in 1673. She had also deduced that Aleksei and Khrisanf had a common grandfather, named Emil'ian. "This would make them cousins," she explained. "But I suppose Khrisanf could also have been Aleksei's godson."

Nina had also managed to follow Aleksei and Khrisanf's offspring through the latter half of the eighteenth century. All that was lacking to close the gap was the seventy-five to one hundred years between those descendants and her husband's ancestors. She had come up with a mysterious Ilia Inkov, who floated in that lacuna, and who she suspected was a crucial link. "I would love to figure this all out," said Nina, "but I would have to go to St. Petersburg to look in the archives, and I don't have the money."

It was a sad measure of the provinciality of Mezen that, although both women knew of the existence of Le Roy's *Narrative*, neither of them had ever seen a copy. When we showed them our Russian edition from the Harvard library, they were beside themselves. Ascertaining that there was a single photocopy machine in town, in the office of the local newspaper, we promised to Xerox the text for them before catching our midday flight to Arkhangel'sk.

Genealogy aside, the widows Inkova proved to be repositories of vast funds of local lore. During the magical two hours that ensued, as I brought up one puzzling detail from Le Roy after another, the women leapt to explications wrung from their lifetimes in Mezen, and from the stories oldsters had told them when they were children.

Although Nina's husband, Yuri, had been a crane operator, he had inherited the Inkov passion for the sea. "Boats, boats, boats—always fishing," she recalled. "He took me often to the sea."

From their husbands, the women had gleaned the story of a heroic ancestor, Ilia Jacovlevich Inkov. On a 1902–03 expedition somewhere in the Arctic, the team leader was Aleksandr Kolchak. During the Civil War from 1919 to 1920, Kolchak would become the supreme leader of the Whites who opposed the Bolsheviks; after the communist victory Kolchak was executed. But almost two decades earlier, Kolchak had nearly perished in the Arctic. "They were walking on pack ice," said Nina, "jumping across leads. Kolchak jumped and fell into the water. They couldn't see him—he disappeared under the ice. Ilia Jacovlevich got him by his hair and dragged him unconscious onto the ice."

Ilia had died only in 1948, so Elizaveta had known him as a child. The two women had built a memorial to the courageous sailor. "We keep the weeds off it, keep it painted," said Elizaveta. "We were there renewing it just last week."

I brought up the astonishing ingenuity of the sailors on Edgeøya, fabricating lances to kill polar bears out of driftwood and nails. The women were not surprised. "It was very natural to use the nails and driftwood," said Nina. "Even today we have all kinds of people in

Mezen who do wonderful things with their hands. There is a man who carves wooden birds and makes boxes out of shells, just to decorate his house."

Nina had a fresh take on the sailors' feat of keeping the calendar through six years and three months. "Most likely," she said, "they wrote this down. If Aleksei was a pilot, he had to do all kinds of things with ship's logs, et cetera. Even if he was illiterate, he could draw the squares and circles he needed for navigation."

Time for a Mezener was less a matter of clocks than of an intuition in the blood. "For example," Nina went on, "living here on the river, we just know when the high tide or the low tide comes. We do not need watches or tide tables, even though each day the tide changes by an hour. We live with the river. People say, 'The big water is coming.'"

I asked about reckoning dates by the saints' days. Elizaveta grew animated. "For seventy years," she declared, "we couldn't officially believe, we were persecuted [under the atheistic Soviet regime]. They tried to make us forget the saints' days. But for three years now, we have a church, now we try to teach ourselves again. But the saints' days—oh, of course, those we knew all our lives from childhood. John the Baptist, Elijah, Saint Catherine, Ascension—we never forgot this."

Nina chimed in. "We just casually say, 'Oh, this year by Saint Elijah's Day, I had to . . .' The old wisdom was that on Saint Elijah's Day, August 2, the first half of the day is summer, the second half is autumn."

This saying suddenly stirred a memory of Masha's, from her own far more recent childhood in Novgorod. "We were not supposed to swim after Saint Elijah's Day," she said. "This was not a superstition—the water became too cold then."

Elizaveta continued: "There used to be churches in every village, each one devoted to a different saint. On the saint's day, there would be a big celebration in that village. People came from other villages all around."

So our parlay progressed. The sailors had killed twelve reindeer with only twelve shots from their musket? "That's usual," said Nina. "They couldn't miss. There were always good hunters from Mezen." Could their hut really have been eighteen feet high? Nina frowned: "That would be hard to heat. The normal height is eight feet. But what about their furs? They had to dry them somewhere. And to smoke the meat. My sons-in-law still smoke fish this way in the winter, hanging up high inside. The whole purpose of hunting [on Svalbard] was to make big supplies to keep all winter. And to keep away from the polar bears."

I drifted into a reverie. I would never find Klingstedt's notes. Why had I even hoped I might? On several occasions, I had burrowed through cardboard boxes stacked in my storage room at home, searching in vain for notes I myself had taken eight or ten years before. If I couldn't find my own jottings, how could I expect to lay my hands on Klingstedt's, relegated to Russian oblivion 251 years ago?

Yet here, in this Mezen coffee shop, I had blundered upon the next best thing. The knowledge of the widows Inkova came from the tail end of a local oral tradition so rich we Americans could scarcely imagine its equal. Because Mezen lay so far from the cosmopolitan world, its dependence on old sayings, on memories of other people's memories, remained all the more crucial to daily life. *Pace* Drannikov, museums and books were less important in Mezen than gossip and twice-told tales. And in the widows Inkova, I had discovered the two souls who, of all the living people in the world, were closest to the four shadowy castaways whose trail I had been following for most of a year.

I brought up the sailors' theories about how to prevent scurvy. Nina said, "Of course. We still eat raw meat in winter, and we still drink warm reindeer blood."

Elizaveta concurred. "My husband, when he slaughters a sheep, he cuts its throat and sticks a cup under it." She spoke in the present tense, as if Iakov Fedorovich Inkov were still alive. "He drinks it straight down. And he loves it."

Nina added, "We were nine children in my family. When there are nine, you don't waste anything. If we did not drink the blood, we mixed it with water and oil and fried it."

I asked about scurvy grass. *Cochlearia* seemed unknown in the Mezen area, but another herb, called Bogorodskaia grass, was a tried-and-true antiscorbutic. "The name means 'born by the mother of God,'" explained Elizaveta. "We still dry it out and make a tea from it. It is good not only for scurvy, but as a remedy for other things—liver disease, high blood pressure, and so on."

I could have talked to the widows Inkova all day, but the hour of our flight back to St. Petersburg was drawing near. I brought up Aleksei Inkov's remarkable deed of finding the Mezeners' hut by dead reckoning. This too was unsurprising to the women. Said Nina, "Well, there was no radio or TV then. The only way to communicate was to tell each other. The sailors came home and said, 'We went here, we went there. . . .' Of course, Aleksei had a compass, so he had a good idea where the ship had been blown to."

Smiling, she put her hand on my sleeve. "For us," she said, "it's sensational that Aleksei found the hut. But for our children, it will be sensational that an American came to Mezen."

Vasily was waiting to drive us to the airport. We dashed off to the newspaper office to photocopy Le Roy. When we returned to Nina's house, which was nearby, Elizaveta handed Masha a bowl of fresh strawberries. As we packed our bags in the gloomy hotel, we gobbled them down. They were the most delicious strawberries I had ever eaten.

As we loaded up Vasily's Lada, Masha walked back to Nina's house to return the strawberry dish. She found Nina on her hands and knees on the floor. The Xeroxed pages of Le Roy lay spread all over the couch and the carpet. "I'm reading it," Nina said breathlessly. "I'm almost done. It's so exciting. I was going to write you a letter. Thank you, thank you!"

"No," answered Masha. "Thank *you*."

8: Halfmoon Island

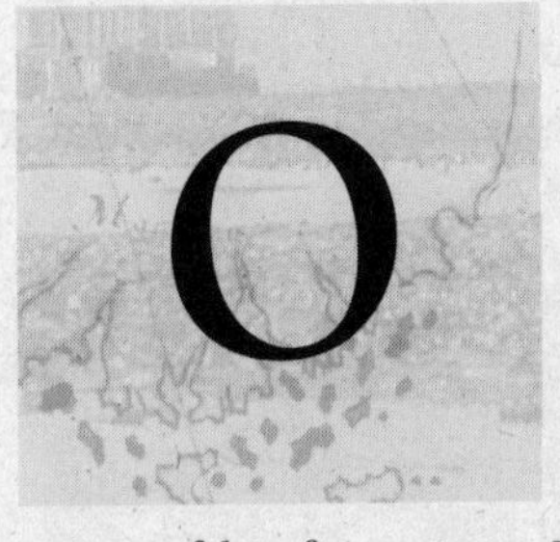

On the morning of August 14, I met Vaughn Hadenfeldt as he came out of security at Charles de Gaulle Airport in Paris. His normally genial face, seamed and weather-beaten by all his years as a climber and guide in the Utah canyons, looked drawn and haggard. It was not simply the disorientation of his first trip to Europe, or jet lag eight time zones from his home in Bluff: Vaughn had just been plunged into a personal crisis that had almost prevented his joining me for our Svalbard trip. Just weeks before, his father had been diagnosed with a terminal illness. There was a fair chance he would not survive the three or four weeks of Vaughn's absence. Yet when Vaughn had visited his father's bedside in the hospital in Fort Collins, Colorado, his father had insisted that Vaughn go ahead with his journey.

Sleep-deprived and distracted though he may have been, it was only a few hours later, as we drank beer at a café near our hotel, that Vaughn made the first of scores of canny observations that would prove just how valuable an ally he would be in my quest. Putting down his mug, he uttered, out of the blue, "What I just don't get is why you'd build a hut a mile and a half inland."

By this point, I must have read Le Roy's *Narrative* twenty times without being caught short by that sentence: "They began with exploring the country; and soon discovered the hut they were in search of, about an English mile and a half from the shore." (I had yet to unearth Le Roy's original German text, which placed the hut only a mile inland.)

"What's the advantage?" Vaughn went on. "You need driftwood for firewood. You're not going to find driftwood inland. And think of how much work it would be to haul all those logs they brought from Russia a mile and a half to build a hut—how big was it?"

"Thirty-six feet by eighteen feet by eighteen feet tall," I recited.

"Give me a break."

The moment Vaughn had spoken, I recognized the judiciousness of his critique. It was the pragmatic guide in him speaking, the man used to hauling supplies about as part of his job; I was perhaps too abstract in temperament, too bookish, to notice such an obvious implausibility. Later, making a careful scrutiny of the excellent modern maps of Svalbard, I could find only a tiny handful of little black squares (marking buildings) any distance from the coast—and those, I would deduce, were modern hunting cabins reached by dog team or snowmobile. Of the six black squares indicated on the map of Edgeøya, all six were smack on the coast.

The next day, Michel Guérin arrived by train from Chamonix. Michel and Vaughn had never met before, but I sensed that they would hit it off, despite a language barrier serious enough so that during the trip I would effectively serve as interpreter between the two. (In all fairness, Michel's English was almost comprehensible, despite its wildly idiosyncratic flourishes. For Vaughn, French was a closed book, though by the end of our journey he was murmuring the occasional "*Bonjour*" or "*Entrez.*")

Over lunch, Michel delivered one of his characteristic apothegms. Touching, successively, the four fingers of his left hand with the index finger of his right, he said, *"Nous sommes quatre—l'écrivain, l'oeil, le tireur. . . ."* I was the writer; Vaughn was the eye, for I had told Michel that I had never met anyone who could spot an artifact in the dirt the way Vaughn could; Mats Forsberg, our Swedish guide, was presumably the sharpshooter who would keep the polar bears at bay. *"Et moi,"* concluded Michel, *"le branleur."*

I burst into laughter. Vaughn gave me a quizzical frown, pleading translation. Easier said than done. A *"branleur"* (the word is not found in your standard *Larousse* or *Cassell's*) is a goof-off, a lazybones, but also a masturbator, a "jack-off." We finally decided that "fuck-off" was the aptest rendering. Though a characteristically self-mocking categorization, *branleur* would turn out to be far from Michel's role on Svalbard. He would prove instead to be a kind of oracular skeptic, Voltaire crossed with Rimbaud.

Vaughn, who, as a former hunter, had a healthy respect for polar bears, had hoped to bring his own rifle to Svalbard, but we had given up on this plan after learning that it was virtually impossible to get a firearm through French customs. He was not reassured to learn that, for our self-defense, Mats had rented four World War II vintage Mausers. Now Michel offered a rueful old Gallic definition of Mauser: "A German gun for killing French rabbits."

That evening, at a party of Parisian friends, two guests independently dubbed Vaughn, with his sandy shoulder-length hair, his pendulous gray dewlap of a goatee, "Boofalo Beel." I was bemused to realize that, among all our American Wild West heroes, only that overblown circus performer William Cody conjured up an image in the French mind. But they were right: Vaughn could easily have played Boofalo Beel in a B-movie shoot-'em-up.

The next day the three of us flew to Tromsø, in northern Norway. Situated on an island in the center of a deep fjord at 69½° N, Tromsø is not only a perfect natural seaport, but has served for centuries as its country's principal gateway to the Arctic.

Mats Forsberg met our plane and drove us to a handsome downtown hotel, perched on the harbor's edge. In the lounge, we drank the first of what would be many bottles of Ringnes (Norway's leading beer) and talked logistics.

Even on such relatively tame junkets as an inn-to-inn skiing trip in Vermont or a caving jaunt in Bermuda, I have always felt a certain malaise at that pregnant moment when the group meets its guide for the first time. Accustomed to organizing and leading expeditions myself, I find it hard to submit to someone else's outdoor style and rules, even when the expertise required lies beyond my credentials.

Here, with Mats as the guide I had hired via telephone and e-mail, loomed the most serious trip I had ever undertaken with someone else in the driver's seat. Over the Internet during the past half year, Mats had talked a good game; but I realized that I knew very little about his background and wilderness experience.

Forty-three years old, Mats was a solidly built Swede with tousled, graying hair that looked as though it had seldom been combed, and a three-days' growth of stubble on his chin and cheeks (which managed, during the upcoming weeks, to maintain its degree of scruffiness intact, like a well-maintained first cut of rough on a golf fairway). He spoke in a forceful, almost declamatory voice. From that first moment, I sensed in Mats an undercurrent of anger against the world, camouflaged beneath a practiced charm.

His first performance in that hotel lounge was not one to inspire confidence. I think I had never before witnessed such a tightly wound combination of sheer manic anxiety with utter distractedness. (I later wrote in my notebook: "completely hyper, digressive, scattershot.") Mats had put together, I had to admit, an admirable structure for our journey, and that had not been easy to pull off. We would fly the day after next to Longyearbyen, the capital of Svalbard, where we would buy our groceries and rent our gear. A cruise ship sailing three days later, on August 20, would take us on as passengers for three more days, until we drew near Edgeøya.

Off the shore of Edgeøya, the cruise ship would deposit us and our gear in our single rented Zodiac, then steam away, leaving us on our own. Almost two weeks later, another ship, a Norwegian research vessel called the *Lance,* would gather us up as its last duty on Svalbard, then head straight south across the Barents Sea back to Tromsø. A sizable hunk of the hefty fee I had advanced Mats bought our passage on these two ships.

Having outlined this itinerary in the hotel lounge, Mats suddenly grew stern, scolding us like the wayward ditherers he already seemed to think we might be. "We absolutely *have to be* on Halfmoon Island for the September third pickup," he lectured. "The ship will not wait for us, and the Sysselmannen will not do a rescue if we fuck up and miss the pickup. In that case, we must take the Zodiac all the way back to Longyearbyen." Mats fixed us with a monitory scowl.

Our guide adjourned for dinner with his wife and kids. Michel, Vaughn, and I headed out to a nearby restaurant, where Michel scandalized Vaughn by ordering whale steak. We discussed the bizarre performance in the hotel lounge. "He is like a beginner," mused Michel. "We must keep him focused on our goal."

The next morning, we window-shopped. Vaughn lingered in front of a gun store, staring longingly at three or four rifles whose makes he knew well, and which he would certainly have chosen over a half-century-old Mauser. In the window of a sports shop, we beheld an inflated Zodiac. It looked big enough to hold one passenger and a couple of duffel bags. The dicey nature of our transport along the shores of Edgeøya began to come home to me.

The bookstore window was dominated by a big poster of a polar bear sauntering toward the camera, snout in the air. The text was in English:

> It attacks without warning—KEEP YOUR DISTANCE! Always carry a weapon with you in areas where polar bears may be encountered. Stay calm if a bear approaches. If you think the situation is becoming dangerous, toss away your mittens, hat, scarf, or something similar. The bear might stop and sniff at the garments, giving you a chance to get to safety.
>
> Aim toward the chest or shoulder, rather than the head, which is easy to miss. The attack often comes very quickly. The bear takes a course directly toward the prey at a quick trot, or in big bounds.

I looked at Vaughn and Michel. One of us—it might have been me—emitted a nervous giggle.

Mats picked us up after breakfast and took us to Polaria, the exhibition hall of the Norsk Polarinstitutt, where a show of his photographs had recently been hung. He told us, in fact, that he made most of his living as a photographer rather than as a guide. The man had calmed down considerably from the evening before: his manic air had evaporated.

The pictures, large blowups of Arctic scenes, were excellent. It was the captions I relished, however, for Mats had annotated his photos in Norwegian and English. These bite-sized editorials gave me some insight into the guide we had met only yesterday. A gang of walruses lounged on a rocky shore: "On the beach they spend the time sleeping, bickering, farting and burping, just like you and me."

A man (apparently Mats himself) staring up at a towering iceberg occasioned a philosophical reflection: "A place where I succeeded to release my self from traditional western thinking and instead have the opportunity to slide into a self-realized state." "Polar Bears Sex," on the other hand—a real photographic coup, I thought—taught a lesson in humility: "It was a most gentil approach and contact that lasted for at least 1 hour. I think we humen have a lot to learn from polar bears."

After Polaria, we paid a visit to the town's Polar Museum, which was strong on Arctic history. A number of Russian artifacts from the nineteenth century were on display, including a pair of thick-handled wooden oars from a *lodja* or *kotch.* What interested me most, however, was a diorama illustrating the classic fox trap used in the Arctic. It was simplicity itself. A grid of boards about two and a half feet square was laid on the ground. A matching grid was tilted up at a 45-degree angle, with heavy stones resting on its upper surface. A single thin stick kept the upper grid perched, like an open jaw ready to snap shut. The fox took the bait, which was attached to this trigger stick, thereby dislodging it. The stone-heavy grid collapsed, crushing or at least immobilizing the fox.

Mats told us that traps just like this one, some of them very old, abounded on the shores of Svalbard. This raised a question I had puzzled over for a while. Le Roy makes no mention of fox traps. Instead, he insists, the sailors on Edgeøya used their bow and arrows to kill "no less than two hundred and fifty raindeer, besides a great number of blue and white foxes."

Surely, as hunters, the Mezen men were familiar with the simple design of the fox trap. Is it possible they lacked the proper driftwood boards and nails to concoct such snares? Or was this another of Le Roy's misunderstandings? The fact that fox traps were still in common use on Svalbard well into the twentieth century argued convincingly that they were a more efficient way to bag the animal than shooting it with a rifle; and surely, killing a fox with a bow and arrow was a far more difficult feat than plugging one with a modern gun. If the Mezen sailors had truly hunted the fox with bow and arrow, then it must have been because they lacked the materials to build the simple traps—which in itself, given the Pomori's skills as craftsmen, seemed unlikely. Mats went on to point out that the blue and the white fox were one and the same, blue (really a blue-gray sheen) simply designating the animal's summer coat.

At lunch, Mats told us a little bit about his background. In 1982, he had started working on a cruise ship called the *Explorer* as a deckhand. Eventually he had graduated to leading Zodiac shore excursions for the clients. He was a classic autodidact, not only as naturalist and historian, but as photographer. Mats's mood today was the obverse face of yesterday's: he seemed subdued, even self-effacing. Gone was the belligerence of his initial briefing in the hotel lounge.

"I'm not academically educated," he said at one point. "I'm nothing—I'm just Mats. But that's okay—I have a good life." It occurred to me to wonder whether the three over-schooled outdoorsmen he had been hired to guide posed a certain threat. Was the bluff, hectoring style Mats had exhibited yesterday a compensation for feeling somewhat intimidated—both by us and by the difficulty of our quest?

Although I had explained the nature of that quest to Mats as early as the previous January, he had, in one sense, failed to do his homework. Right there in his hometown (I would later learn), in the library of the Norsk Polarinstitutt, there were several editions of Le Roy, including the English. Yet by the time we arrived, Mats knew the story only through Sir Martin Conway's garbled résumé of it in *No Man's Land.* It was not until halfway through our trip that Mats sat down and actually read the photocopy of Le Roy's *Narrative* that I had brought with me.

This bespoke not laziness, I sensed, but the self-taught man's distrust of books. During our stay on Edgeøya, time and again, when I would read a passage from one of my texts out loud, Mats would say, "This is all bullshit." It was at such moments that the buried anger came to the surface.

The first of these outbursts occurred that second day in Tromsø. Out of the blue, Mats suddenly pronounced, "David, I'm going to have an argument with you. These guys were Inuit. I don't think stupid Christian white people could survive this long."

I was nonplussed. Inuit? What in God's name did Mats mean? The Inuit, or Eskimo, had never come anywhere near Svalbard.

It turned out that "Inuit" was Mats's all-purpose designation for "natives." He meant, I suppose, that the Inkovs, Sharapov, and Verigin must have been Samoyeds. "I don't think so, Mats," I said, then launched into what I had learned in Russia. I mentioned Nina's family tree linking the Inkovs back to their Novgorod origins.

"An Inuit could be named Inkov," Mats insisted. "It happens all the time." His verdict was inflexible. "Stupid Christians, they would die the same way as Franklin and Scott did." Where, I wondered, did this chip on Mats's shoulder come from?

Tromsø seemed an appealing, civilized, thoroughly European village, even though it lay three degrees north of the Arctic Circle. Michel, Vaughn, and I thus felt a certain ambivalence about leaving behind our spiffy hotel, the sophisticated downtown restaurants, the excellent bookstore (where I found a facsimile reprint edition of Sir Martin Conway's 1906 *No Man's Land,* out of print and extremely rare in the U.S. and U.K.).

In its own way, the Norwegian seaport was preparing us for our sojourn in the deep north. Every other hotel and supermarket lobby seemed to showcase a stuffed polar bear. Michel paused as if paralyzed beneath one brute that had been mounted on its hind legs, fangs bared, forepaws extended to seize the unlucky Frenchman who had blundered near its den. The crown of the bear's head towered a good four feet above Michel's.

On the plane to Longyearbyen, Mats translated out loud a story in the local newspaper. It seemed that an old female bear, previously tranquilized and tagged by a Canadian researcher, had taken up residence in the outskirts of Longyearbyen, where she made a living robbing cabins. Svalbardians might have taken this nuisance in stride, but the bear had recently given birth to two cubs. "They have become hut bears," reported the journalist. "They specialize in breaking into huts. She trains the young ones." So, just the day before, local wardens had shot all three bears with tranquilizer darts, loaded them onto a helicopter, flown them to Edgeøya, and set them loose, where they ought to bother no one.

"Oh, great," said Vaughn; then, affecting a drawl I had come to know on our Utah hikes, that of the Swedish ranchers on the Nebraska plains among whom he had grown up: "Them bears gonna be *real* pissed off 'n they wake up."

Late on the afternoon of August 18, we landed on the coastal runway just outside Longyearbyen. At 78° 15', the town lay nearly seven degrees of latitude farther north than I had ever before been. For Vaughn too, it was a new farthest north; Michel, however, had once skied to the North Pole, after landing by plane on the ice sixty miles away, on a commercial junket led by his good friend Christian de Marliave.

The landscape was bare and severe: the town nestled around a valley mouth made of gravel, patched with sedges and scraggly tundra, without the hint of a bush sprouting anywhere. Glum schistose hills loomed to the north and south. As we took a taxi into town, I surveyed the boxy, workmanlike houses, walled with sheet iron painted bright colors to relieve the universal drabness. Our hotel, however, the Spitsbergen Funken, turned out to be a semiluxurious gem, whose rooms and lounges mingled chrome and unvarnished blond wood in a tasteful Scandinavian design.

With a population of 1,400, Longyearbyen is the most cosmopolitan of Svalbard's five towns. Along with a handful of far-flung research stations, those five hamlets comprise the bulk of the archipelago's meager population of about 3,300 souls. All of Svalbard's residents are confined to Spitsbergen proper. The other three main islands, Nordaustlandet, Barentsøya, and Edgeøya, are uninhabited.

Tucked in a cove of the Adventfjorden, a small arm of the spacious Isfjorden (Ice Fjord), Longyearbyen claims a well-sheltered nook some fifty miles inland from Spitsbergen's west coast, itself gentled by Gulf Stream currents. The weather can often be atrocious, but when we arrived, a wan northerly sun gleamed over the fjord, and the temperature was a fairly balmy 40° F, making the place seem almost attractive.

In its glory days through the 1920s, Longyearbyen produced more than ten thousand tons of coal per year. Today the mines are all but abandoned, and the town's raison d'être is a blend of science and tourism. Almost all of the latter consists of summer jaunts on spartan cruise ships that make leisurely circumnavigations of the archipelago. On one such ship, a Russian vessel called the *Professor Moltanovsky,* we would set sail two days hence. In the meantime, we needed to dash about Longyearbyen in a beat-up Toyota Tercel Mats had borrowed to buy and rent our supplies. Because we would be picked up after two weeks by the Norwegian ship *Lance,* which would head straight for Tromsø, everything we had brought with us to Longyearbyen had to go on the cruise ship, and then to be offloaded by Zodiac and carried to our camp on Edgeøya.

Over the months, Mats and I had refined my wildly ambitious original plan. I had at first hoped to disembark near Hvalpynten, where Keilhau and Löwenigh had visited the large Russian settlement in 1827. From there I hoped to poke along Edgeøya's south coast, combing the shores of Tjuvfjorden, rounding Negerpynten, visiting Halfmoon Island, then finishing with a jaunt up the narrow strip of southeast coast called Stones Forland, up to the point where it abrupted in the massive Edgeøyjøkulen, the icecap spilling into the Barents Sea. I had imagined moving camp every day, shuttling our gear in the Zodiac, pitching our tents on the seashore.

Mats, however, had made it clear that this itinerary was impossible. Quite aside from the distance involved—ninety to a hundred miles by protractor, at least 130 as the boat would have to wend—the shallows and submerged rocks off the south coast of Edgeøya made navigating there treacherous. To get from one shore landing to another, we might have to head straight out to sea for several miles, traverse east in certifiably deep, safe water, then pick our way hypervigilantly back to shore. There was no way to carry all our goods in one load on the Zodiac, and ferrying supplies would create logistical chaos. On top of this, as I was to see firsthand, a tent camp on the Edgeøya coast was an open invitation to a disastrous and possibly fatal attack by polar bears.

Now we drafted Plan B. Mats had scored a coup with the Sysselmannen by winning permission for us to stay in two huts on Edgeøya, historic buildings that had been renovated to serve as emergency shelters. Normally the few visitors whose expeditions to Edgeøya were approved were not allowed to camp in these huts, but Mats had argued that our quest required exceptional help.

The two huts were at Andréetangen, on a jetty some fifteen miles north of Negerpynten, and on Halfmoon Island (see map, page 191). Mats asked my preference. Remembering Keilhau's cryptic prediction that the place to look for the Mezeners' hut was on Halfmoon Island, I chose the latter. It was, after all, an easy decision, since by prearrangement the *Lance* would pick us up on September 3 on Halfmoon Island. Should we choose to base ourselves at Andréetangen, we would still need to get ourselves and all our gear to Halfmoon by the 3rd—a distance of some twenty-five miles across often perilous seas.

Thus instead of the mobile expedition I had first envisaged, we would set up a base camp at Bjørneborg ("Bear Castle"), as the hut on Halfmoon was named. From that cabin, we would make day trips along the coast, looking for traces of the long-vanished Pomori. The single (though significant) disadvantage of this plan lay in the fact that, in dense fog or heavy seas, we would effectively be trapped on our island, able to explore only the four-by-one-mile surface of its crescent-shaped mass.

Another factor weighed in my decision. Back in July, shortly before leaving for Russia, Masha Olmsted had had a last phone conversation with Viktor Derzhavin, the archaeologist whose popular article in *Mir Severa* had put us on the trail of the enigmatic Vadim Starkov. According to Derzhavin, Starkov's own search for the castaways' hut, some fifteen years ago, had planned to focus "on the eastern part of Edgeøya, toward the south." The savant added, "Starkov was confident that where he had already looked, the hut was not there. But Starkov was never willing to go inland."

These were puzzling remarks, as if embedding a riddle within their calculated ambiguities. Then, on our last day in St. Petersburg, Masha had succeeded in reaching Starkov in Moscow, at last returned from the Lena delta and on the eve of heading off himself to Svalbard. Since Starkov and I could not search for the hut together, where ought I to look?

According to Masha, Starkov's response oozed sincerity. (Later I would wonder.) "My first choice," the man said, "would be to the northeast of Halfmoon Island." This description specified the narrow coastline, Stones Forland, pinched between the great icecap of the Edgeøyjøkulen and the Barents Sea. "My second choice would be from Negerpynten up to the delta." This meant a good thirty-five miles of coastline facing the Tjuvfjorden from the east, a stretch that included the refurbished hut at Andréetangen. "I have definitely searched the coast from Halfmoon Island to the south cape at Negerpynten," Starkov went on. "The hut is not there. David will see that it is not there. There are no triangular-shaped mountains there."

What in the world did Starkov mean? Le Roy never mentions triangular mountains—only "many mountains and steep rocks of a stupendous height," a description that looked on the map as though it could apply to any stretch of Edgeøya's south coast. And when had Starkov searched the shore between Halfmoon Island and Negerpynten? Apropos of the lost hut, Derzhavin's article had stated, "Several years ago, an archaeological expedition from Moscow carried out a research mission in this region of the archipelago, but stopped a few kilometers short of this island [Halfmoon], on account of a tight work schedule, and so missed the opportunity to investigate this out-of-the-way place." Was Starkov trying to lure me away from the ground he himself was most keen to investigate?

By August 18, Starkov was installed in Barentsburg, only twenty miles west of Longyearbyen along the coast of Isfjorden—the traditional center of Russian research in Svalbard. Aboard our cruise ship, we would sail within sight of the town as we headed out to the open sea off the west coast of Spitsbergen. But, as Mats made abundantly clear, "Take me to Vadim" was a command that would fall on the deaf ears of the captain of the *Professor Moltanovsky,* even though he himself was Russian. The cruise ship had its own itinerary to observe.

So, from Longyearbyen by telephone, through a bilingual aide in Barentsburg, I had my first and only "conversation" (such as it was) with the sibylline Starkov. After apologizing for not being able to meet the archaeologist in Barentsburg, I played it straight. "I plan first to search the shore northeast of Halfmoon Island."

"Okay," he answered through his interpreter.

"Then, if there is time, from Negerpynten north."

"Okay."

"Do you think this is a good plan?"

"Yes. Fine."

Especially through the screen of an interpreter, these deadpan responses were unreadable. I hung up more perplexed than ever.

At the supermarket in Longyearbyen, Mats ran into an old friend named Hallvar Holn, a schoolteacher who had taken a keen interest in Svalbard's history. Holn knew Starkov's work well. The great thrust of the archaeologist's research, according to Holn, was to prove (as before him M. I. Belov had sought to prove) that Russians had reached Svalbard before the official discovery by Barents in 1596. "Starkov found a piece of wood," said Holn, "that was dendro-dated to the 1440s. But you always have the 'old wood problem.'" I knew about the old wood problem from Anasazi sites in the Southwest. A log carried by ship from Russia to Svalbard might well bear tree rings that proved the tree was alive in the 1440s, but this did not prove the journey had taken place during those years. The sailors could well have carved timbers in Russia from a long-dead tree. "And Starkov says he found an inscription from 1592," Holn continued, "but this could be a fake"—not Starkov's forgery, he explained, but some anonymous sailor's. Nonetheless, these hints of archaeological chauvinism on Starkov's part gave me further pause about his advice as to where to search for the Mezeners' hut. If the man was determined to prove that it was his countrymen, not Dutch or Icelanders, who had discovered Svalbard, why would he be willing to help an American he had never met snatch the prize of the lost hut from under his nose?

Mats seemed to know half the residents of Longyearbyen, thanks to his many sojourns here as a tour guide on the cruise ships. He kept bumping into cronies on the streets, with each of whom he would engage in a long dialogue in Norwegian. For a day and a half, Michel, Vaughn, and I played tourist. We hiked up to one of Longyear's abandoned coal mines, gaining an eagle's-eye view of the town huddled below. A pair of glacial tongues snaked down the valleys to the northeast and southeast, ready to obliterate the village during the next Ice Age.

In town, a good portion of the populace carried rifles whenever they walked the streets, even on a three-block jaunt to a café. Although there are far fewer polar bears in west Spitsbergen than on Edgeøya, they pose a constant threat to the locals. It seems, however, a universal human tendency to tame the monsters that haunt our collective imagination by turning them cute. Longyearbyen was awash in polar bear kitsch. The mascot of Mack Arctic Light beer, emblazoned on the big white trucks that delivered it, was a lumbering ursine straight out of a petting zoo. In the supermarket sat a big stuffed bear doll with a cowboy hat on its head and a tag that read (in Norwegian), "Hi! My name is Isak, and I would love to live with you." The price: 2,500 kroner, or about $280. Between Isak's legs sat a baby bear with a baseball cap on its head.

The weather was holding magnificently: our first taste of Svalbard thus seemed benign. Mindful that we had arrived during the warmest time of year, I asked a bartender about the long winter. "The first sun comes on March 8," she answered. "There is a big party for one week. If you stand by the church on March 8, you can see the sun for twenty seconds."

Michel and I pondered a grid of burnt stumps protruding from the ground, the gloomy ruins of a large building the Nazis had burned during World War II. (How, I wondered, could remote Svalbard have been a pivot point in that war?) We scared up our first fox, who ran to safety up a talus-strewn hillside above us. With Mats, we visited the cemetery, a small forest of simple white crosses. Half the dead had perished during the great influenza epidemic of 1917–20. From these graves—of miners too poor or unfriended to warrant shipping their remains back to their native Norway—American researchers within the last decade had performed the remarkable feat of isolating the still viable virus that had unleashed the greatest plague of the twentieth century.

Two of the graves belonged to friends of Mats, ages twenty and eighteen, who had been killed in accidents. One lad, he told us, had been riding his Zodiac back from Barentsburg when it hit a wave and he fell out. He had a survival suit on, but the boat spun out of control in wild circles, and as he tried to climb aboard, the propeller cut open his suit. Water rushed in and the fellow drowned. The other was the last to leave a hut across the Adventfjorden after a winter party. His snowmobile broke down on the near shore. Trying to walk back to town, he floundered in deep snow. High tide came in and soaked him. He struggled on into the night, crawling under a full moon, before he collapsed only a hundred yards from a dog pound. His corpse was found the next day.

Despite these touristic interludes, a tension hung over our two days in Longyearbyen. The *Moltanovsky* would embark at 7:00 P.M. on August 20, and we had damned well better have our logistical act together by then. Yet hour by hour, as Mats ran around town in our car trying to round up supplies, the doubts that he had left in the wake of his manic performance in the hotel lounge in Tromsø magnified. For all his experience on cruise ships, Mats seemed utterly disorganized in the face of our expeditionary needs.

I accompanied our guide during a long parlay in the office of one Edwin, an old friend who had agreed to rent us a Zodiac. The two men bantered in Norwegian with all the laid-back garrulousness of septuagenarians reminiscing on a park bench as they fed pigeons bread crumbs. But the upshot of the dialogue was alarming: the engine on the Zodiac Edwin had reserved for us wasn't working. He would tinker with it overnight, but if he couldn't get it running, we would have to borrow or rent an engine from some villager.

In the excellent supermarket, Mats strolled the aisles, tossing packages of frozen fish and loaves of bread into his carriage in apparently random fashion. I prided myself on the ability to shop for an expedition without a grocery list, and I had sometimes assembled provisions for five for a month in Alaska in just the same fashion. But something about Mats's casualness bothered me. "How many days' food are you buying?" I asked.

"Nine."

"But aren't we going to be on Halfmoon for thirteen?"

Mats paused, seeming to count in his head. "I think you are right." He resumed his package tossing with renewed zeal.

Later Vaughn accompanied Mats on his second round of grocery shopping, to ensure we bought enough food. And he helped Mats choose our gear out of an outfitters' warehouse. This exercise, too, did not inspire confidence. After Mats had thrown a few cooking pots into a bag, Vaughn said, "How about cups?"

"Yeah, that's a good idea."

Later Vaughn pleaded, "Don't we need an axe and a saw?"

"Don't worry, I'll get to that." In the end, however, he forgot. On board our cruise ship, Vaughn was perplexed to overhear Mats trying to borrow an axe and a saw from crewmates, who looked nonplussed.

A beer drinker by preference, Vaughn bought several cases of Ringnes. It fell to Michel and me to select our wine. To our astonishment, the supermarket had a decent selection of middle-range French wines at about the same prices as obtained in France (Longyearbyen, we learned, was a duty-free town). With our carriage groaning under the weight of thirty bottles of pinot noir, Mouton Cadet, Graves, and Sancerre, we approached the cashier—and narrowly averted disaster. The Japanese couple in line ahead of us, their faces stricken, were in the process of returning all their bottles to the shelves. We deduced that there was a law (or at least a rule) against cruise ship passengers buying their own wine and liquor to carry on board—clearly a way of ensuring that tourists would buy all their cruise booze from the bar on the ship.

When it came our turn, the woman behind the counter eyed our carriage and asked sternly, "You are not going on a cruise?"

"Oh, no," I said.

"You arrived in Svalbard by airplane, and you will leave by airplane?"

"Exactly."

Something looked fishy, nonetheless. "I am a writer," I explained. "We are going on an expedition, to look for a hut from the eighteenth century—"

She interrupted me with an impatient wave of the hand. Scientists were always doing crazy things in the field. Our wine stash was home free.

The contrast between the cushy style of our own expedition and the dire circumstances of the sailors in 1743 was not lost upon us. On Halfmoon Island, to be sure, we would be out of contact with anyone else in the world. The only radio we would carry was a two-way walkie-talkie, good across at most six or eight miles. But we would have the crash beacon to set off in case of an emergency, sending our distress call via satellite to Paris and (in theory) launching a rescue from Longyearbyen. Despite all these hedges against catastrophe, despite our wine and beer (and some Armagnac Michel had brought from Paris, in lieu of the "konjak" Mats had demanded), we hoped to gain in a mere two weeks some kind of empathic glimpse into the trials the Pomori had faced two and a half centuries before.

Only three hours before the *Moltanovsky* was scheduled to leave port, however, our whole journey was in jeopardy. For some reason, the survival suits that Mats thought he had reserved for us were not available. Mats would not explain what the glitch was, though Vaughn learned that the imminent onset of the reindeer hunting season had left the suits in short supply. Instead, we drove from one office to another, waiting politely like job applicants in the lobbies until each functionary told us that no, he was sorry, he didn't have any suits he could rent or lend us.

In Arctic seas, a life jacket is of no use, for in water near the temperature of freezing, one succumbs to hypothermia in less than an hour. The survival suit is a heavy, uncomfortable, one-piece garment, colored orange for long-range visibility, that encases the body like an astronaut's uniform. Hoods and clunky rubber boots are built into the suit, and one dons thick rubber gloves, so that, fully garbed, a survivor exposes to the elements only a sealed-shut ring of flesh around the eyes, nose, and mouth. The suit has abundant flotation built into its fabric. In theory, in a survival suit one can bob on one's back for up to twenty-four hours in 32° seas before hypothermia takes its inevitable toll. Quite a few victims of Zodiac flips and accidents have been plucked by helicopter from otherwise certain death because they were wearing survival suits.

We were not going to attempt two weeks of shuttling between Halfmoon Island and the coast of Edgeøya without the suits. With Mats unwilling to force the issue or explain the problem, I grew exasperated. "For Christ's sake," I said, "if we have to, let's *buy* some goddamned suits." They cost, I learned, upward of $1,000 each, but I had already poured so much moolah into my wild-goose chase, what was another four grand?

"Don't worry, David," Mats placated unconvincingly, "I will work something out."

I lost it. "Why the fuck didn't you have this all sorted out months ago?" I yelled. Mats did not answer.

Vaughn, whose taciturnity precluded such an outburst, was at least as upset as I was. Since arriving in Paris, he had been having a hard time sleeping, the combined effect of jet lag and agony over his father's illness. Now, as our deadline crept closer by the minute, his stomach was tied in knots. As he later told me, "If I'm guiding a trip, the day before the expedition, my clients ought to be able to just lie around and do nothing." Michel confided darkly, "I think Mats has never before done such a serious expedition. I fear the worst."

It seems to go against Norwegian notions of civility to express anger or even urgency—which explained why, instead of bursting into offices blaring, "We have to find survival suits!" (as I would have done), we waited patiently, for example, as the headmaster of the local college finished his business with a student before telling Mats that unfortunately he had no suits to lend. Once I had unloaded on him with all the fury of my frustration, Mats refused to let me accompany him on his search.

An hour before departure, Mats returned with a big smile on his face. "We have the suits," he said quietly.

"What happened?" I asked.

"I do not often get angry," Mats said cryptically, "but this time I did."

In a big warehouse, we picked out the first suits at hand (none of them would fit very well, so bulky and shapeless were they), then dashed for the cruise ship. As the *Moltanovsky* sounded its horn and crept away from the dock, we felt a relief more akin to emotional collapse than joy at the commencement of our journey. During the next two weeks, I would come to admire many of Mats's talents, but in a sense, the ambience of our group never recovered from the impact of the guide's sorry performance in Longyearbyen. Throughout the trip, a three-against-one undercurrent subtly pervaded the air inside our hut on Halfmoon Island, and whenever two of us hiked out of Mats's earshot, we discussed his character and his decisions.

A few years before, for a magazine assignment, I had spent three weeks aboard the *Professor Molchanov*, the *Moltanovsky*'s sister ship, as it carried clients from an American travel company to Antarctica. With the collapse of the Soviet Union (and of its research budgets) in 1991, these icebreakers built for science turned to Arctic and Antarctic cruises to pay the bills. Now both ships (as well as a small flotilla of kindred vessels) spent each northern summer circumnavigating Svalbard, each austral summer poking south from Ushuaia, Argentina, across the Drake Passage and along the Antarctic Peninsula.

So similar were the two Russian ships that as I prowled the corridors of the *Moltanovsky*, I felt as though I had returned to a favorite hotel. And, as I had on my previous jaunt, I quickly grew addicted to the hearty meals served by zaftig Russian women in heels and stockings, to beers at any hour in the comfy bar, to the lordly views from the bridge (to which, unlike the protocol on most cruises, passengers were given unlimited access).

I had found in Antarctica, however, that the ship routine ran the risk of trivializing the wilderness we glided through. So safe and snug was the icebreaker that the landscape began to seem like a video projected onto some sky-to-sea VCR screen. The Antarctic cruise had been billed by the travel company as "the adventure of a lifetime," but it really wasn't adventurous at all. At periodic intervals, we were taxied from ship to shore in Zodiacs, then allowed to putter about photographing penguins or to take tea at an Argentine research station. I was forbidden to hike out of earshot of the paranoid group leader, who insisted that sudden katabatic winds could turn our little picnics into catastrophes.

The same drill obtained aboard the *Moltanovsky.* The cruise was underbooked, with only twenty-nine passengers for sixty berths, most of the clients hailing from the Netherlands. The ship's crew was Russian, but the tour leaders were cocky Scots, some of whom ordered about the Zodiac drivers and serving ladies with all the arrogance of the colonial imperialists their forefathers had no doubt been. The captain was a gruff bear of a Russian who refused to acknowledge our presence on the bridge. Said Vaughn, "He looks like Khrushchev. Looks like he's drunk a lot of vodka in his life."

A few hours into the cruise, we sailed in sight of Barentsburg, tucked inside the mouth of the Grønfjorden. From the deck, I waved, "Bye, bye, Vadim!"

Oddly, in their initial briefings, the tour leaders made no mention of the special errand the four of us were embarking on; they did not even acknowledge that we would be dropped off on the third day. The other passengers, as we told them one by one our story, were fascinated by our quest, but the Scots running the trip seemed embarrassed at having let us come on board. As one of them awkwardly explained to me, as we were preparing to leave the ship with the greatest possible haste, "It's important not to compromise the experience of the other passengers."

For two days, we had no duties but to relax. The interlude was blissfully welcome. Slowly we floated down the west coast of Spitsbergen, gazing from the railing at seals lounging on ice floes, at flocks of barnacle geese arrowing through the golden sunlight. In Hornsund, a deep fjord toward the southern end of the island, the captain pulled the standard Arctic cruise trick of creeping up close to the sixty-foot-high cliff of a glacier (the Hornbreen), where it spilled into the sea. We passengers gathered on the foredeck and rooted for bergs to calve.

Later that day, we took a two-and-a-half-hour hike among the hills behind the Polish research station at Isbjørnhamna. The weather was as fine, I guessed, as it ever gets in Svalbard: blue skies feathered with mackerel cloud bands, the temperature in the 50s. At our backs across the fjord loomed the sharp, graceful mass of Hornsundtind, at 4,694 feet the third highest mountain in Svalbard. Our guide, Jason, told us the peak had been climbed only a handful of times (he himself had failed on a winter attempt).

But for our putterings around Longyearbyen, this was our first hike on the archipelago. I had been worried that the terrain might resemble the hideous muskeg of Alaska—a swampy morass of tussocks, mud, and fetid pools; but now we walked easily across swaths of green moss and gray scree. Auks and skuas wheeled in the bright air, alighting on ridge crests not far from us. A fox stalked the birds from a talus slope above. We crossed a divide and saw three reindeer (a mother and two young) several hundred yards away: curious, they trotted toward us before thinking better of it and loping away.

If this weather should hold, I thought, and if Hornsund were representative of the country, then Svalbard promised to be an elysian place, our trip a hiker's delight. Yet the skeptic in me recalled the climatological forebodings of the guidebooks (on average, one day of clear skies in the whole month of August in Longyearbyen, by all accounts a milder place than Edgeøya). I decided to enjoy these few hours of paradisiacal strolling as if I were sipping the last drops of a rare nectar. Tomorrow, when we would be dropped off near Halfmoon Island, would take care of itself.

Back on board the *Moltanovsky,* we pored over the texts and maps I had brought along. I had photocopied both the English and French first editions of Le Roy; now Michel studied the latter with the assiduity of a biblical scholar.

In the bar that evening, as we each downed a third can of beer, Michel put his finger on a critical paradox in Le Roy, one that had floated for months on the periphery of my consciousness. "I think this must have been a small island the sailors were on," he said to me in French. "They toured it, they knew it, the pilot names it Aleksei's Island. And they find the clay for their lamp *vers le milieu*—toward the middle—of the island. I do not think they could have gone to the middle of Edgeøya."

"But what about the 'many mountains and steep rocks of a stupendous height'?" I rejoined. The phrase was identical in the French edition.

"This is a problem."

We reexamined both texts, and a possible solution dawned on us. Le Roy does not exactly say that the crucial phrase refers to the island of the sailors' refuge. He says instead that he asked the Inkovs to describe "the island of *East-Spitsbergen.*" The sailors may well have taken the question literally, for from Halfmoon Island (or any of several other small islands off the south coast) Edgeøya is prominently visible.

Once again, Michel raised the question of how much Russian the chronicler understood. "If Le Roy comprehended Russian as well as I comprehend English," he half joked, "then his book is a novel."

That evening we stayed up late, raiding our precious Armagnac, acutely aware that it was our last night to enjoy the amenities of the *Moltanovsky.* In the penumbral hours around midnight, the ship rounded the southern cape of Spitsbergen and steamed east across the Storfjorden toward Edgeøya.

We woke, hungover, on August 22 to a different world. The sky had turned to lead, and a raw breeze raked the ship's deck. A few low islands, the leading edge of the Tusenøyane, humped brown and shapeless out of the water. A Russian Zodiac driver saw our first polar bear on one of these islands, but the beast slipped into the sea before the driver could alert the passengers.

At last Martin, the Scot in charge of our briefings, explained to the group at lunch that the four of us would be dropped off on Halfmoon Island. He winked at Mats, adding, "There's always bloody bears on Halfmoon."

Undercutting our anticipation was a vague dread, an anxiety about being abandoned by the ship on which we had grown so comfortable in only three days. At 2:45 P.M., the ship halted off the west cape of Halfmoon. All we could see of the island was a low basalt bluff teeming with birds. The Russian crew hurried to hook our Zodiac, with Mats standing inside it, to a crane that lifted it over the railing and down to the water. Then, one cargo-net-load after another, the crew winched our supplies down not only to our Zodiac, but to two of the *Moltanovsky*'s boats. It seemed slightly appalling that we had nearly a ton of gear and food, including a fifty-gallon drum full of boat fuel. (Again, the contrast between our lavishly appointed expedition and the Pomori's meager roster of belongings came home to me with a vengeance.) We put on our survival suits for the first time, then climbed down a ladder hung off the ship's railing and stepped into our Zodiac. With no further ado, we were off. The passengers on the *Moltanovsky* waved as the ship dwindled behind us.

It took a mere twenty minutes to cover the six nautical miles between the ship and the inner crook of the crescent of Halfmoon. The Russians sped ahead of us, as if drag-racing. We turned a corner, and suddenly, there before us, stood a trim gray-green building: Bjørneborg. We pulled onto shore and ran the Zodiacs up the stony beach. As quickly as they could, the Russian drivers helped us dump all our gear on the ground. No doubt Martin had warned them about the risk of compromising the other passengers' experience with any untoward delay. We tipped the men $20, shook their hands, and pushed their boats back into the water. They sped away, and were soon out of sight. All of a sudden, we were alone.

We shucked off our survival suits and started lugging our supplies up to the hut. Mats detached the outboard motor from the Zodiac, then told Vaughn and me to lift it by the rear pontoons so he could affix a rigid metal carriage that sprouted a small solid rubber wheel. With this gizmo in place, it was an easy matter to pull the boat up the beach to well above the high-tide line, where we tied it off to a big driftwood log. After we had gotten all our gear up to the front porch of the cabin, Mats took out a tool kit and strung thin wires a foot and a half off the ground in a triangular fence surrounding the Zodiac, affixed at the corners to nails he pounded into yet other scraps of driftwood. Then he attached magnesium flares to the wires, each armed with a little pin, like a hand grenade.

This clever setup was standard procedure in polar bear country. One bite out of our Zodiac by an inquisitive ursine could sabotage our

Opposite: Halfmoon Island and the southeastern shore of Edgeøya.

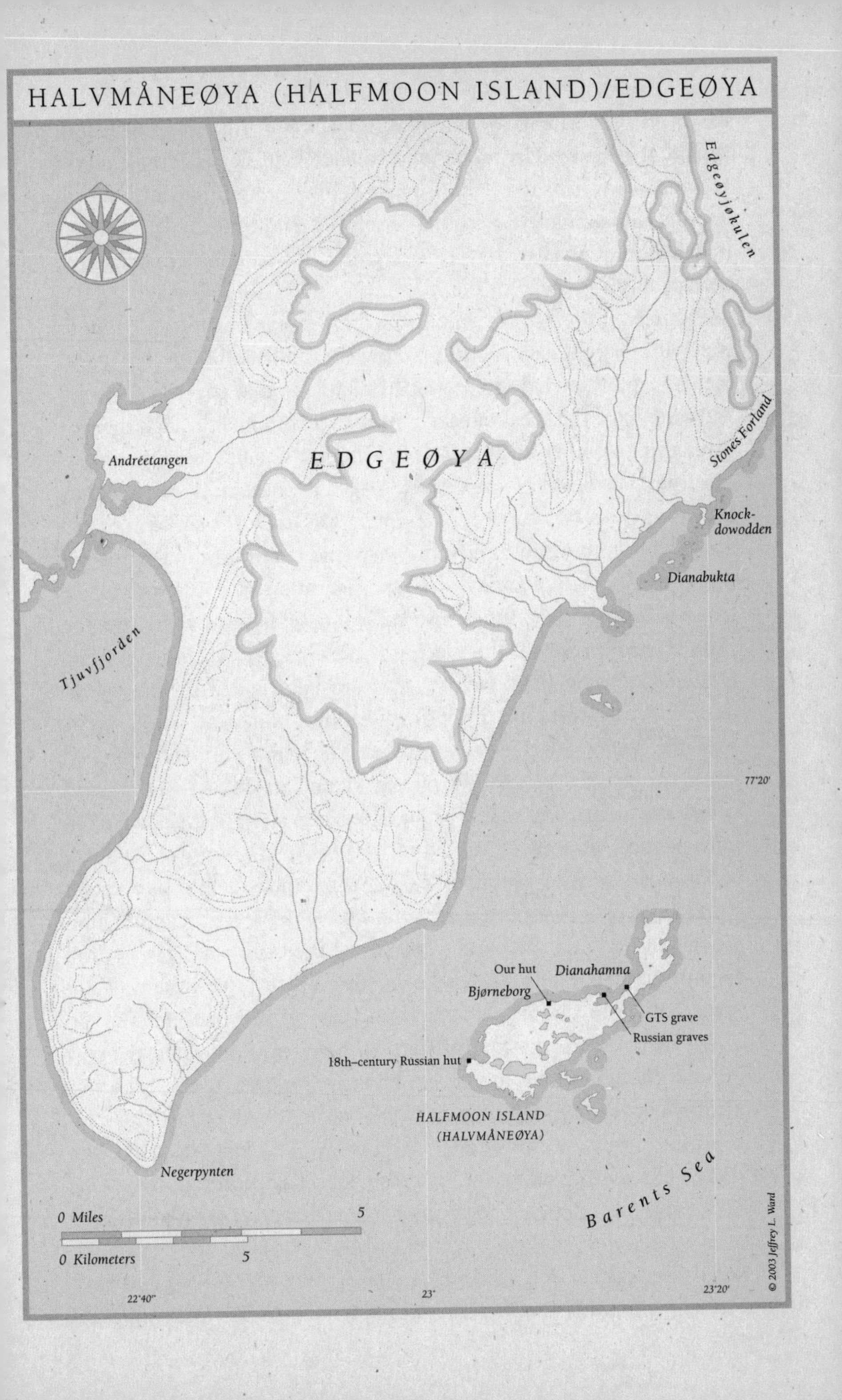

HALVMÅNEØYA (HALFMOON ISLAND)/EDGEØYA
Edgeøyjøkulen
Andréetangen
EDGEØYA
Stones Forland
Knock-dowodden
Dianabukta
Tjuvfjorden
77°20'
Our hut
Dianahamna
Bjørneborg
GTS grave
Russian graves
18th–century Russian hut
HALFMOON ISLAND
(HALVMÅNEØYA)
Negerpynten
Barents Sea
0 Miles 5
0 Kilometers 5
22°40''
23°
23°20'
© 2003 Jeffrey L. Ward

whole journey. The wire fence meant that a bear ambling near would trip the flares, each of which would explode with a considerable report and a steady jet of red flame—presumably sending the startled bear into headlong flight. Of course once the Zodiac was thus booby-trapped, we ourselves had to be careful not to stumble across the nearly invisible wires.

Bjørneborg itself had been likewise bear-proofed by its last previous occupant. Now Mats took out a crowbar and pried loose the boards that covered the windows, unslatted the plank that covered the door, and assembled the sheet metal chimney that sprouted through the roof from a small potbellied stove inside. The hut was not terribly impressive from outside, but I was pleased to see how neat and expertly refurbished were its two small rooms. There was even a stack of chopped firewood leaning against one inner wall. And to our great relief, the hut was equipped with an axe and a saw. Two hours after our arrival, we had a fire going inside the stove and were cooking our first dinner. "The true loneliness of the place is somewhat overwhelming," I had written in my notebook shortly after we had landed on the beach. Now, however, with the opposing windows admitting a soft Arctic light, the inner door closed to isolate the living room-cum-kitchen where we would spend most of our waking hours, the hut seemed warm and cozy. How much better, I realized at once, than a pair of tents pitched forlornly on the shore.

Mats had been to Halfmoon two or three times before, as a cruise ship guide. There was a ledger on the kitchen table that recorded previous visitors. Nineteen parties had signed the book since 1997, all of them either cruise ship parties passing by on their brief shore walks or inspectors from the Sysselmannen. All had arrived between July 26 and August 27, during the brief late-summer window when the seas around Halfmoon were free of ice. Yet only one party had spent a single night inside the hut in the last thirty years.

All of Edgeøya, including Halfmoon Island, had been made a nature preserve in 1973, ending for good the polar bear hunting that, along with the hunt for walrus, reindeer, and fox, had been the island's principal attraction for almost three centuries—as well as the original reason that huts such as Bjørneborg had been built. The longest and most interesting entry in the ledger had been written by Per Johnson, a legendary hunter whom Mats had already told us about. Under the dates August 26–27, 1997, Johnson wrote in Norwegian, "I have been here with Denmark Radio and TV to make a documentary on the hunting life, skin preparation, hut life. . . . We have walked over the whole island. . . . Incredibly interesting to be back."

Johnson, we realized, as Mats translated on, had been the last hunter to occupy Bjørneborg.

> The winter of 1970–71 [Johnson wrote] was the first year with a quota on polar bears. And then, when I had caught my twenty-five, I left the station. Since then the hut has been left by itself until the History/Culture Department on Svalbard repaired it in the summer of 1996. . . .
>
> I left the island on 15 February 1971; I nailed the door and the windows shut, and drove over to Longyearbyen with my dogs. It took fourteen days.

This laconic résumé of the last overwintering on Halfmoon Island—a solo one, at that—took my breath away. Mats and I spread out my map and plotted the course by which Johnson must have dogsledded to Longyearbyen in the dead of winter: across the pack ice of Tjuvfjorden and Storfjorden, up the Hayesbreen Glacier to the Spitsbergen divide, down the Von Postbreen Glacier, and back on sea ice across Tempelfjorden, Sassenfjorden, and Isfjorden—a distance of 150 miles at a minimum, most of it performed in the dark of night. The ledger entry put our own timid and sybaritic outing in perspective, while it furnished a living link to the mythic deeds in the tradition of Svalbard overwintering, of which the Pomori from 1743 to 1749 had written the most extreme chapter.

Shortly after arriving, Mats had insisted that each of us shoot a practice round with both our Mausers and our flare guns. I had fired a 30.06 rifle only once before, in preparation for an expedition to the Brooks Range in the late 1960s. Michel was equally inexperienced. Aiming out over the empty sea, bracing the butt of the gun firmly against my right shoulder, I fired. The report was deafening, the tiny splash almost invisible.

The Mausers were our weapon of last resort, to be used only in the direst straits of self-defense. Should we have to kill a polar bear, we would face a stern and thorough investigation back in Longyearbyen. Now Mats demonstrated the flare gun, our first line of bear-discouragement. It was a snub-nosed lightweight pistol with a large bore that held a cartridge that looked like a wax candle encased in brass. The gun made a loud bang as Mats triggered it. Whistling through the air, the cartridge arced some fifty yards, coming to earth with another explosion in a burst of brown flame. You could hit a bear directly with the flare without injuring it, but the more humane tactic was to try to land the cartridge at the bear's feet.

Exhausted from the week's preparations, I crawled into my sleeping bag and fell asleep, with the stove crackling softly in the far corner of the living room. The other three went out for a midnight stroll, carrying a Mauser and a flare gun apiece. A soft rosy afterglow hung behind the high plateaus of Edgeøya in the north, across the two miles of sea that separated Halfmoon from the main island. The others were gone for less than an hour, but when they came back, waking me, Michel was afire with a revelation that had come to him as he stood on a low ridge a few hundred yards behind the hut.

Gazing around him in the half-light at the alien landscape, Michel had tried to imagine the experience of spending more than six years on Edgeøya. Reflecting on comparable trials, he had thought of the deportation of the Jews from France in World War II. That thread led him to a more personal memory.

Michel's grandfather—his mother's father—had been killed in 1914 in World War I. Only one year old at the time, she had never known her father. As she grew up, however, she grew increasingly curious about the man and about his demise. She began seeking out other veterans of the Great War, to ask them about their own experiences.

"She always said to me," Michel reported with animation, "that these men were almost incapable of talking about the war. For example, it took her more than twenty years to learn what was meant by the phrase, 'clean the trenches.' It meant to kill everybody with bayonets, then cover their bodies with shoveled dirt.

"So I think, the *Relation* of Le Roy is so frustrating maybe for this same reason. Perhaps these Russian sailors, who had had such a difficult time, who had become closer to animals than to people, found it very hard to relate what had happened to them, especially only four months after their rescue. When you go right to the limits of being human, it's very hard to recount it when you get back. Maybe the frustration of Le Roy is not his fault. For the sailors, this was not an adventure. It was an ordeal."

It was an intriguing thought. Certainly the orotund style of Le Roy's prose did not bespeak a man of few words. Perhaps the digressions that had so maddened me on each reading of the narrative were Le Roy's padding, to make up for a paucity of firsthand testimony. Perhaps that January 8, 1750, when the academician had received the Inkovs in St. Petersburg, the sailors were still in a state of what we now so trendily call "post-traumatic stress disorder." After all, "shell shock" had been discovered in the same war that had taken the life of Michel's grandfather. Perhaps the Inkovs had been all but speechless before Le Roy's questions.

All of Halfmoon Island, as we would see in our ramblings, is composed of a brown basalt—not the sharp-edged columnar stuff of Devils Postpile in California or of cliffs all over Iceland, but a weathered, lumpy, undistinguished stone. The highest point on the island scarcely rises 150 feet above sea level. Peering out the south-facing window of our cabin, we saw only a watery tableland punctuated with low ridges. The "many mountains and steep rocks of a stupendous height" of Le Roy's report could not by any stretch of the imagination be made to apply to Halfmoon.

But looking out the other window, the one above the kitchen table, we saw, across the two miles of ocean between us and Edgeøya, a series of stern gray ridges, their summits a good thousand feet above the sea, with dull white fingers of the Kvitkåpa icecap stretching into view out of high valleys that interrupt the massive, scree-strewn cliffs frowning over the shore. Le Roy's phrase is supremely apt for this apparition, which never left our sight except when fog enshrouded our universe. Hornsund on Spitsbergen, where we had taken our hike with the cruise ship passengers, was a beautiful landscape. But there was nothing beautiful about this part of Edgeøya. "Bleak," "desolate," "empty" were the adjectives that came from my pen as I tried to capture the mood of the place in my notebook.

By morning on August 23, a stiff wind was blowing out of the northeast. The swell on shore had turned into sizable waves, whitecaps curling toward us before they broke to pieces on the polished stones of our harbor. We had hoped to make our first excursion over to the mainland, but now Vaughn and I had our doubts.

A confession is in order here. Despite flailing around in the shallows of many a pool in my childhood, despite having had to pass a remedial class to graduate from Harvard, I have never managed to learn how to swim. Sheer counterphobic obstinacy has led me to participate, as a white-knuckled passenger in rafts rowed by experts, on first descents of the Tekeze River in Ethiopia and of part of the Tua-Purare in New Guinea; but a primal fear of water still haunts my waking nightmares.

In this respect, Vaughn is a kindred soul. He can enact a kind of thrashing crawl in calm water, but boats and oceans tend to terrify him. A few years before, on a warm day in May, I had talked Vaughn into sharing a motorboat rental with me on Lake Powell, so that we could shortcut a whole day's drive to reach a side canyon of the Escalante River. Surrounded by water-skiing frat boys, by coeds in bikinis drinking beer on the decks of their houseboats, we motored slowly and vigilantly down what used to be the Colorado River, the only two mariners on the lake with our life jackets buckled tight around our chests.

Michel, on the other hand, had no such qualms about the sea. And Mats was in his element in a Zodiac. So when Vaughn and I wondered whether the surf was a bit too boisterous for our first ferry over to Edgeøya, Mats scoffed at our timorous bleatings and insisted the launch would be a piece of cake.

So much a piece of cake, in fact, that he didn't bother to give us landlubbers clear directions. At noon we wheeled the boat down to the water's edge and disassembled its carriage. We loaded the Zodiac with supplies for a day's outing, including a tent and stove in case we got stuck by weather on Edgeøya. "Wait for a small wave," Mats shouted over the surf and wind, "then run with the boat and jump in."

We were standing up to our knees in the sea. In my survival suit, I felt extraordinarily clumsy. A few waves splashed over us; then Mats yelled, "Now!"

Laden with so much gear, the boat was sluggish, nearly immobile. In front on opposite sides, Vaughn and I tried to run as we pulled hard on the ropes strung from the Zodiac's pontoons. When the water reached my waist, I crawled awkwardly up over the side of the boat, like an obese child trying to shimmy onto a ledge. Later Mats told us that both Vaughn and I had jumped in too early. Suddenly all four of us were aboard, and Mats was screaming, "Paddle!"

This command had not been part of our pre-launch briefing. By the time Vaughn and I had located the paddles, wedged beneath a spare engine and duffels full of gear, the Zodiac had started to fill with water from waves breaking over its bow. Vaughn and I pulled with all our might, but we could hardly move the swamped craft. A big wave hit us and turned the boat sideways. We had lost control. A surge of panic swept through me, as I imagined losing the Zodiac altogether to the angry sea.

"Get out!" yelled Mats. "Back to shore!" When we jumped out, the water reached our chests. Seizing the ropes, we tried to haul the recalcitrant raft back to the beach.

Our struggle was chaotic. With each wave, the boat made a violent surge toward shore, dragging us with it, but the subsequent undertow swept us back out. Slowly, however, we gained on the land. Vaughn had maneuvered himself so that he stood directly in front of the rubber beast we were wrestling with. Just as he planted his left foot and prepared to haul, the Zodiac surged forward with a big wave. Vaughn screamed a curse and crumpled in pain. The dead weight of the water-filled boat had caught him directly on the side of the knee. Because his foot was planted, his leg had been bent severely in a direction it was not devised to bend.

At last the boat was safe. We sat on shore, gasping for breath. Vaughn tried to stand up, and collapsed again with a cry. In our collective panic, unaware of the danger of trying to pull the surging boat from a stance directly in front of it, he had suffered the same kind of injury that happens to a football player when, cleats planted, his leg is buckled by the tackle of a three-hundred-pound lineman. Perhaps he had torn ligaments in the knee; at the very best, he had suffered only a bad sprain. But, although it would take weeks to learn how serious the damage might be, both Vaughn and I at once foresaw a grim scenario. Thinking of the football player analogy, I heard the TV announcer's pat phrase: "career-ending injury." Vaughn's own career depended utterly on being able to hike and backpack in the Utah canyons.

Our first effort on Halfmoon Island, then, had turned into a complete fiasco. Exhausted, we pulled the boat back up to its driftwood anchor and unloaded it. Mats reconfigured the trip wire triangle. We retreated to our cabin for a dispirited lunch.

Mats was in a strange mood. He could not quite conceal his disappointment, even disgust, at our ineptitude: it ought, he had said that morning, to be "easy" to run over to Edgeøya in what was only a middling surf. Yet he seemed to recognize that much of the blame was his own. And I had lashed out in a petulant moment as we sat defeated on the beach, "Mats, we should have gone over the drill a lot more carefully before letting this happen." Now he fussed in the kitchen, compensating for the botched launch by fixing us a hot meal.

Michel tried, as always, to be philosophical. "We have not," he said in English, "to cry on the spelt milk." Vaughn sat silent, kneading and flexing his knee, a grimace of pain deepening the creases on his face.

Though the wind stayed strong and the sea roily, gradually the day improved, as sun broke through a thin layer of clouds. In midafternoon, we decided to salvage what we could of our first full day on Halfmoon by going for a walk. We headed toward the southwest cape, the one we had first seen in the distance as we had prepared to depart from the *Moltanovsky*. Vaughn knew that he ought to stay in the hut and nurse his wounded leg. He even recited to us the acronymic wisdom of all the first-aid courses he had taken, as to how to treat such an injury: "RICE," or rest, ice, compression, and elevation. But he couldn't bear to be idle. "Maybe I can walk it off," he rationalized as he laced up his hiking boots.

Our five-hour-long loop stroll turned out to be the closest thing to an idyll we would enjoy during our two weeks in the field. I decided to leave my Mauser at the hut and carry only a flare gun: the cumbersome rifle weighed an annoying eight pounds, and if anybody had to shoot a polar bear, it was work best left to Vaughn and Mats. For that reason, I made sure not to wander off with Michel and put any real distance between us and our designated shooters. Just by observing the way my French friend carried his firearm, balanced by the barrel over his shoulder like a hobo's knapsack, I concluded that in a showdown with a bear, I would be better off running away than counting on his cartridges to keep us alive. An image from some French romance I had read in adolescence came to me unbidden. "You look like a Zouave," I told him. Michel burst into his characteristic laugh, an ear-to-ear rictus, his head bobbing up and down, without the slightest sound emerging from his throat. It turns out that "Zouave" referred not only to any of a species of reckless and dashing French soldiers dressed up in dandyish Oriental garb, but, by extension, to a clown. "All through my childhood," said Michel, "my father tells me, *'Ne fais pas le Zouave!'*—'Stop playing the fool.'" ("Quit goofing off!" an American dad might have said to the budding *branleur* he had had the misfortune to sire.)

The basalt underfoot was swathed with a black *Umbilicaria* lichens, crinkly to the tread when dry, but, as we would soon learn, a slimy, treacherous carpet when soaked with rain. In the damper hollows, the rock gave way to gravel, out of which spread scraggly cushions of an impossibly green moss. We passed a clump of fragile, pale yellow Arctic poppies, their earnest blossoms bent heliotropically to follow the course of the milky sun in the west. They would be almost the only flowers we saw in two weeks.

Here and there we stumbled across reindeer antlers among the rocks, their tangs well coated with gray-green lichens. We found our first fox trap, the upper grid collapsed upon the lower, the deadly rocks still in place. Starting to merge with the tundra itself, the weathered slats of the trap looked very old. After about a mile, we came to our first whale bones—huge curving ribs and massive jawbones. These were not, Mats explained, the detritus of any whaling operation, but the scattered remains of whales naturally beached over the ages.

Some of the whale bones, however, lay inland as far as half a mile, at heights approaching fifty feet above the sea. As we stood over one such set, I asked Mats, "How could beached whales have ended up here?"

He had a gleam in his eye. "This is a very interesting question, David," he answered. "These bones are very old. They are from the warm climatic intervals after the last Ice Age, when the sea level was much higher."

I was inclined to take Mats's explanation with a grain of salt—another wild myth from his autodidact's trove of lore. But later I met a

German scientist who had studied similar bones found on the north coast of Norway. Mats was dead right. The German had carbon-dated some of the bones to between 3000 and 6000 B.P. (before the present), but had reason to suspect that others could be as old as forty thousand years. So well preserved were these bleached ribs and vertebrae, it was hard to fathom their great age.

Near the coast we came upon the first of scores of bear traps that we would find on Halfmoon Island. The trap's design was fiendish simplicity itself. Atop a wooden sawhorse, a parallelepiped-shaped box was mounted. The back half of the box was closed, except for a small hole out of which the last few inches of a gun barrel protruded. The front half was open. The box stood at about the level of a bear's head. A piece of bait would be laid inside the open front of the box, connected by cord or wire to the gun's trigger. The bear seized the bait in its jaws, triggering the firearm, and received a point-blank blast directly in the face.

The efficacy of the old trap, which stood sagging and decrepit, was evinced in a jumble of bones scattered among the rocks. Before 1973, when hunting was outlawed, Mats told us, a veteran such as Per Johnson, upon finding a bear dead in front of one of his traps, would have skinned it on the spot. He would have fed the meat to his dogs, then left what he could not conveniently pack on his sled as carrion. It was the pelt that was the point of the hunt.

As the sun lowered in the west, it etched the dark and dramatic outline of Negerpynten, the southernmost cape of all Edgeøya, about seven miles away. There, cliffs soared more than a thousand feet straight out of the water. We wandered across talus piles of brown rock, photographing whale ribs and reindeer antlers. Vaughn limped along, his binoculars dangling on his chest. Every three or four minutes he would raise them to scan the horizon, the hunter for whom vigilance was second nature. Michel and I clumped along, oblivious as Zouaves.

Mats had been staring across the sea toward the gray cliffs of Edgeøya. Now he raised a hand, as if commanding silence.

"What?" I asked.

He had a smirk on his face that I was already getting to know—the guide's relish in a discovery to parcel out to his clients. "Bear," Mats whispered.

So familiar was the man with the signature of a distant polar bear projected upon the drab gray screen of the Svalbardian universe—that speck of white, a subtly different shade from snow—that Mats had spotted our first such creature with the naked eye, at a distance of three miles. We spent ten minutes studying the bear in our binoculars, as it browsed on moss, then lumbered sideways across a gully choked with scree. "Nice spotting, Mats," I murmured.

Even with the sea between us and that huge beast, even knowing that the bear had no inkling of our presence, I felt a frisson of awe tinged with fear. The animal looked so completely at ease in his domain, so lordly in his supremacy, that it underlined just how thoroughly we were the intruders.

By the time we had regained the hut, around 8:00 in the evening, the day was at its warmest, at least 40° F. We took off our boots and lounged, out of the wind, against the westward-facing wall of Bjørneborg, drinking cans of Ringnes. Life seemed a simple delight. Had we known that that was the last time during our whole stay in Svalbard that we would see the sun, we might have tried even more fervently to soak up the clarity and comfort of its golden rays.

We woke on the morning of August 24 to the sound of rain on the roof. The wind was still streaming out of the north. Whenever one of us ventured outside, even just to urinate in the backyard, he carried at least a flare gun and sometimes a Mauser with him. Now we discovered that the rain was half snow, pelting us in a slanting blizzard. If anything, the waves crashing on shore were bigger than the ones that had defeated our pathetic launch the day before.

Plainly, the weather dictated a rest day. We fired up the stove and cooked hot cereal. Vaughn now realized the folly of his hike: his leg throbbed with pain, and as he hobbled around the cramped cabin, it felt weaker than ever. "It's ligaments," he said quietly. "I hope only strained or stretched." Then, under his breath, "Man, I've never done anything like this to myself."

As cozy as it seemed, the hut in a storm could foment a certain stir-crazy restlessness. Pulling on my foul-weather gear, I volunteered to fill our water pail. Our drinking supply was a freshwater pond a few hundred yards inland from the hut. Here on Halfmoon, there was no need to treat or filter it. It was the first time in decades—maybe since my last

Alaska expedition—that I had drunk from a lake or stream anywhere in the world without treating the water with iodine tablets or pumping it through a filter.

The ground all around our hut was littered with several generations' worth of debris: nails, coils of wire, spent rifle cartridges. A second structure closer to the beach had served as a boat shed. Inside it we found the broken pieces of a dogsled—perhaps Per Johnson's. An overturned wooden rowboat lay near the shed, mocking our own trip-wired craft as it reminded me that tougher men than we had regularly cruised the shores of Edgeøya in an age before Zodiacs and survival suits had been invented. There was also a small crate made of logs, which Mats said was a trap for capturing baby bears alive (the hunters would carry them back to Norway, then sell them to zoos).

There was so much driftwood on the shore that we could not have burned it all in our stove, I thought, in a year's stay in Bjørneborg. Poking among the waterlogged timbers, I tried to imagine their blind journey from the headwaters of Russian rivers. Mingled among the driftwood was more modern debris, cast off by passing ships: metal and plastic fishnet floats, plastic bottles, pieces of Styrofoam. The junk strewn all around us pointed up a giddy paradox. Here we were, as Mats had said, in one of the hardest places on earth to get to, and yet the tawdriest products of our modern civilization lay scattered all around, reminding us how difficult it was to turn our backs on the material culture that ruled our everyday lives.

Just before noon, Mats and I went out, despite the blizzard, to poke about the ruins of an old stone structure that we had noticed, only a hundred yards from Bjørneborg, perilously close to the high-water line. Now, as we perused the ruins, we saw that banks of piled stones had walled in a building made of upright planks, all but disintegrated over the years. Clearly this had been a hut, but when we measured its interior dimensions at a mere ten feet by twenty-five, we recognized what a claustrophobic shelter it must have been. A few forlorn objects scattered about bespoke a human presence—the rotting green leather of a boot far too thin for winter, a lump of rope grease (a kind of wax once used to keep ropes supple).

I had brought along the photocopied pages of Gustav Rossnes's *Norsk Overvintringsfangst På Svalbard, 1895–1940*, the only semicomprehensive guide to historic overwinterings by Norwegians in the archipelago. Here Mats discovered the key to the hut's identity. He translated Rossnes's laconic note:

> In 1898–99, four men, Karl Møller, Hammerfest; Ibenhart Jensen Fladseth; O. Engvik; and Henrik (last name unknown) erected main station. . . . Møller and Fladseth overwintered here, died in the winter, and are buried in the vicinity. The other two overwintered on Kong Ludvigøyana [an island group thirty miles to the west].

Later I would find a fuller source for this grim story, which quoted several passages from Fladseth's diary, found with the corpses by Engvik and Henrik when they rejoined their companions at the beginning of July 1899. Møller and Fladseth had been, apparently, the first Norwegian attempt ever to overwinter on Halfmoon, and something had gone dreadfully wrong. The two were dropped off on August 31, 1898. Already, by September 20, Fladseth wrote, "Karl is sick." On December 19: "I am sick, and it's 20° below zero [minus 4° F] outside." On a loose piece of paper, their companions found a longer note from January 26, 1899: "The light is now coming back. 4 hours of shooting [i.e., hunting] light. Cold very severe: 20–27 below [minus 4–19° F]. Climate is very heavy and depressing. The time is going very slowly. Haven't been out [of the hut] for 10 weeks, since Nov. 16. That day we shot 2 polar bears."

This passage gave me a vivid image of the squalor of the men's desperate predicament, as I pictured them lying in their own feces inside the hastily built hut. On February 6, the two invalids made a game attempt to rally themselves: "Went on walk, almost eaten by polar bear because rifles didn't work. At last moment, I got rifle to work and shot polar bear." Perhaps the meat briefly restored the men, although on February 9, Fladseth wrote: "Headache and stomach pain. Trying to hold out." On the 18th, they tried to ski to Kong Ludvigøyana, but quickly gave up. A few weeks later, perhaps sensing that something was wrong, the moribund men's companion Engvik tried to ski to Halfmoon from the island group to the west, but was stopped by open water.

On March 27, Fladseth wrote, "Both sick, and I am very bad." March

30: "We are suffering many pains." April 4: "We have a good day today. Minus 12° [10° F]." But the next day: "Back in bad conditions again."

Curiously, only once does Fladseth's diary mention scurvy, of which ailment surely both men believed they were dying. The last entry was written on April 6: "Ice fog. Westerly wind. Minus 14 to minus 15° [3° to 5° F]."

Later, writer and Arctic expert Lawrence Millman would point out to me that Møller and Fladseth might well have died of trichinosis from eating undercooked polar bear meat. "Trichinosis mimics the symptoms of scurvy," Millman noted. "In fact, many deaths in the Arctic attributed to scurvy are the result of trichinosis."

It was only in July that Engvik and Henrik, sailing rather than skiing, were able to make their way to Halfmoon Island and discover their dead colleagues. "We found them both in their beds," Engvik later wrote, "in terrifying and horrible conditions." A few weeks later, the Norwegians returned with other hunters and buried Møller and Fladseth in a single grave.

Mats was prowling among the boulders uphill from the ruins of the 1898 hut. He let out a cry. I walked over and saw, squeezed into a natural aperture in the basalt, a sizable wooden box, overgrown with moss and piled under with stones. Mats was on his hands and knees, his eye pressed close to the only corner of the box not blocked by stones. "Look at this, David," he said softly.

I took his place. It required a minute for my eyes to adjust to the darkness within the box, and in that span, as I crouched miserably in the driving sleet, the full balefulness of our surroundings came home to me. As I stared into the dank, umbral interior, I saw, lying on its side, the bleached skull of either Karl Møller or Ibenhart Jensen Fladseth grinning back at me.

9: Wet Search

By 1898, sailors and hunters in Svalbard had a century and a half's worth of collective experience in the Arctic to add to the folk wisdom the shipwrecked Pomori had carried inside their heads in 1743. In particular, by then it was well known that citrus fruits were an effective preventive against scurvy. Yet Møller and Fladseth had succumbed to the disease in their first winter on Halfmoon Island, the former man falling ill within the first month of his stay in the cramped hut the men had thrown together near the shore.

Assuming that the illness that took the life of Fedor Verigin, after having "passed almost six years under the greatest sufferings," was in all likelihood something other than scurvy, what explains the Mezeners' extraordinary success in avoiding the vitamin deficiency that took so many lives in the Arctic? Could a steady diet of scurvy grass, reindeer fat, and reindeer blood really have kept them healthy all those months?

For various reasons, Norwegian hunters did not begin to frequent Svalbard until around 1795, at least a full century after the first Russian incursions. It was not until the 1820s that the Norwegians first dared to overwinter. In the pages of such historians as Rudmose Brown and Sir Martin Conway, I had read many a vivid account of these bold and often fatal adventures. The upshot was clear: the Russians were simply better at overwintering than the Norwegians ever became, despite the opportunity on the latter's part to learn valuable lessons from their predecessors' failures. The all-time virtuoso among Russian hunters was a fellow named Staratschin, described as "a lively, ruddy little man with white hair and of patriarchal appearance," who was reported to have spent a total of between thirty-two and thirty-nine winters on Svalbard at the end of the eighteenth century and the beginning of the nineteenth. Yet even this hardy veteran's endurance cannot be compared to that of the Pomori from 1743 to 1749, for every one of Staratschin's winters was spent in the hut he had built on relatively benign Grønfjorden (near today's site of Barentsburg), with a winter's supply of food and gear carefully laid up in the autumn.

Writing in 1920, Rudmose Brown concludes that "The chief resort of the Russian trappers was Edge Island, where for over a century there were probably always winterers on the south-east coast." Yet with all the accumulated wisdom of their annual campaigns, the Pomori never succeeded in perfecting the formula for surviving even a single winter. James Lamont, an English sportsman who sailed along the coast of Edgeøya in 1858 (he was perhaps Svalbard's first tourist), writes in his delightful memoir, *Yachting in the Arctic Seas,*

> Many of these hardy fellows, however, succumbed to scurvy and the hardships they endured, and many hundreds must have thus miserably perished, as the traveller in these awful solitudes frequently comes across the ruins of a small log-hut, with two or three mounds or cairns of stones in front of it; and it is also common enough to see the skeletons of the hapless Russians bleaching alongside of those of the bears and reindeers they had killed and eaten.

Within the previous decade, Lamont learned from local informants, a colony of eighteen Russian hunters had perished en masse near Hvalpynten, the southwest cape of Edgeøya. As Lamont heard the story, the men had successfully overwintered and were awaiting their relief ship out of Arkhangel'sk, but that vessel was lost en route. The other parties in Svalbard knew nothing of the stranded Pomori at Hvalpynten, and even if they had, the usual sea ice prevented a near approach. It was not until August that a ship carrying Norwegian sailors happened upon the Russian settlement. Writes Lamont, "On reaching the huts they were horror-struck to find the inmates all dead. Fourteen of the unhappy men had recently been buried in shallow graves in front of the huts, two lay dead just outside the threshold, and the remaining two were lying dead inside, one on the floor and the other in bed." The last to die had kept a diary, in which the details of the terrible attrition were laid bare. The corpses lying before the hut had been dragged there by the last two survivors, who were too weak to bury their comrades. Those two then reentered the hut and resigned themselves to a similar fate. "When one of them died, the last man—the writer of the journal—had only sufficient strength remaining to push his dead companion out of the bed and onto the floor, and he soon after expired himself, only a few days before the Norwegian party arrived."

After 1852, the Pomori stopped coming to Svalbard, in large part because the industry of such towns as Mezen and Arkhangel'sk turned to the timber harvest. But in their absence, in the latter half of the nineteenth century, Norwegians flocked to the archipelago. The failures of some of their overwinterings make for just as gruesome reading as do those of the Russians.

Writing only three years after it had taken place, Lamont summarizes the fate of a Norwegian crew of thirteen, who, without intending to winter over, were trapped by early sea ice on Mitra Hook, a cape in northwest Spitsbergen, in September 1872. Another Norwegian vessel sent to relieve the men the next summer found them all dead. Five lay on the beach underneath a cloth. The men had a hut (probably built by earlier overwinterers), but it did them little good. Six corpses were found inside the hut, "horribly disfigured by the ravages of scurvy." Beside the dead men, the would-be rescuers found their last, unfinished meal: three biscuits, five packages of sugar, and "a parcel of dried vegetables" (which latter might have been of some small avail against scurvy). The other two sailors were never found.

Once more the last to die had kept a diary. In October, the trapped men had managed to kill two bears, two foxes, and some reindeer, but with the onset of winter darkness they gave up all efforts to hunt. By December 21 all thirteen men were ill with scurvy. The first two died on January 10; others followed soon after. On February 23, the diarist desponded, "There is now only one sound man to keep us all. May the Lord have pity on us!" The penultimate death came on April 19. Writes Lamont, "The last survivor left the only testimony of his death in throwing his weakened body across the [storage] chest in the sudden agony in which this awful malady often terminates."

Despite the superstitions that clung to the illness well into the twentieth century, scurvy is not a matter of luck, of lack of exercise, of failing to stay awake nineteen hours out of twenty-four (as many Russians tried to do all winter), of poor morale, nor—as far as we know—of lack of faith in divine providence. Whatever allowed the Inkovs, Sharapov, and Verigin to avoid the malady that condemned so many other hunters within their first winters on Svalbard (even those amply provisioned beforehand), that allowed all but Verigin to flourish for more than six years in good health, remains one of the central mysteries of the Pomori's extraordinary tale.

All day on August 24, the sleet and wind never let up. We hung around inside the hut, killing time. Vaughn kept massaging his sore knee, as if he could magically knead it back to health. He told us that he had realized that yesterday—the day of his accident—was his wife's birthday. That triggered a memory of the closest call in all his prowlings through the Southwest. "It was five years ago," he said, "and the day was Marcia's and my twentieth wedding anniversary. I was guiding an Earthwatch group in Grand Gulch, recording rock art. I was a hundred fifty feet off the deck, heading for a panel between Collins Canyon and Bannister Ruin. Here I am nonchalanting it along this narrow ledge, when a chunk of the ledge breaks off. Both my feet skid off the edge, and I land on my knees, barely in balance." Vaughn grinned ruefully. "When I got back to my feet, I nearly threw up."

So Vaughn, like most of us, like all those Svalbard overwinterers who had preceded us, had some kind of superstitious hunch that fate was less than random. But what was the moral to be drawn? Stay in bed on anniversaries and birthdays? (Make the right wish when you blow out your candles?)

Michel and I endlessly discussed Le Roy. That day we came up with a pair of bilingual *jeux de mots*, more or less by accident. Apropos of my yearlong quest for the sailors' half-lost story, I tried to translate the phrase "wild-goose chase," which seemed to have no exact equivalent in French. *"La chasse pour l'oie sauvage,"* I rendered it literally. *"Mais oui,"* answered Michel in a blink. *"La chasse pour Le Roy sauvage."*

Likewise, as we discussed Verigin—clearly the *branleur* among the Pomori's group of four—Michel spontaneously renamed him *"le vrai Guérin,"* the true Guérin. After that, *le vrai Guérin* became a richly loaded epithet. Sometimes it meant the "very heavy" and "lazy" sailor who liked to loll in the hut and couldn't swallow warm reindeer blood; sometimes it meant Michel at his most endearingly or maddeningly characteristic.

What, I wondered, had the various Svalbard hunters done to kill the endless time of their hut-bound winter vigils? Conway's Russian informant, Charitonow, emphasizes the obsessive antiscorbutic rite (designed to prevent sleep) of knot tying: "Like automata, each [hunter] ties a rope into an endless number of knots, and again unties it, and thus, now tying the knots, now undoing them again, spends nearly half the winter." I doubted that the overwinterers spent much time reading books, assuming they had any—especially if most of them were illiterate. No doubt, like fishermen in Newfoundland or Iceland, who used to while away the winter mending their nets, the Pomori spent many hours resewing their clothing, or crafting booties out of reindeer skin, or carving pretty knicknacks out of driftwood.

James Lamont found among the debris of one Russian settlement on Edgeøya a wooden bat and a set of balls, which Rudmose Brown later speculated had been used in some scurvy-preventing athletic contest. At the big Russian settlement north of Hvalpynten in 1827, Keilhau found among the ruins both playing cards and a checker board.

Learning that Michel and Mats were players—Vaughn had never learned the moves—I decided to make a chess set. Pulling on my foul-weather gear, armed with my flare gun, I pottered around among the debris surrounding our hut, gathering materials. First I found a square wooden plank of the appropriate size. Then I filled my pockets with dark- and light-colored junk, out of which to craft the black and white pieces.

Inside the hut, we drew a grid of sixty-four squares on the plank.

Within an hour, I had the board set up. The kings and queens were rifle cartridges of different lengths. Bishops were kittiwake feathers mounted on wooden pedestals. Twisted wires served as knights, walrus vertebrae as the white rooks. Pawns were black pieces of coal and tan chips of bone.

Since Mats, Michel, and I were players of approximately equal strength, our games grew surprisingly serious. In the claustrophobic living room, hunched over our board as the sleet drummed monotonously on the roof, we cared far more about winning than we would have in civilization. I found, as an even middle game slipped into an endgame with chances on both sides, that I could feel my heart thumping with adrenaline. Michel took several losses very hard: he seemed to feel that, in falling for some swindle I had tempted him with, he had betrayed the trust of the boyhood friend who had taught him the game, Christian de Marliave (himself an expert at chess as well as the Arctic).

It was only our third day on Halfmoon Island, and yet a single storm confining us to Bjørneborg could elicit the first glimmerings of cabin fever. The intensity of our chess games—the desperate need to win—was not simply a by-product of three rather competitive natures: it was an instinctive emotional reaction to being cooped up together.

On one of my expeditions, a fifty-two-day marathon in the previously unexplored Revelation Range, my companions and I had endured the worst weather I had ever seen in Alaska. On about the thirtieth day, four of us had played "hole ball"—an aggressive sport that I had invented, involving two men to a team, a football, and, as goals, a pair of pits we had dug in the glacier some thirty yards apart. This particular contest went down to the wire, and suddenly we were throwing vicious body blocks on players who were among our best friends in the world, as well as arguing like spoiled NBA rookies over rule infractions we ourselves had to referee.

My team won 23 to 22. Afterward, I felt so ashamed of my overinvestment in the victory that I went off alone for several hours and made the first ascent of an easy peak. It was a slightly foolhardy thing to do, with crevasses and avalanches lurking all over the range, but it seemed to purge the mood of violent willfulness that hole ball had unleashed.

Only three days into our cushy expedition on Svalbard, we were starting, albeit in relatively harmless ways, to get on each other's nerves. There was only one sleeping bunk in the two rooms of the cabin. The first night, I had thrown my sleeping bag down there. Mats had slept on the floor by the stove, while Michel and Vaughn had laid out their bags on the floor of the much colder antechamber, in which the front door opened onto a multitude of storage shelves. Obviously my berth was the prime spot, and after the first night I offered to swap with the others, but they declined. Out of some odd inertia, we kept the seemingly random sleeping positions of our first night invariable throughout the trip, as if we had been assigned quarters according to our ranks in some four-man navy.

There was a host of minor nuisances attendant upon our sleeping arrangement. If Mats or I had to go out in the night to urinate, we stepped over the recumbent Vaughn and Michel, often waking them up. The hut's john, because we were in bear country, could not be a detached outhouse, but was rather a one-holer built into a larder annexed to the antechamber in which Vaughn and Michel slept. On first arriving, Mats had suspended a double garbage bag beneath the toilet seat. As required by the Sysselmannen, we would pack out all our excrement and toilet paper from Halfmoon Island. Slowly our deposits grew into a sizable burden. A door closed off the larder from the storage room, but at intermittent times, the odor of the toilet wafted into the rest of the cabin.

Another nuisance derived from the fact that Mats and Michel proved to be herculean snorers, but Vaughn and I were not. There might thus have been a certain logic in pairing the snorers in one room, the silent sleepers in another, but, without ever discussing the matter, Vaughn and I stuck to our berths and struggled nightly to slip into dreamland despite the chain saw racket emanating from our companions.

Did any of this give me insight into the interpersonal tensions that must have afflicted the Inkovs, Sharapov, and Verigin, confined to their hut not for two weeks but for more than six years? Le Roy spends not a word on the subject, except to mention the unfailing solicitude that the three healthy sailors showed toward Verigin, feeding him "like a new-born infant" when he could no longer raise a spoon to his mouth. The absence of any such commentary is not surprising, for "cabin fever" had not, so to speak, been invented by the mid-eighteenth century.

Indeed, throughout the history of exploration literature, perhaps the most neglected subject of all is the extreme psychological vicissitudes suffered by adventurers forced together in close confinement under miserable conditions for months at a time.

On Paulet Island in Antarctica, for example, I had visited the ruins of a hut erected by a Swedish team in 1903. After their ship had been trapped in the ice and sunk, the team had rowed in whaleboats sixteen miles to the island, the nearest piece of terra firma. Knowing they would have to winter over, they gathered flat stones and built a rude hut in a week. Paulet abounded then, as it does today, with penguins, but the Swedes knew the birds would all migrate north within the next two weeks. To lay in provisions for the winter, the sailors went on a mad orgy of penguin killing, eventually stacking some 1,100 frozen carcasses beside their hut like so much firewood.

For eight months full of darkness and intense cold, twenty men lay in a chamber only twenty-four feet long by twenty-two feet wide. The ceiling, made of sailcloth and sealskins, was so low that only next to the central ridgepole could a man stand upright. As I puttered about the gloomy remnants of the hut, I could see firsthand that for eight months the men must have lain elbow to elbow, disturbing one another's sleep with every toss and turn, inhaling a musty fog of collective exhaled breath. The stones of the hut were chinked with penguin guano; the mattresses were rotten penguin skins.

Miraculously, only one man died. Yet the official account of this ordeal, written by one C. J. Skottsberg, barely hints at the interpersonal tribulations of that overwintering. "If anyone happened to move the bundle [of penguin skins]," Skottsberg notes in a rare vignette, "a terrible odor at once filled the room."

Cabin fever is a serious business. NASA, anticipating manned voyages to Mars, has begun contemplating the question (as a *Boston Globe* headline put it) of "how humans can colonize space without killing each other on the way." According to the *Globe,* the Russian cosmonaut Valery Ryumin, veteran of four prolonged journeys aboard the Mir and other spacecraft, reported that a trip of only two months with two astronauts in a space station fulfills "all the conditions necessary for murder."

Why is exploration literature so silent about this universal phenomenon? A partial answer had come to me decades before, in the wake of my own worst experience of cabin fever. With my best friend, Don Jensen, I failed on an attempt on the unclimbed east ridge of Mount Deborah in the Hayes Range in 1964. For at least half our forty-two days, we were stuck during storms inside Don's tent, which he had built especially snug to save weight. Soon everything we did drove each other crazy. I needed abundant conversation, while Don crawled for hours into a cocoon of placid silence. At mealtimes, the very sound of Don's chewing drove me up the wall. If the feet of our sleeping bags accidentally touched, it felt like a physical assault. Fed up with going out in the storm to pee, I started urinating into plastic bags and tossing them out the door. It took Don several days to voice his complaint about the odor of urine that lingered in the air. By the end of our trip, every word we exchanged was freighted with unspoken accusations.

Cabin fever on Mount Deborah nearly cost Don and me our friendship. Yet when I sat down to write about the experience, it took me months to see that the bickering, the resentments, the mute distrust, the mannerisms that loomed as blatant affronts were as much a part of the story as pitches led or gear loads ferried. For after we had returned to civilization, Don and I each felt ashamed of our obsessive pettiness on the glacier. We were like a married couple waking up the morning after a drunken fight, incredulous to recall what trivial matters we had screamed about the night before.

I suspect that all explorers, confined together under trying conditions, later feel a deep shame about their cabin fever behavior. It is as if it were their own failures of character, their own childishness, greed, and stubbornness that had produced the tensions—not storms and discomfort and too little space. For the myth of adventure is one of perfect teamwork, of personal quirks subsumed in a common goal, of "the brotherhood of the rope."

About the cabin fever the Pomori must have suffered from 1743 to 1749, I could only speculate. The single glaring clue adhered around Verigin's prolonged decline. Just as, in a far less serious way, a subtle three-against-one alignment had from the start infected our partnership on Halfmoon Island, so there must have been, for all their compassion and solicitude, a three-against-one split among the Mezeners. How could it not have driven the healthy three to distraction when, despite all their pleadings, Verigin refused to drink warm reindeer blood? If, as Le Roy states, for fear of bears the men never dared leave their hut alone, then Verigin's indolent refusal (even before he became ill) to go out on the hunt or to gather driftwood must have severely taxed the others' patience, as well as limiting their logistical options. (Among a healthy and active quartet, for instance, two could have hunted reindeer far afield while the other two went in search of scurvy grass.)

Within our own group of four, another tension revolved around the ineffable joys of tobacco. Though every sip of our wine and Armagnac was liquid élan vital to me, I had had the good fortune never to fall under the spell of demon nicotine. Not so my three colleagues. The year before, Vaughn had kicked a chewing tobacco habit that had spanned a quarter century of his life. During his months of abstinence, he had put on weight, and his normally laid-back equanimity had been troubled by uncharacteristic fits of pique and petulance. He confessed that not a day passed without his having to quell intense cravings.

With his father's serious illness, alas, Vaughn had resumed his habit. To Svalbard he had brought ten cans of Skoal, and in Longyearbyen, just to be safe, had picked up a stash of some cheap Norwegian stuff. Now he was rail-thin again, and his day-to-day serenity had reconstituted itself—even under the pall of his crippled left leg.

Mats and Michel, on the other hand, were in trouble. Both steady cigarette smokers, they had independently vowed to quit on our trip. Michel was wearing a nicotine patch, but in Longyearbyen, on impulse, he had bought his last four packs of Marlboros to dilute his withdrawal over the trying weeks ahead. In hopes of literary reinforcement, he was reading a French edition of Italo Svevo's novel *Dernières Cigarettes.*

Mats had made no such hedges against deprivation. Even on the *Moltanovsky,* he had proved himself an inveterate bummer of cigarettes, soliciting everyone in sight who shared his habit. Now, on Halfmoon, he shamelessly and regularly turned to our *branleur,* demanding, "Michel." (He pronounced the name "Mitchell.") "Got a cigarette?"

Michel was unfailingly generous, but so far Mats had smoked more of his precious Marlboros than Michel himself had. At last Michel inveighed in English, "Mats, you have to stop before I stop." To me, this quirk of Mats's was little more than an annoying peccadillo. To Vaughn, however, with his appreciation of the narcotic pleasures of the weed, Mats's filching was the least forgivable of all his faults. Out of earshot of Mats, he kept murmuring, "I can't get over the way he keeps bumming Michel's cigarettes. It's unbelievable."

In this tawdry melodrama, playing itself out in Bjørneborg day by day, there lay another link to the Pomori in 1743. Going ashore to search for the Mezeners' hut, carrying the barest minimum of vital gear, the four sailors had not neglected to bring along, in Le Roy's phrase, "a bladder filled with tobacco, and every man his wooden pipe." No doubt the tobacco had not lasted long, and when it was gone, another cruel privation had descended upon the castaways.

The literature of polar exploration, in fact, is full of paeans to tobacco, and concomitant laments upon its absence. A homely entry, for instance, in the diary of Alexander Konrad, Albanov's sole fellow survivor in the epic recounted in *In the Land of White Death,* written as the men desperately struggle to reach Franz Josef Land, grumbles, "I think that leading the kind of life that we lead in the polar land must probably seem pretty vexing, because I have 15 rubles on me and I can't spend them on anything, not even on tobacco, without which we have been suffering for over a year already."

On August 24, with the sleet pelting down outside, Mats at last began to read the English version of Le Roy. For Michel, Vaughn, and me, the four Pomori in the narrative inspired unmitigated awe. For Mats, however, a certain ambivalence laced his evaluation of the sailors' deeds. On the one hand, as he had said in Trømso, their survival was so extraordinary that he could not believe the men were "stupid Christians": they must instead have been "Inuit." On the other, he implied that any resourceful outdoorsman could have pulled off some of the survival tricks of the Pomori.

To demonstrate the latter proposition, Mats now set to work starting a fire with a homemade drill and bow, as native cultures all over the world had done for eons. It took him several hours to make a bow out of a piece of bamboo and a cord he found inside the hut, the drill out of driftwood pine, pine shavings for tinder, and a baseboard in which he had whittled a cuphole to hold the shavings. As we watched intently, Mats squatted on the living room floor, holding one end of the drill to the cuphole, the other in his mouth, as he vigorously sawed the bow to spin the drill and turn friction into fire. Before he could produce even a hint of smoke, the drill suddenly broke in half. I made the mistake of guffawing. (In Mats's defense, a good drill-and-bow apparatus uses hardwood for the drill, soft for the tinder. The pine was simply too soft.)

During the previous year, among all the friends and acquaintances to whom I had related the outlines of the sailors' story, only one had pooh-poohed their survival. Like Mats, the man was an autodidact: he also happened to be an intensely competitive world-class mountaineer. "What's the big deal?" he said when I had finished. "The Inuit did that kind of thing all the time."

The man's stricture troubled me for months. Had I, in my runaway enthusiasm for what I believed to be the most extraordinary survival story I had ever heard, unconsciously condescended toward native peoples, whose own survival skills were too easy to take for granted? (I had written a book about the Chiricahua Apache under Cochise and Geronimo from 1861 to 1886. Those warriors could routinely run a hundred miles in a day—something no white soldier at the time ever accomplished.) Was the Pomori's six-year survival on Edgeøya merely "pretty good for Europeans"?

Eventually, I decided my friend's canard was beside the point. Culture was everything. In the Mato Grosso of Brazil, I had watched Suya Indians shoot fish I could not even see in murky water with a bow and arrow. But plunk a Suya in the middle of Manhattan, and he would have a hard time crossing 42nd Street without getting run over. (One of the tribe's elders had indeed recently been killed by an auto trying to cross the street on his first trip to a big city, Goiania.) Given the skills that, as northern Russian sailors and hunters, the four Mezen men had carried to Svalbard in their heads and hearts, their six-year survival was unmistakably a miraculous accomplishment. The proof lay in the fact that no other European overwinterers ever came close to duplicating their feat; that even today, the Pomori still hold the record for the longest survival of shipwrecked men in the Arctic by more than two years, their nearest rivals being sailors such as some of the English parties searching northern Canada for Sir John Franklin's lost expedition in the 1850s. Those teams, whose own ships got irretrievably stuck in the ice, had the inestimable advantage over the Mezeners of tons of supplies and food salvaged from their vessels, as well as the aid of other searching parties who came to their rescue.

In the same spirit of experimental archaeology that had driven Mats's fire-starting attempt, Vaughn, out for a short walk in the storm, had gathered up a gob of loamy clay. Now he kneaded it into a flat patty, then laid it on the stove top to cure. A few hours later, he dubiously handled his clay concoction. "It's pretty marginal," he said. "Maybe if you added flour." Only after boiling some of their flour into a starch with which they had lined the clay had the Pomori crafted a lamp that worked. Vaughn placed his creation back on the stove top. "Once you get it made, if you don't bang it around too much . . ."

Despite the poor visibility, on a short walk of his own, Mats had spotted another bear across the sea on the cliffs of Edgeøya—or perhaps the same bear as the day before, having ambled a couple of miles east. So far, to our relief, we had detected no signs of bears on Halfmoon itself—no recent pawprints, no piles of fresh excrement.

Rummaging in a storage cabinet, Mats found several gunny sacks filled with coal, obviously imported from elsewhere in Svalbard. He was quite sure that this fuel dated from Per Johnson's last overwintering in 1970–71. We mixed coal and driftwood in our stove, and produced a hot, slow-burning fire.

"Ten years ago," Mats mused, "the Sysselmannen would never have given us permission to stay in a hut. Then they have the attitude that all the old huts should just fall apart, or be burned down." Once more I pictured us camped miserably in tents encircled by trip wires, listening for the dull thump of a bear lumbering near. If Mats had done nothing else, he deserved the highest credit for convincing the Sysselmannen that we might base ourselves in Bjørneborg without compromising the hut's function as an emergency shelter.

Belated though it was, Mats's reading of Le Roy produced dividends. (Here was one more example of the fruitful principle I had discovered in Russia—that rather than search for another primary source for the old story, I might benefit from asking a number of readers with different kinds of expertise to peruse Le Roy.) Michel and I had been discussing the nagging question of whether both Klingstedt's and Le Roy's interviews of the sailors had been conducted as much in the spirit of a judicial investigation as out of admiring curiosity. Le Roy admits that at first he had his doubts about the truth of the three survivors' tale, and, apropos of Klingstedt's interview with the men, uses the phrase "sent for and examined them very particularly."

Now Mats put his finger on a detail Michel and I had overlooked. The very first sentence of the narrative proper begins, "In the year 1743, one JEREMIAH OKLADMKOF, a Merchant of *Mesen,* a town in the province of *Jugovia* and in the government of *Archangel,* fitted out a vessel, carrying fourteen men." Vexed that Le Roy never names the ship or its captain, I had paid little attention to Okladmkof. In the Arkhangel'sk Area Archive I had learned that the name (usually spelled Okladnikov) had been very common in the Russian north, and Hugh and I had combed the register looking for any record of a ship outfitted by that merchant, but found none. Le Roy never mentions Okladmkof again.

Now Mats made an inference based perhaps on his own experience as a guide hired by a company to produce a satisfactory result. "This guy Okladmkof," he said, "why wouldn't he be pissed off? He is the man who pays for the expedition. Then the sailors come back with all this booty, these furs and reindeer fat and so on, and they give it all to—what is the name of the pilot who rescues them?"

"Kornilov," I supplied.

"Yes, Kornilov, and then they give more things to Count Shuvalov. If I am Okladmkof, I am pretty pissed off. Maybe I call for a criminal investigation."

The speculation hung in the air, tantalizing me. Like so many hunches about the reality behind the fugitive story, it hovered ambiguously, an untestable hypothesis. But in my imagination, the scenario played itself out. Okladmkof's ship vanishes without a trace. The Pomori are gone so long that in the 1748 Mezen census, they are officially listed as dead. Then suddenly, three return—not as starving wretches, but as affluent hunters with spoils worth many rubles. All this flies in the face of the collective Pomori wisdom about how hard it is to overwinter in Svalbard, let alone after surviving a shipwreck. Yes, if I were Okladmkof, I might very well call for an investigation: hence, perhaps, the prosecutorial tone of Klingstedt's and Le Roy's interviews with the sailors.

By 4:00 P.M. on August 24, the mist had closed in so tight we could no longer see any part of Edgeøya across the two miles of foaming sea. We sat reading in the hut, listening to the steady sleet on the roof, punctuated every five or six seconds by the crash of a wave on shore. When at last we went to sleep that night, I was convinced that another rest day was in store for us on the morrow. As glad as I was to lie in a dry sleeping bag inside a coal-warmed hut, I had the gloomy premonition that weather could severely curtail our movement, turning our two weeks into a vigil rather than a genuine search. In a footnote in Conway's *No Man's Land,* I found a quote that matched my mood, from an English pilot in the early seventeenth century: "This is the worst and coldest region of the world, everywhere cliffs, mountains and rocks. . . . The amount of ice is enormous and the ice-mountains so many that they seem to have been accumulating even ever since the birth of Christ. The abundance of snow surpasses belief."

By morning, however, the rain had stopped, and though a heavy ceiling of clouds cut off the Edgeøya cliffs at about five hundred feet above sea level, the wind had shifted from the east and the surf was down. Mats thought we ought to be able to get over to the mainland. Vaughn and I had our aquaphobic doubts. Vaughn's leg was, if anything, worse than the day before, proving to him that he had not simply sprained it: there had to be damage, possibly permanent, to the ligaments. He could not even move around the hut without hobbling.

A little after 10:00 in the morning, we boarded up the doors and windows of our hut to bear-proof it—as we would have to do every time we left it, even for a one-hour walk. Then we wheeled our Zodiac down to the shore and prepared to launch it. To make the boat more manageable, we loaded it up with much less gear than two days before, omitting the emergency tent, sleeping bags, and extra food. To our great relief, we got the boat off shore without mishap. Mats fired up the outboard engine, and we churned steadily toward Edgeøya, survival suits sealed tight. In only thirty-five minutes we arrived, pulling into a cove formed by the crook of a rocky jetty named Skotteneset on the map. We were about six miles due north of Bjørneborg.

Mats gentled the boat toward the pebbly beach. We hopped out and waded on shore, pulling the Zodiac by its pontoon ropes. For the first time, we stood on Edgeøya.

We had chosen this precise destination in part because of its shape on the map. The coast of Edgeøya northeast of Halfmoon (which Starkov had urged as the first place to look for the lost hut) unfolds as a featureless, almost straight line up through Stones Forland, the strip of beach trapped between the sea and the icecap of Edgeøyjøkulen. Only around Skotteneset is the coast interrupted by small islands and by a two-mile-long bay called Dianabukta, which looked to Mats like a perfect natural harbor.

Moreover, in Gustav Rossnes's guidebook to Svalbard overwinterings from 1895 to 1940, Mats had found mention of two Norwegian huts located in Dianabukta, one built in 1906, the other in 1936. It was thus an eminently logical place to look for even earlier vestiges of Russian overwinterers.

Having trip-wired our Zodiac, we set out along the beach, hiking northeast from the neck of Skotteneset. We spread out across several hundred yards, hiking in parallel to canvass our surroundings, Michel and I on the seashore, Vaughn and Mats atop a headland plateau some 150 feet above sea level, each of us carrying both a Mauser and a flare gun, except for Mats, who lugged along his .357 Magnum.

Surprisingly, we found nothing human—except the usual flotsam washed up at the high-tide line. Soon, however, I had stumbled across a fresh reindeer track in the sand. The print looked much like that of a deer, but for an extra percussion point at the rear, imprinted by a flexible appendage at the back of the hoof that apparently aids the animal's purchase.

I hiked on, tracking the reindeer. Michel had joined Mats and Vaughn atop a promontory overlooking the vast delta of the Dianadalen, where a major river flowed into the harbor from a deep valley heading in the icecap. So much, I thought, for Le Roy's remark that the island of the sailors' exile "has no river, but a great number of small rivulets."

Moving on, below and ahead of my three companions, I topped a gentle rise to see five reindeer browsing on the moss about two hundred yards in front of me. During twenty magical minutes, I walked very slowly toward the animals, who had discovered me right away. I wanted to see how close I could get without spooking them. Every other minute, the five craned their necks in unison toward my intrusion, then trotted off for a few yards, before returning to their mossy feast. I froze, then crept forward again. I managed to get within twenty yards before all five took off running up the valley.

From the promontory, Vaughn had watched my stalking in his binoculars. As I rejoined him, I asked, "How hard would it be to shoot a reindeer with a bow and arrow from twenty yards?"

"It depends on how good the bow is," Vaughn answered. "I've seen a lot of bow hunters miss at twenty yards."

Mine would be the closest encounter of our trip with reindeer. Because the species found on Svalbard (*Rangifer tarandus platyrhynchus*) is unique to the archipelago and to Novaya Zemlya, and because it bears a closer similarity to Canadian caribou than to the reindeer of Russia and Scandinavia, we know that the animals must have migrated to their present home a very long time ago. By 1920, they had been hunted almost to extinction on Svalbard, but a foresighted government declared them a protected species in 1925. Since that date, they have flourished and multiplied. Biologists estimate their population on Svalbard today at about ten thousand to twelve thousand, of which 2,500 exist on Edgeøya and its neighboring island, Barentsøya. On Edgeøya, they remain a protected species, although since 1983, the hunt for reindeer has been reauthorized on Spitsbergen proper, with a quota of 100 to 150 per year.

The reason the five reindeer had allowed my approach to twenty yards, I later learned, was that they have poor eyesight, and must rely on scent to identify an intruder. Despite that handicap, the animals are superbly adapted to the harsh environment of the high Arctic. Browsing ceaselessly on mosses and ground plants in summer, they store up reserves of fat that allow them to get through the winter. They easily cross glaciers and swim short distances in the sea. The main cause of death among the reindeer, curiously, is starvation after having worn out their teeth grazing on plants clogged with sand and gravel.

Unlike North American caribou, the Svalbard reindeer never gather in large herds. Five is ordinarily the largest number that will be found traveling together. This trait may be an adaptive mechanism, to spread the animals across the largest possible area, so that no particular region ever gets overgrazed.

From the promontory, in binoculars we watched our five reindeer trot slowly inland. It was obvious that the unnamed river northeast of us, draining the Dianadalen, would require a serious ford; even getting close to it, we would most likely get soaked above our knees in tributary channels and sloughlike marshes. With the temperature barely above freezing and a steady wind from the east, we were not keen to tempt hypothermia.

Where, however, were the Norwegian huts Rossnes had indicated on the shores of Dianabukta? Vaughn, whose eye for ruins is sharp, swept the barren delta for long minutes with his powerful binoculars. "I don't see a damn thing," he murmured.

We decided to head inland, testing Le Roy's assertion that the Mezeners' hut had stood as far as a mile from the shore. Mats pointed out a low cliff that overlooked a small canyon: if you were to build a hut inland, that looked like a logical place to position it, with drinking water nearby, an open vista to the south, and a mountain slope at your back to block the north wind.

We trudged along a gray waste of plain, gravel and sand interspersed with gray-green tussocks. The sky was dark, the cloud ceiling still around five hundred feet, and the wind felt raw. Even hiking vigorously, I was none too warm with all my clothes on, including gloves, wool hat, Gore-Tex parka, long underwear, and rain pants. A vague feeling that I had carried in a corner of my mind for the last two days all at once burst into words: *This is the most godforsaken place I have ever been.*

We started to climb the gentle hill that led to the low cliff. All the way inland, the five reindeer had paralleled our march, maintaining a distance of several hundred yards. Michel had wandered off to the right to admire them.

Suddenly Mats stopped and raised his hand. In a soft but urgent voice, he spoke: "Mitchell. Get over here."

What was going on? In the next moment, I got my answer. From behind the cliff, at a distance of 150 yards, a polar bear suddenly came into view, ambling straight toward us. Mats had caught a glimpse of telltale white a few seconds before the rest of us saw the bear.

At once Vaughn pulled the bolt on his Mauser, slipping a cartridge into firing position. Michel and I just stood there. Mats raised his flare gun and fired. Two seconds later, a brown flame burst with a loud bang from the rocks just in front of the polar bear. The animal wheeled and ran uphill, then slowed to a walk, turning now and then to stare in our direction before vanishing behind the cliff.

The encounter had written a finis to our inland search. You could hardly say that we had been in any real danger, yet now I tasted the residue of adrenaline on my tongue. Michel had a sheepish grin on his face. *"Formidable!"* he declared.

We climbed to the top of a nearby prong of rock and sat down, staring intently at the last place where we had seen the bear. Abruptly, it reappeared on the other side of the low cliff, walking across a snowbank. "It's a female," said Mats, peering through his binoculars, "and she's big."

For the next half hour, as we glued our binoculars to the scene, we were treated to an inimitable display. The bear kept peering at us, but approached no closer. It was not fear of us that kept her on the snowbank, however, but another agenda. In a climate where we needed all our clothes to ward off hypothermia, the bear, with all her fur and bulk, was overheated. Rolling in snow was one of the few ways she could cool off during the balmy Arctic summer.

In what looked like an orgy of self-gratification, the bear lay on her back, legs raised, and slid down the bank, then got up and climbed to the top again. She rolled over and over, squirming with cool relief. The snowbank was impregnated with a reddish orange algae (a common phenomenon in Arctic and alpine regions): slowly but steadily, the bear's pure white coat turned a color halfway between peach and strawberry. A red-orange bear: Vaughn, Michel, and I had never seen the like, though Mats had several times before. My anxiety dissolved into sheer delight, and for half an hour, Edgeøya seemed anything but godforsaken.

—

There is no accurate count of the numbers of polar bears in Svalbard. Informed estimates range between two thousand and three thousand. Since 1973, the animal has been protected throughout the archipelago, but it reproduces so slowly that the population has only gradually increased over the past three decades. Nowhere in Svalbard are polar bears more numerous than around the south coast of Edgeøya.

The largest bear ever killed in Svalbard weighed a little over 1,500 pounds. The average late-summer weight of a female is about 800 pounds, the average male 1,100. Polar bears are prodigious travelers, routinely covering a region 650 miles in diameter in a single year. One bear tranquilized and tagged in Svalbard in the late 1960s was recaptured in southwestern Greenland, having traveled almost 2,200 miles in a year and a half. Bears routinely walk fifty miles in a day; they ride ice floes as if they were pleasure yachts; and as swimmers, they are the Mark Spitzes of the mammal kingdom. They feed almost exclusively on ringed and bearded seals, which they catch on the ice. Because of this cycle, by late August, the bears are entering the time of year when they are hungriest, having gone as long as several months since their last solid meal—a fact that was not lost on us as we watched our overheated companion frolicking on her snowbank.

Polar bears live about twenty to thirty years. They mate in April and May, but a process called "delayed implantation" means that the female's egg does not begin to develop until September or October. The pregnant female builds a den at the end of autumn, inside which she gives birth in December to between one and four cubs, and reemerges in the following March or April. The cubs follow their mother for two and a half years, during which period she does not mate.

In the mid-1990s on Edgeøya and on Hopen Island farther south in the Barents Sea, a Canadian scientist named Andrew Derocher performed some remarkable research that produced an unexpected and disturbing result. In 1996, he discovered that two of the bears he had tranquilized had "dual genitalia" and no Y chromosome. They were, in Derocher's phrase, "female pseudo-hermaphrodites." The condition was previously known, but thought to be exceedingly rare. During the next two years, however, Derocher found six more bears on Svalbard with the same hermaphroditic aberrations. Extrapolating from his sample, he estimated that 4 percent of Svalbard's polar bears might be afflicted by the condition.

Casting about for a possible cause, Derocher and colleagues concluded that PCB contaminants might be the culprit. Except for Russia, northern European countries have banned PCBs since the early 1970s, but the chemicals take a very long time to break down and have an insidious way of getting stored in the fat of animals—including seals.

The diet of the Svalbard polar bears might thus have included inordinate amounts of PCBs during the previous two decades, wreaking havoc with the reproductive systems of a certain number of them. Like the ozone hole growing over Antarctica, here may lie one of the most vivid examples of the far-reaching impact of our industrial proliferation—that on Edgeøya, one of the most pristine places on earth, invisible PCBs unleashed into the environment a quarter century ago may be threatening the survival of one of the noblest and hardiest of animals on earth.

Sublime though our half hour of bear watching had been near the inland cliff, we had kept our Mausers close at hand, firing chambers loaded. I could not help imagining Sharapov and the Inkovs, off hunting reindeer in such a place as this, only to have a bear come lumbering out from behind a cliff. No flare guns in the 1740s: at such a moment, the men must have clutched their two homemade lances and prayed. Sometimes the prayers had not worked, and the bear had charged. Try though I might, I could not visualize myself wielding a lance effectively enough to kill a polar bear without suffering grievous injuries in the process.

It would not be until well into the twentieth century that hunters in Svalbard were able, thanks to technology, to tip the scales significantly in favor of humans in the immemorial combat with the polar bear. It would have been a tragedy had Svalbard not banned bear hunting in 1973, by which date repeating rifles and snowmobiles had raised the specter of extinction for *Ursus maritimus*. And yet I also harbored a deep admiration for the courage and resourcefulness of the last overwintering hunters, men such as Per Johnson.

Upon my return to the U.S. in late September, I got hold of Johnson by telephone. I expressed my astonishment at his solo wintering in 1970–71, his success in killing twenty-five bears, his two-week dogsled jaunt back to Longyearbyen in February.

"Oh, but that year there was a quota," he said. "In 1969–70 I also overwintered. There were three of us. Two lived on Halfmoon Island, and I overwintered alone at Andréetangen. That year there was no limit on bears."

"How many did you get?" I asked.

"I'm not sure I should tell you," said Johnson.

"Please."

"I killed 140." In the old man's voice, I thought I detected a mixture of pride and embarrassment. But the former won out, as Johnson proceeded with nostalgic zest to describe the "enormous work" of the hunt. "To preserve the skins over the winter, we dig into the snow on the leeward side of the hut," he said. "The snow drifts higher and higher. We keep putting new skins in. In the spring, we dug up ten skins at a time. We had to melt the ice chunks out of the fur." It was curious, I thought, that Johnson used the first person plural for his solo deeds.

"Oh, the blubber cutting! It takes a special knife. We cut the blubber in small strips, put it in thirty-gallon oil drums. We brought back twenty tons of blubber. In Tromsø they pay us two kroner per kilo."

Thinking of the thin walls of the hut at Bjørneborg, I asked how warm a man could stay in winter there.

"No, it is not warm," Johnson chuckled. "The hut is not insulated."

I asked about the Pomori in 1743. "This is the first story I hear, when I first come to Svalbard in the 1960s. But where did this happen? It is impossible now to tell."

My account of our own stay on Halfmoon Island had stirred up Johnson's memories. "Oh, it is a good thing I did not go with you," he said in closing. "Otherwise I should never stop talking!"

Another old-timer, Odd Lønø, had gradually evolved from one of the most skilled bear hunters into a self-taught natural historian. In 1970, Lønø, who had first overwintered on Edgeøya in 1946–47, published a lengthy monograph that remains the definitive work on the history of the Svalbard hunt as well as on the behavior of the archipelago's polar bears. After our trip, I found a copy at Harvard: mercifully, the work was in English.

Lønø had combed every Norwegian source he could find. (The earlier Russian history of hunting in Svalbard, as Rudmose Brown had bemoaned, is lost to human record.) Since the Norwegians did not start coming to Svalbard until 1795, the early testimony was spotty. A captain in 1828 wrote, "Bears are shot when seen, but are not hunted specifically." In Hammerfest, with Tromsø one of northern Norway's two principal seaports, Lønø found records of bear catches on Svalbard between 1824 and 1829. Among the entire Norwegian fleet, the most pelts brought back in a single year was thirty-two, the fewest only one.

It was not until late in the nineteenth century that Norwegians began to hunt polar bears in earnest. The pivotal event was the invention of the "spring-gun trap," whose origins remain obscure, but which Lønø thought dated from the 1890s. Originally the trap was a big wall of logs or stones behind which a rifle was mounted, its barrel protruding through the wall, its trigger tied by cord to a piece of bait, usually seal blubber. These first spring-gun traps "were not very effective," wrote Lønø. "If there was snow in the trap, the bear stood too high up, and the shot did not hit where it was supposed to. Any snow covering the bait prevented the bear from finding its way to the spring-gun."

In 1920, a hunter named Gustav Lundquist invented a brilliantly efficient new type of spring-gun trap—the parallelepiped mounted on a sawhorse, with a sawed-off rifle barrel protruding from a hidden rear chamber—the remains of which we would find scattered all over Halfmoon Island. With the ready availability of cheap Remington army surplus rifles (discontinued for military use in 1904), this killing machine entered its heyday. In Lønø's first overwintering, in 1946–47, his team killed eighty-seven bears with spring-gun traps; it also hunted down and shot another fifty-one. Eventually, in Lønø's estimate, 75 to 85 percent of all the polar bear catch was accomplished with Lundquist's fiendish invention.

Early in the century, poisoning was also tried, with a piece of seal blubber laced with strychnine dangled from a tall pole. The trouble was, it took the bear five to ten minutes to die, during which time it typically wandered out onto the sea ice, from which it was all but impossible to retrieve the carcass. Some bears vomited up the poison at once, indicated Lønø; others walked miles after eating the bait, vomited, then marched on with no ill effects. Poison was outlawed in 1927, but its use continued on Svalbard "for a long time."

Lønø's monograph also clarified the purpose of another structure we had found on Halfmoon. Close to our hut, a fifteen-foot-high pole had been mounted on a tripod wedged among the rocks. Mats had told us that bears are naturally attracted to any tall object: the pole (and others we found scattered around the island) had the opposite effect of a scarecrow. But Lønø indicated that a piece of bait was dangled from a pole erected near a hut, with a line fastened to a tin can suspended inside the hut. The bear took the bait, rattling the can, and alerting the hunter, "who then shoots the bear through a hole in the door."

No place in all of Svalbard saw more bear killing than Halfmoon Island. The apogee came in 1964–65, when a single pair of hunters overwintering there took 145 bears. Lønø believes that by 1970, seventy years of steady hunting had reduced the bear population of Svalbard by only 25 percent. But before the Sysselmannen outlawed bear killing altogether, the snowmobile had begun to revolutionize the hunt. A pair of bears was even shot from a helicopter, before the government forbade such tactics.

Reading between the lines of Lønø's monograph, I realized that, no matter how much one might deplore the hunting of the magnificent *Ursus maritimus,* that near century of overwintering in pursuit of the valuable white pelts had been a campaign of heroic proportions, that hunters such as Odd Lønø and Per Johnson were mythic figures. The Svalbard hunt cries out for a Norwegian Herman Melville to sing its epic deeds, before they vanish from human memory. As Mats had said to me one day, "There are only five or six men like Per Johnson still alive who know this story well. They know this country as no one else—where the seals are having pups, where you find some kind of duck, where the reindeer have their feeding places. When these men die, this whole knowledge will be gone."

In Lønø's monograph, I found glimpses of that unwritten epic: the firsthand testimony, for instance, of hunters who, half a century before, had watched a female bear build her den, or who had crawled into the den in spring just after the mother and cubs had left it. And I found a host of fascinating and surprising facts gleaned from those veteran observers. It is commonly said that a polar bear has no natural predator to fear; but according to Lønø, walruses (and even hooded seals) in the water had been known to kill bears. Also, "adult bears sometimes kill one another"—fighting, for instance, over dead seals. I had wondered whether reindeer had little to fear from polar bears, because they could easily outrun them, but according to Lønø, "The polar bear shows no interest in reindeer whatsoever"—a matter, presumably, of taste.

For me the strangest affirmation in Lønø's text, repeated several times, was that "in the summer the bear is rarely found on land." Given that all the bears we saw during our two weeks in the wilderness were on land, not one in the water, I began to wonder whether the animal's behavior had changed during the thirty years since Lønø wrote. In the Canadian Arctic, I knew, within the last decade polar bears were facing serious threats to their existence, thanks to the diminishing of the ice pack (probably a result of global warming). If the ice that normally surrounds Edgeøya were similarly shrinking in recent years, perhaps the bears were forced onto land in summer in a desperate search for food. Perhaps the reddish orange female bear we had delighted in watching as she rolled in the snow had reached the very edge of starvation.

From our inland prong of rock, we hiked slowly back to the Zodiac, then huddled wretchedly in the rocks while Mats cooked up a lunch of ramen noodles and leek soup. Having come so far, we felt that we needed to make a further reconnaissance of Dianabukta, so we pushed the boat back into the water, then motored northeast two miles to another promontory called Knockdowodden. Here we made a minor miscalculation. Having pulled our Zodiac up onto shore and rigged it once more with trip wires, we discovered that a small tidal channel separated the promontory from the mainland. There was little choice but to wade it in our survival suits—a scary proposition for Vaughn and me, as the water came up to our chests and the footing, among slimy, invisible rocks, was treacherous. All day Vaughn had made no complaints about hiking on his bad leg, but I knew he was in constant pain.

The gray ceiling of clouds had begun to lower, and out at sea, fog had started to roll in. I was alarmed to notice that we could no longer see Halfmoon Island. Mats was unperturbed, for before leaving Bjørneborg, he had plugged in its precise latitude and longitude on a global positioning system he carried inside his survival suit. In pea-soup fog, he insisted, he could find the hut just by homing in on it with the GPS.

On principle, neither Vaughn nor I had ever used a GPS. In the Southwest, the gadgets have spawned a new kind of backcountry tourism, as guidebooks increasingly give GPS coordinates for trailheads, peaks, and even archaeological sites. Novices who cannot read a map, who have little sense of how to find their way around canyon country, simply plug in the numbers and stumble toward their objective. Not only did this seem like cheating to Vaughn and me; the GPS had been known to get hikers in trouble, either when it failed to work or when it led them into cul-de-sacs they might, with common sense and dead reckoning, have otherwise avoided.

Here the GPS posed a different threat. In the seas around Svalbard, everybody uses the devices. But it disturbed Vaughn and me to put so much faith in a fallible electronic gizmo. What if the batteries went dead? What if Mats accidentally dropped the GPS into the sea? Then nothing but blind chance might prevent us, heading through fog back toward Halfmoon, from missing the island altogether and plowing on out into the Barents Sea. Mats did not even carry a compass, though I did.

So, with the weather deteriorating, we made only a hasty search around Knockdowodden. The shore was barren in the extreme, a limitless shelf of fine gravel and mud, with only a few clumps of bog saxifrage, its tiny yellow blossoms dancing in the wind, to relieve the monotony. Once more we found no signs of human presence, save the ubiquitous ship debris washed up by the waves. If huts had been built in Dianabukta in 1906 and 1936, nothing must be left of them.

Hiking along the beach, we crossed the tracks of a polar bear. Where our boots sank only an inch into the mud, the bear's paws had left deep oval indentations, some half filled with pools of water.

Returning toward the Zodiac, we started slipping in a particularly fine mud. "More clay," muttered Vaughn. I whipped out a plastic bag, scooped a couple of handsful of the stuff out of the ground, and dumped it in the bag.

All the way back, as Mats held the outboard motor and we plunged through whiteout, I felt a deep anxiety, though I kept my mouth shut. Both Vaughn and I peered into the blowing mist, hoping for a glimpse of low shore that would herald Halfmoon Island. Mats looked completely relaxed. Sure enough, the GPS worked. Only in the last few hundred yards could we at last see land, and we came to shore directly in front of our beloved hut.

By the time we were ensconced in our sanctum, cooking up dinner, the fog had completely closed in, the thickest we had seen in our four days on Halfmoon. Exhausted but exhilarated after our eight-hour day on Edgeøya, we lounged in the living room, sipping beer while a coal-and-driftwood fire crackled in the stove. Vaughn took the gobs of clay I had gathered and patiently kneaded them into a shallow cup, then placed the vessel on top of the stove. "That's a lot better stuff than what I messed around with the other day," he said.

Michel had smoked his last cigarette. On a nicotine-deprivation jag, he washed a huge pile of dishes, cooked three times as much frozen steak as we could eat, then went out in the drizzle to saw driftwood for an hour.

I had been musing on our lack of discoveries in Dianabukta. If that harbor was the likeliest place on the northeast shore of Edgeøya for human settlement, and yet no sign of occupation remained, then perhaps the whole shore from Halfmoon up to the great Edgeøyjøkulen icecap—the very shore Starkov had urged me to investigate—was barren. On the other hand, in eight hours we had not really performed a thorough search. In particular, we had made only one tentative probe inland (where, according to Le Roy, the Mezeners' hut lay), that one thwarted by the sudden appearance of the she-bear. I thought back to the blithe plan I had formed in my Cambridge study the previous winter, of covering the south coast of Edgeøya in a series of hikes supplied by Zodiac ferries. Searching the Svalbard shores was about ten times as difficult as I had imagined it might be.

The next morning, I was awakened at 6:30 by a sudden commotion. Groggily I fancied that it was only Mats starting the fire in the stove. It turned out instead that he had gone out into the yard to urinate, for once not bothering to carry his flare gun or his revolver, only to discover a bear a mere fifteen yards away, between himself and the decrepit boat shed. "Not a big one," he said later, "but not a cub, either." The bear headed toward Mats, but when he hissed sharply, it paused. Mats hastily reentered Bjørneborg and seized his flare gun, then returned and fired a shot over the boat shed. This only provoked the bear to approach the cabin. A second shot, almost point-blank, finally sent the creature running, but straight in the direction of our Zodiac. Mats ran after it, shouting, until the bear veered off and disappeared among the rocks south of our cabin.

Still half in our sleeping bags, Michel and I never saw the bear, though Vaughn had leapt up in time to catch sight of it as it fled along the shore. "I wouldn't be surprised if he comes back," Mats said. "He's hungry."

One question had been settled. Our fond hope that the bears were confined to Edgeøya proper had been dashed. Not only did they range Halfmoon Island as well, but they apparently had no qualms about approaching our hut, from which enticing aromas no doubt wafted, despite our best efforts to contain our trash and keep the place clean.

That morning the fog was still tight to the ground, and the wind was strong out of the east. We decided, rather than force another Zodiac journey in marginal conditions, to hike to the northeast tip of Halfmoon Island. In particular, we were eager to search another bay, called Dianahamna, an apparently even more ideal harbor than Dianabukta over on Edgeøya, since it lay curled inside the protective crescent of Halfmoon itself. Gustav Rossnes's guidebook to Norwegian overwinterings indicated that huts had been built in Dianahamna, although one of them, he claimed, was the rude dwelling in which Karl Møller and Ibenhart Jensen Fladseth had died of scurvy in the winter of 1898–99. That hut, of course, lay only a hundred yards from Bjørneborg, not in Dianahamna at all. The suspicion would grow upon us that Rossnes's records were not very accurate or authoritative, and we became convinced that, among other lapses, he had confused Dianabukta with Dianahamna.

There was another compelling reason to visit the latter harbor. Back in Longyearbyen, only hours before boarding our cruise ship, we had visited a scientist named Kolbein Dahle at the Sysselmannen office. To our surprise, Dahle revealed that just a few months before, a government team had made a very cursory archaeological survey of the southeast coast of Edgeøya, including Halfmoon Island. In frantic haste, I had copied some field notes off Dahle's computer, which the man quickly translated into English. On my annotated map, I had marked the spit that forms the western arm of Dianahamna with the note: "Graves—7 + 4."

The fine drizzle of the last two days had soaked the *Umbilicaria* lichens that swathed the basalt boulders across which we clambered. Ours was a slimy, awkward progress, full of opportunities for sprained knees and ankles, as well as a sore trial for Vaughn. What with constant stops to survey the blurry horizon with our binoculars (now a far more urgent chore, after our bear visit that morning), we proceeded at a pace of only about a mile an hour.

Everywhere we saw tall bear-attracting poles, some still erect, some collapsed in the talus. Each had at least one spring-gun trap beside it, usually surrounded by a liberal scatter of bones.

Mats called us over to examine a plant at his feet. A scraggly, undistinguished clump of shiny green leaves with a sprinkling of white flowers met our gaze. "That's scurvy grass," said Mats. "*Cochlearia officinalis.* Taste it."

I seized a few buds and blossoms and popped them in my mouth. The plant, indeed, tasted like a vitamin C tablet. "Grows in damp or not too dry places," commented a flower book I later consulted back in the hut. "Very common in Svalbard." So this was the stuff, I mused, that had saved the Pomori—but why, then, had all those later Norwegians such as Møller and Fladseth not had the wit to gather enough of the plant to ward off scurvy?

We had almost reached Dianahamna when Mats paused, binoculars raised, and held out his left hand. "There's another one," he whispered. "The biggest yet."

For the first time I sensed Vaughn's frustration that he (who quietly prided himself on the eye I had bragged to Michel about) had not yet spotted a bear. All five that we had encountered had been Mats's discoveries. Now we trained our binoculars. The bear was a good two hundred yards ahead, lying on its side among a pile of boulders. For five minutes, it did not move, prompting Mats to wonder whether the bear might be dead, rather than asleep. We did not, however, plan to walk up to it to ascertain the truth. Unfortunately, the bear lay right above the beach at the center of the harbor of Dianahamna. Our path would pass just in front of it.

We crept stealthily forward, never taking our binoculars off that lump of white in the rocks for more than a minute or two. Soon we found the spit. Sure enough, laid out among the debris of a spring-gun trap were neat piles of rock, each about six feet long by two feet wide. The graves were in two clusters, four in a kite-shaped pattern to the west, the others—I counted eight, rather than seven—mostly lined up in a row that angled toward the point of the spit. Nervous about the bear, we took only a perfunctory look at the graves before moving on. We would save a careful perusal for the way back.

With Mats and Vaughn carrying their guns with chambers loaded, we sidled wordlessly along the beach. The bear never stirred.

On the far, eastern end of Dianahamna, we found further signs of human passage. The skull of a beached whale sat, a four-foot-high lump of porous white bone, on a patch of moss. Hunters had carved their initials in it. I made out "ALJ" and "IPSS" and "LK and "AS." As these were Latin letters rather than Cyrillic, they had no doubt been carved by Norwegian visitors. Not far from this landmark we came upon a solitary grave, across which lay an old plank on which had been carved the initials "GTS." Another hapless Norwegian, no doubt—but the initials matched none of the overwinterers recorded by Rossnes.

Half a mile farther on, I made a thrilling discovery. A large, odd-shaped piece of wood lying in the grass caught my eye. As I approached, I saw that the object had been carefully hewn to shape, apparently by axe-blade, with rusted strips and bolts of iron holding it together. Suddenly, thanks to the Maritime Museum in Arkhangel'sk, I knew exactly what I beheld. It was the rudder from a Russian *kotch* or *lodja.* Vaughn and I lifted the thing up and propped it on end, in the position it would have occupied on the boat it had once steered. The rudder was remarkably heavy, taller than our heads.

Mats came up to see. As I would later realize, in his competitiveness, relishing his role as guide, he was not particularly pleased if someone else discovered anything interesting. A bit grudgingly, he acknowledged my find, and he agreed with Vaughn that the rudder could well date from the eighteenth century. It was the first unmistakably Russian artifact we had come across.

A bit farther on, we won another confirmation of a long-ago Russian presence. A mossy stretch of shoreline was littered with bones. "Walrus skulls," Mats said, prodding one with his toe. "This is the true sign of an old Pomori hunting ground." Mats had seen the like on other parts of Svalbard. As Sergei Terent'ev, the nautical historian we had bumped into by accident in Arkhangel'sk, had shrewdly divined, these were the animals (not whales, as Le Roy states) that the four castaways in 1743 had come to Svalbard to hunt.

After three hours, we headed back. The bear lay exactly where we had last seen him. Once more we sneaked past without arousing him. Mats ventured the opinion that the bear might indeed be dead. But several days later, when we made another jaunt to the northeast tip of the island, he was gone. Evidently at the time of our first passage, the huge beast had simply been indulging in a power nap.

Back on the western spit of Dianahamna, I paused for half an hour to study the graves. By law, we were forbidden to move even a single stone of these mounds (or of any other archaeological site). Peering close, however, I thought I could glimpse the weathered remains of upright boards—crosses?—in two of them, as well as possible remnants of wooden coffins beneath the rocks. But I knew that often on Svalbard the dead had been laid to rest coffinless in shallow trenches gouged out of the permafrost, then covered with stones to keep the bears from ravaging the corpses.

Who had these twelve men been? Rossnes's guide made no mention of the graves, but did quote an earlier historian, Arvid Moberg, who asserted, "On Halvmåneøya [Halfmoon Island], there are Russian graves."

The strangest thing about this scene—the most mournful prospect I would behold during our journey—was that there was not a trace of a hut, or of any other structure, anywhere near the graves. Surely the twelve had died of scurvy in some overwintering tragedy, but if so, where had they lived?

During the very last Russian overwintering of all, from 1851 to 1852, twelve of the eighteen hunters had died. I was tempted to wonder whether the graves we had found were the mute testimony of that debacle, but for the fact that both Conway and Rudmose Brown record it as having taken place in Red Bay, which is nowhere near Edgeøya. Given that all the authorities agreed that no Norwegians had overwintered on Halfmoon before 1898, I was certain that the twelve graves were Russian. Yet how had a disaster of this magnitude not caught the ear of so perspicacious a listener as Sir Martin Conway?

Unless some archaeologist digs up this forlorn cemetery, I concluded, the mystery of the dead men's identities will linger on.

10: The Edge of the Ice

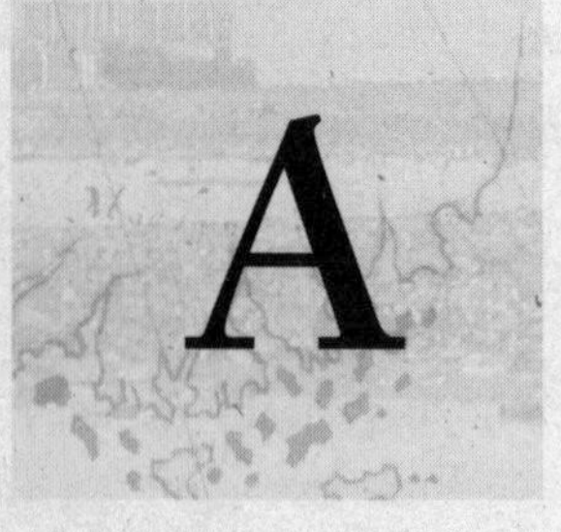

As always, we were glad to get back to Bjørneborg, pry off the boards covering the windows, start a fire in the stove, and dry out and get warm. Vaughn found that his clay vessel had hardened nicely on the stove top, without even being properly fired. Outside, the fog was slowly lifting, though the wind continued to blow hard.

Despite the gloomy weather, despite the desolation of our Arctic shore, I slept on Halfmoon Island as soundly as I ever have anywhere—that night, nine and a half hours without waking, untroubled by the snorers' wheezes and snorts. August 27, however, dawned on the foulest conditions we had yet seen in our six days on land: a bitter wind out of the northeast driving a spray of fine rain, the temperature about a degree above freezing, with fog once more tight to the ground. Edgeøya was invisible, and on the water offshore for the first time we saw genuine whitecaps. Even Mats, the veteran mariner, said, "This is definitely not a day to be out at sea in a little rubber boat."

It was not a day, we decided, to go anywhere. We loitered inside our hut, reading, playing chess, and counting the minutes until the next meal. Mats was in one of his surly, aggressive moods. When I read out loud Charitonow's remark (in Conway) that "bears were afraid to cross the track of snow-shoes," he muttered, "That is a very stupid idea.

Whoever wrote that didn't know what he was talking about." Our discussion drifted to the *Jeannette,* a disaster that had unfolded in 1881 when an American ship was frozen into the pack ice north of Siberia. Mats categorically declared, "That was a stupid expedition." Though he had lost more of our chess games than either Michel or I, Mats drove me crazy by kibitzing loudly when Michel and I squared off.

Brooding upon the twelve graves we had examined the day before, I came across an intriguing passage in Conway that I had not noticed on first reading. Summarizing the disastrous last Russian overwintering in 1851–52, when twelve of the eighteen hunters had died of scurvy at Biscayers Hook in Red Bay (near the northwest corner of Spitsbergen), Conway remarks that he himself had visited the ruins of the hunters' hut in 1896, then adds, "but the tragedy connected with it was already forgotten by the Norwegian sailors who accompanied me. They told a somewhat similar tale, but associated it not with Biscayers Hook but with Keilhau Bay in Edge Island." Keilhau Bay (no longer an official name) lies close to Hvalpynten on the southwest coast of Edgeøya, thus not very close to Halfmoon; but I could not help wondering if Conway's Norwegian shipmates, whom he thought merely confused, had not caught the distant echo of a Russian tragedy on Halfmoon, the sole memorial of which was the cluster of a dozen graves we had discovered the day before.

Vaughn had been rereading Le Roy. Now he produced some penetrating queries. Out of the blue, as was his wont, he said, "How do you store two thousand pounds of reindeer fat?" That amount, says Le Roy, the sailors had with them when rescued by Kornilov in 1749. "What do you keep it in? It's not like they had fifty-gallon oil drums. How do you keep it away from the bears? Do you keep everything—fat and furs—inside the hut?" I could only nod in puzzled agreement.

A few minutes later, Vaughn said, "Why would Kornilov change all his plans and go back to Arkhangel'sk, for only 80 rubles? Why wouldn't he go ahead and winter over, like he planned?" This too was hard to answer.

Later we were discussing driftwood. Mats insisted that timbers would float only two and a half weeks before becoming so waterlogged they would sink. Vaughn grasped the implications at once. "So all this driftwood on Edgeøya is carried here by the ice?" Mats nodded. "So when the sailors found the driftwood with the nails and bolt in it, only after the meat from their twelve reindeer was almost gone, it must have just melted out from the land-fast ice."

"How long could four men live on the meat from one reindeer?" I asked.

Vaughn did a calculation in his head. "This is a wild guess, but let's say you get a hundred pounds of meat from a reindeer. That's ten days per reindeer, if they eat two and a half pounds per man per day. Twelve reindeer, a hundred and twenty days, four months."

"So if they were shipwrecked," I ventured, "in May 1743—that's six years and three months before the day they were rescued—they found the crucial driftwood around September."

"Makes sense, in terms of when the ice would melt."

We had not seen the sun in five days, but despite the nearly constant rain and fog, in less than a week we had become vividly aware that each night was slightly longer and darker than the previous. We were near that time of year, climaxing at the autumnal equinox, when the hours of daylight most rapidly decrease. With this perception came an instinctive dread, an anticipation of the coming winter that we could feel in our very bones.

It was in that sense a perfect time to visit Edgeøya, for it must have been about now—at the end of August and the beginning of September—that for six years in a row the Pomori had seen their hopes of salvation, which they had patiently nourished through the endless previous winter, begin to turn to ashes. With each September would come the sea ice, ending another year's chance of rescue. The growing darkness was the harbinger of another terrible winter to be endured.

Indulging in a sort of wistful empathy, Michel composed a ballad about his quasi-namesake, Fedor Verigin:

Le pauvre vrai Guérin:
Qui ne voit plus rien,
Qui ne pourra pas lire,
Et qui voudra mourir.

("The poor *vrai Guérin:*/Who can no longer see anything,/Who won't be able to read,/And who wanted only to die.")

Mats, whose personal grooming bordered on the slovenly, had lavished some nice domestic touches on our hut. He had brought along a pair of paper tablecloths for our dining table. When we changed one, I discovered, carved into the tabletop, the name "Odd"—surely the "Kilroy was here" of the master hunter turned naturalist, Odd Lønø. Beneath the two windows, Mats placed rows of votive candles, which kept the panes defrosted while they lent a certain holiday cheer to the room. For chairs, he had turned spring-gun bear traps we found in the yard on end: they worked perfectly.

Partly to kill time, I made a detailed floor plan of Bjørneborg. Besides the two main rooms, there was a pair of small annexes attached on the west and south: the larder-cum-toilet, and a kind of work room that had a loophole in the wall, out of which hunters might have shot bears that took bait hanging from the pole that stood off the back corner of the hut. I calculated the total floor area at about six hundred square feet, of which the living room occupied a mere two hundred. The hut had evidently been much remodeled over the years.

According to Gustav Rossnes, Bjørneborg had been built in 1935 by two hunters named Henry Rudi and Gunnar Knoph, who had taken apart a hut on distant Nordaustlandet (the northernmost main island of the archipelago, almost completely glacier-covered), transported it by boat to Halfmoon Island, then rebuilt it and spent the winter inside it. When I later talked to Per Johnson, however, he told me that Rossnes's account was completely wrong. To straighten me out, he sent me a photocopy of a chapter from a memoir by one of the pioneer Norwegian hunters, Arthur Oxaas, called *Svalbard Var Min Verden* (*Svalbard Was My World*).

I had the chapter translated into English, then read it through in one enthralled sitting. It is worth quoting Oxaas at some length, for his text not only gives a detailed description of Bjørneborg—it also remains the most vivid account of a Svalbard overwintering that I came across anywhere.

In August 1906, Oxaas sailed from Tromsø as part of a crew of eight, under Captain Petter Trondsen. Trondsen seems to have been of a mercurial, indecisive disposition, for he had his team unload vats of salt

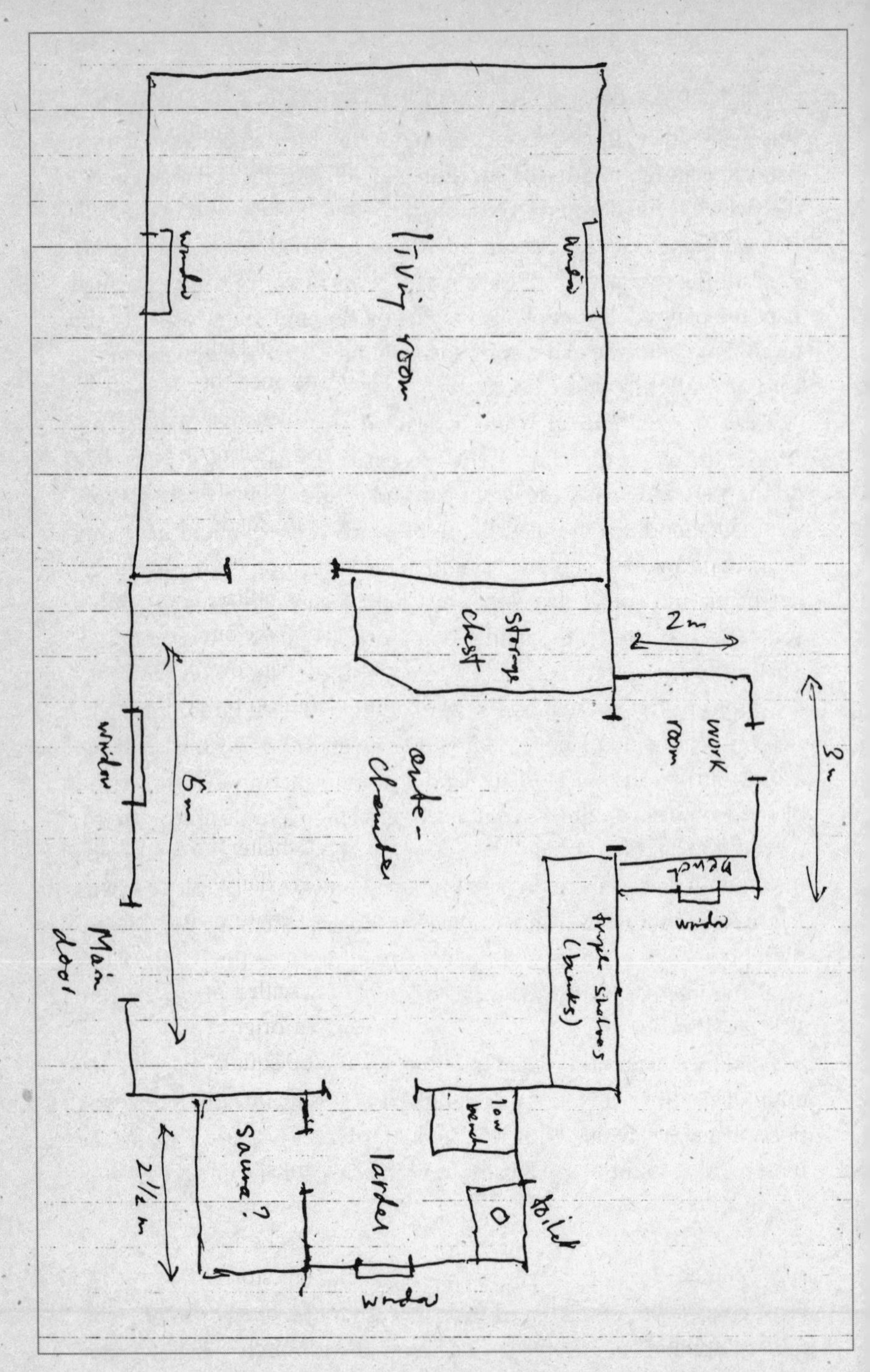

Floor plan of Bjørneborg today, originally built in 1906. (Courtesy of the author)

and coal at Negerdalen on Edgeøya (about three miles due west of the southwest corner of Halfmoon) before he changed his mind. The ship pushed on east toward Dianabukta, where the four of us had searched in vain for any signs of old buildings. They unloaded all their gear at Dianabukta, before Trondsen once more changed his mind and decided to investigate Halfmoon Island. The weary crew reloaded the ship and headed south.

Anchoring in the curving harbor near the center of Halfmoon's crescent, the Norwegians came on shore to scout. At once they found the "moss-covered remnants" of the small hut in which Karl Møller and Ibenhart Jensen Fladseth had died only seven years before. Oxaas must have had their grim story from the teammates who discovered the corpses, for he furnishes details not elsewhere published:

> Because of lack of space in that small room, and to utilize the heat to the utmost, they had shared the bed. It looked as if the one lying farthest out had died first, since the other one had bent over his chest and was lying headlong with his fingers in a butter tub placed on a shelf beside the bed. They were buried in a large cairn a little ways from the hut.

Trondsen chose a site not far from the fatal shelter, partly for its proximity to the same pond from which we now daily gathered our pails of drinking water. Like the Mezen men two centuries before, the Norwegian crew had brought their own lumber to build their hut. They got a framework up quickly, then covered it with boards about an inch and a half thick. According to Oxaas, this original Bjørneborg measured twenty-four square meters, or about 260 square feet—a little larger than our present living room. Affixed to one outside wall was a storage shed measuring another 170 square feet.

Inside the hut the men built four sleeping bunks, a table, a pair of benches, and a kitchen cabinet, and installed a stove in one corner. To insulate the hut for the winter, the men stacked rocks around the outside walls, inserting a layer of moss between stone and wood. (Bjørneborg today is surrounded by such a girdle of stones, reaching halfway up its walls.) They covered the roof with birch bark (brought, along with the boards themselves, from Norway). Oxaas says that as the men dug up the moss, they uncovered a multitude of old fish and walrus bones—unmistakable evidence of an earlier Russian occupation.

It was now well into September, and the ship that had brought the men to Svalbard had headed home. Now Trondsen revised his plans once more. Perhaps it had become obvious that the hut was too small for eight men. Back to Dianabukta, six miles away, the men hurried in their rowboat, to build a second hut on the mainland of Edgeøya. (So Rossnes had been right after all about the hut built there in 1906, of which we had found no trace.) Oxaas and two others were appointed to winter over in this second structure, while they hunted fox and bear. None of the three had overwintered before, so Trondsen gave the men some quick lessons.

If Oxaas was irked by his captain's haphazard planning, he kept his feelings to himself. One vexsome chore, entirely the consequence of Trondsen's vacillations, was the hike the three men had to make all the way southwest along the coast to Negerdalen—eighteen miles round-trip—to pick up salt and coal that still sat there in the vats the men had deposited on shore in August. The prospect of spending the coming winter in the hastily erected shelter must have been a daunting one. Writes Oxaas, in his even-tempered way,

> First we had to collect all the driftwood we could find, but not much was to be found. Consequently our wood supply was less than we had hoped for. We did not have a boat, so everything had to be either carried on our backs or pulled by sled.

The men made fox traps out of driftwood, and erected the old-fashioned (pre-Lundquist) kind of spring-gun bear traps. Instead of army surplus Remington rifles, they installed "bottle-nosed cannons" behind stone walls. These firearms shot about fifteen small round balls per charge, like some kind of overgrown shotgun. The men had had no time to hunt seal, so for bait they used less effective "boiled pieces of fatty pork," which for good measure they soaked with strychnine. They also rigged a baited pole attached to a rope that ran inside the hut, which, if jiggled, released a tin can that would alert the men.

For a whole month, the hunting was fruitless. "The days passed without any sign of bears," writes Oxaas. "We had set the fox traps and inspected them daily, often walking as far as Negerpynten, but so far there was no sign of foxes either."

It was not until October 17 that the trio got their first bears. Oxaas's account of that coup is a marvelous rendering of the hunter's eternal ambivalence:

> At 9:00 A.M. on 17 October the tin can hit the floor with a thump. . . . We tiptoed out to the hallway and opened the shooting hatch. What we saw was a she-bear tearing meat off the bait and giving the pieces to the cub next to her. We did not have the heart to shoot right away, but were left standing there admiring this touching display of motherly love. We finally pulled ourselves together and fired. Three shots rang out and two lives were ended. Such are we human beings, it seems, that we are able to do anything for money. But we did get the fresh meat we had dreamt about for so long. And it was both tender and pleasant-tasting, since the she-bear was relatively young.

By November the ice was fast in the sea. The trio at Dianabukta, however, had shot only one more bear. On their jaunts to Negerpynten, they found abundant bear tracks near that southernmost cape, as well as "a well-trod path across [the ice] to the outer side of Halfmoon Island. Once more a reminder of how wrong the placement of our hut was."

In the penumbral gloom of late November, the men had another poignant triumph. A bear cub had nibbled on the poisoned bait, then wandered three hundred yards out onto the ice. The men tracked it, guns cocked.

> It started getting dark, and we could expect an angry polar bear confronting us any minute. We heard a bear snarl and grumble, not too close by, and soon after we saw a dark, large shadow. . . . When we followed the tracks to where they ended, we found the cub dead on the ice. The mother kept close by and only moved away grudgingly. We followed her to get close enough to shoot, but she disappeared in a southerly direction.

In more than three months of hunting, the trio had bagged only nine bears and three foxes—"not exactly," commented Oxaas, "a result to be proud of."

As Christmas approached, the men baked cookies to cheer themselves up. "The cookies were rather simple," notes the memoirist, "but the important thing was that they tasted good." The men were hardly living high off the hog. A week's ration of margarine amounted to nine ounces per man, of sugar, six ounces. The staple foods were canned milk, cocoa, dried apricots, prunes, raisins, and home-baked bread—"not much to brighten the day throughout the year," observes Oxaas. "We . . . could only afford to spread an extremely thin layer of margarine on the bread, barely enough to see." The men drank their coffee black. Dinner was a barley porridge, polar bear meat, and salted fish. Yet, says Oxaas, "We got so used to this simple and dull menu that we did not miss other food."

With the ice thick against the shore at Dianabukta, the men listened for hours as it "cracked and banged" under tidal pressure. Three days after Christmas, Petter Trondsen made a surprise visit, having walked six miles across the ice from Halfmoon Island. It was the first time the two parties had been in touch in more than three months. Trondsen revealed that his own party of five had managed to kill only fifteen bears, allowing Oxaas the meager gratification of realizing that their own catch (three bears per man) was identical to the Halfmoon party's.

Trondsen invited the trio back to Bjørneborg for a belated Christmas feast. It took three hours to traverse the ice pack and enact "a joyous reunion." Trondsen broke out "a case of Christmas goodies." After a lavish meal, the men drank toddies and chatted late into the night.

> Being the guests, we had to spend the night on the floor, of course. The days passed too quickly. This was the kind of re-energizing relaxation we really knew how to appreciate. . . . We played cards, dominoes, and checkers and really enjoyed ourselves. A couple of the guys were handy with the accordion and the guitar, so we did not lack for entertainment.

The upshot of the visit was that Oxaas and one of the Bjørneborg men agreed to change places. On January 3, Oxaas hiked back to

Dianabukta, gathered up his personal gear, and returned to Halfmoon, arriving alone "well into the night."

One of Oxaas's new companions, Hilbert Henriksen, an "old, seasoned polar sailor" who had previously overwintered in Bellsund on Spitsbergen, struck the others as distinctly weird in character.

> Strangely enough, he never liked going out alone, and was actually afraid to do so. . . . Even before leaving Tromsø, he had picked out a pair of unique skis. . . . As a rule, Hilbert had his skis on when he went out hunting, but going home, he took them off and pulled them by a rope attached to the tips. . . .
>
> He also had brought with him a large red-painted box which he used as a clothes chest. It was placed outside, along one wall, and he had sprinkled snow between each piece of clothing.
>
> "Why do you preserve them with snow?" we asked.
>
> "Well," said Hilbert, "experience has taught me that this is the best way to preserve clothes."

Henriksen was, Oxaas concluded, "a very careful guy." Approaching an obviously dead bear in a spring-gun trap, "he always fired off 3-4 shots, 'just to be sure,' he said." Henriksen also had a penchant for firing at a whale jawbone that protruded from the snow, which had become a landmark for the overwinterers, because "always, when nearing the jawbone, he thought he saw a polar bear there."

The January cold was particularly intense. As Oxaas, writing in 1955, modestly explains, "We did not know about windproof clothing then and we had never heard of an 'anorak.' In order to keep the cold out we had to double the layers on windy days." Bitter wind and snow blowing into the men's faces posed their most difficult challenge.

Trondsen put Oxaas in charge of the bear hunt on the southwestern end of Halfmoon Island. One day in March, out by himself, Oxaas discovered two cubs playing near a spring-gun trap. The inevitable mother soon approached. Oxaas threw himself to the ground, fired from sixty yards, and missed. A second shot hit home. Hoping to capture the cubs alive, Oxaas panicked them into flight.

A few hours later, Oxaas returned with several companions, including Trondsen. The cubs were still in the vicinity, but once again "they disappeared like feather fluffs." In anger, Trondsen fired a shot, striking one of the cubs in the foot, but allowing the men to capture the pair. Back inside the hut, the hunters tried to nurse the wounded cub back to health, but ended up having to put it out of its misery. "The other cub," writes Oxaas, "was allowed to roam around inside the cabin and settled in well. We named it 'Prikken.'"

In April, Oxaas and another man discovered a poisoned she-bear near death toward the eastern end of the island. They shot it, then discovered two baby cubs beneath her body, still trying to nurse. Now the men had three pets. They tied Prikken to a chain outside the cabin "where he had lots of play space," then kept the two infants inside a box within the hut. "We had to teach them to drink water from a bottle," writes Oxaas. "It was a welcome change in our routine to care for these cuddly, cozy bearcubs."

During this month, the three men in the hut at Dianabukta ran out of driftwood for their stove. They were forced to abandon their shelter and walk across the sea ice to join their companions on Halfmoon. Eight men now had to sleep, eat, and work inside a hut that had seemed cramped for five. (Our own living room, only sixty square feet smaller than the whole original hut, felt crowded enough with but four men in it. Cooking or feeding the stove, we were constantly bumping into each other, or excusing ourselves as we sidled from table to kitchen counter.)

One of the men from Dianabukta, Imbert Olsen, had contracted scurvy and was now confined to his bed. "How he became ill is a mystery," noted Oxaas, "since we all ate the same kind of food. And besides, Imbert was a lively and enthusiastic fellow."

Cabin fever now descended upon Bjørneborg, exacerbated (as it was among our own quartet, despite the brevity of our stay) by nicotine cravings. Oxaas vividly evokes the mood:

> We were now out of tobacco, a real tragedy. We searched all our pockets and collected any specks we could find, but they didn't amount to much. We tested anything that might be "smokable"; tea, coffee, and moss, but it did not satisfy us, and with the lack of tobacco came irritability. Our spirits were not so high any longer, and to avoid confrontations we started to go out on short solitary walks on the ice.

Imbert Olsen's scurvy alarmed his companions.

> I did his laundry and made his bed every day, and tried to cheer him up. But he was feeling low and looked only at the dark side. We poured orange drink into him, and whatever else we had saved "for a rainy day," but unfortunately we had no vegetables.

The orange drink was probably a powdered beverage, like today's Tang, and thus at best only a meager source of vitamin C; yet the continued health of the seven other men argues that they were ingesting the crucial vitamin—perhaps in the bear meat and fat that were part of their nightly dinner.

By the end of May, no more polar bears were to be seen. The men grew preoccupied (as the Pomori must have been late each spring in the 1740s) with the imminent breakup of the ice pack.

> Idleness dampened our mood. We took daily trips to the highest point on the island and looked through binoculars at the ice. After a while, these trips became our only occupation, and sometimes we would make several trips a day. We always walked there with a sense of anticipation, but always returned without having discovered anything new of interest.

Trondsen had arranged for the ship that had deposited the men on Halfmoon Island the previous August to return as soon as the ice broke up around Edgeøya. The men kept their vigil through all of June and July. "It was really no fun waiting like this," remembered Oxaas, "especially now, when both flour and margarine were in short supply."

August arrived with no sign of the ship. "By then we were out of flour and had only meat for food," writes Oxaas. "I don't know if any of you have tried a diet without bread. It was one of my worst experiences, and I can truthfully say that I would not want to relive this period." (*Tell that to the Pomori!* I wanted to say to Oxaas as I read this passage.)

The men began to prepare for the dire possibility of a second winter in the Arctic, gathering driftwood, shooting newly arrived eider ducks for food. By now the ice had broken up sufficiently that the men could maneuver their rowboat along channels of open water among the floes. The men went out in the boat in threes and fours to hunt reindeer. Oxaas describes one desperate mission, during which he and three comrades, rowing against the wind, managed to round Negerpynten and reach what he calls "the innermost part of the fjord" (perhaps the ample bay where a huge river, the Dyrdalselva, empties into Tjuvfjorden).

Almost immediately after going on shore, one of the men wrenched his back so badly that he was incapacitated. The four hunters bivouacked under their overturned rowboat. Out scouting, one of the men, Kalle Finspong, had shot a reindeer and carried half the carcass back to the shore. "We cooked a large pot of reindeer meat," writes Oxaas, "which gave renewed life to cold, tired bodies. Kalle had shot a nice fat buck and several inches of fat floated on top of the soup. We poured it into our cups and drank fat and ate meat enough to make it hard for us to move."

This touch-and-go foray proved vital to the men's survival, for in three subsequent days, the three able-bodied hunters succeeded in shooting nine more reindeer. A measure of the Norwegians' hardiness, despite their undernourished state, can be gleaned from Oxaas's dead-pan remark, "We each put a reindeer carcass on our back and started on our return trip [to the shore], which proved long and tough." In summer, a Svalbard reindeer weighs between 130 and 200 pounds. No doubt the men cut off hooves and heads, but the feat of carrying the rest of the carcass without a backpack, across muddy and marshy terrain, wading small rivers, should not be underestimated.

In another herculean bout of rowing, the men carried their spoils back to Halfmoon Island. "We had a big feast in the cabin that aftenoon," Oxaas dryly notes.

The water all around Halfmoon and the south coast of Edgeøya was now mostly clear, but from their lookout point, the men could see solid ice pack to the south. Later they would learn that the summer of 1907 had proved an anomalous one, as the pack in Storfjorden never fully broke up, isolating Edgeøya from the rest of the world. A number of ships, including Trondsen's relief vessel, had tried to zigzag their way along the open leads, only to be blocked by impenetrable pack.

During these anxious days, Oxaas had one last, memorable

encounter with a polar bear. Out on a lookout walk to the west without his gun, he had been surprised to see the bear standing on an ice floe not far off shore, eating a seal. Oxaas ran back to Bjørneborg to fetch his rifle and an ally. When the two hunters returned, the bear was still eating its catch. They hid behind a driftwood tree stump and waited for the bear to come onto land.

> When it finally had enough, it threw the rest of the seal into the water. It did not seem to want others to enjoy what it left. Between the large ice floe it was standing on and the shore was newly formed ice, too thin to carry the weight of a bear but too thick for even a polar bear to swim through. It dived in and started swimming underneath the ice. Each time it needed to breathe, it popped up and made a hole in the ice with its head. It finally reached shore only 100 meters from our hiding place.
>
> We were quite frozen by now, but it took its time and walked around sniffing every small thing. . . . We both fired at the same time, but the bullets whizzed past the bear and hit the ground, spraying sand. It turned around and headed straight for us. Our fingers were so cold, it took extra time to change the cartridge in the chamber, so the bear came quite close to us, really only a couple of meters away.
>
> Then I stood up abruptly and screamed "Stop!" at the top of my lungs. And the bear actually stopped! It stood there looking at the strange creature who was standing up in front of it. But by now the cartridge was in place and I took aim. "Bang!"—and it fell down. We spent the rest of the day carrying the meat and pelt up to the cabin.

In late August, out in the rowboat with two companions on a reindeer-hunting sojourn, Trondsen quite by accident met up with the *Elida*, the only ship that (thanks to its small size) had been able to break through the Storfjorden ice pack. The captain was leery of trying to navigate to Halfmoon Island, for the time of year was approaching when new ice was about to form; but he agreed to take the eight Norwegians and their booty back to Tromsø for the sum of 300 kroner, if they could quickly make their way to the ship in a pair of rowboats.

In a frenzy of activity, the men loaded eighty-two bear pelts into the two boats and closed up Bjørneborg. They carried the scurvy-ridden Olsen to one of the boats and made a bed for him of bear pelts. Each man took only a small bundle of clothes, leaving all his other possessions behind, but they brought their three pet bear cubs with them. "After a terribly strenuous trip," Oxaas wrote, the eight reached the prearranged rendezvous site, only to find no ship in view. "I have to admit our blood almost turned to ice," recalled the memoirist. The men waited for "two nerve-racking days" before the *Elida* appeared.

The men's relief at their deliverance is only hinted at in Oxaas's understated narrative. For crew, the ship had a mere five hands, so living quarters were nearly as cramped on the *Elida* as in Bjørneborg. "Imbert got his own bunk," wrote Oxaas, "the rest of us found space here and there. . . . [Captain] Lambert sold us margarine and hard scones and a little pipe tobacco."

The men reached Tromsø on September 10, 1907. Theirs had been a close escape. Olsen would surely not have survived another winter, and, given to what a low ebb the men's fortunes had been reduced, there is a considerable likelihood that all would have perished during the second winter. The Pomori from 1743 to 1749 notwithstanding, the number of hunters who ever survived a second, unplanned winter on Svalbard remains minuscule.

In fact, even a single unplanned overwintering produced a high likelihood of death. In a 1991 monograph, Odd Lønø surveyed the fate of Norwegian hunters trapped by ice and forced to stay for the winter. Before 1892, eight parties comprising fifty-six men suffered such a fate. Of those fifty-six, according to Lønø, twenty-one died of scurvy and fifteen of other causes.

Oxaas's last line sounds the rueful note so many of the overwinterers must have felt, from the seventeenth century on, after returning to Hull or Amsterdam or Tromsø or Arkhangel'sk. Had it all really been worth it? The eight men in Trondsen's crew gained a profit from their eighty-two bear pelts of only 300 kroner apiece. "Not much," reflects the memoirist forty-eight years later, "considering all the toil and effort up there in the ice."

• • •

To relieve my own cabin fever during the days of foul weather, I went out on a series of short solo walks, flare gun in my pocket, Mauser hoisted over my shoulder. It was striking how much more desolate and threatening the landscape seemed when I was alone, even in sight of Bjørneborg. It was easy to empathize with the Pomori's rule of never venturing solo out of their own hut.

As I stood on some basalt promontory and scanned the horizon, hyper-vigilant to detect some distant speck of white, I heard only three sounds: the shrilling of the wind, the crash of waves on the outer shore of Halfmoon (where the surf was always much more violent than on the protected shore facing Edgeøya), and the ceaseless cacophony of birds. The shore cliff nearest our hut, just beyond the ruins of Møller and Fladseth's fatal shelter, often teemed with kittiwakes, and the rocks were coated white with their guano. These birds emitted a screeching, scolding caw. Overhead streamed gaggles of barnacle geese, brent geese, and pink-footed geese. Eider ducks bobbed in the water like decoys, and on the beaches, purple sandpipers scuttled along with their Chaplinesque gaits. Mats, who knew his birds, also pointed out to us Arctic skuas, pomarine skuas, Arctic terns, and glaucous gulls. (Why had the Pomori never been able to feast on birds or birds' eggs, which in summer, at least, must have been as abundant around their hut as they were on Halfmoon? Or was this another of Le Roy's oversights?) The eeriest call I heard was that of the red-throated loon, always at a distance: it sounded like the cry of a woman wailing in grief or pleading for help.

On our first Halfmoon hike, toward the southwest point of the island on August 23, we had paused to ponder an intriguing assemblage of man-made debris. On a high point of land stood a rectangular log structure, its roof caved in, a rusty stove with the Norwegian brand name Olefos still standing in a corner, an axe rusted almost to pieces lying on the floor. The remains of a sledge lay scattered outside. The building, only nine feet wide by twelve feet long and barely six feet tall, was too small to be a proper hut. Mats remembered Per Johnson telling him that such cabins served as bear-watching stations, in which hunters would hole up for most of the day before returning to sleep in the hut they lived in. This station was ideally located, for the chief bear migration route (the trodden track Oxaas had seen leading across the pack ice from Negerpynten to this corner of Halfmoon) ran right through this headland. We guessed that the station dated from the 1930s or 1940s. (Rossnes documented Halfmoon overwinterings in both 1946–47 and 1947–48, the former by a party including Odd Lønø.)

Sure enough, not far from the cabin, a spring-gun trap still stood, before which was strewn the richest scattering of bear bones we would see anywhere on Halfmoon or Edgeøya. Among the boulders nearby, I came upon an intact polar bear skull, both upper and lower jaws still sporting rows of powerful teeth.

This point of Halfmoon was also strewn with the bleaching ribs of beached whales. On a previous visit, Mats had discovered carved inscriptions on two of these massive, curving bones lying in the moss, which he now showed us. One could be partially read as

H CRISSS 1880
AM I E.

The other sported the initials "EMN" and the date "1897."

Clearly these were the graffiti of Norwegian hunters. What was intriguing was that the inscriptions predated by as many as eighteen years the first Norwegian attempt to overwinter on Halfmoon. Like "GTS," whose solitary grave we had found on the other end of the island, we were never able to identity these fugitive visitors.

From our point of view, however, the pièce de résistance of this corner of Halfmoon was the ruins of a much older hut we found near the shore, below both the bear-watching station and the spring-gun trap. Half-collapsed walls of sea cobbles nearly hid the remnants of birch-bark-lined walls made of upright planks, which appeared to have been burned. The notes from the previous summer's cursory archaeological survey, as I had transcribed them off Kolbein Dahle's computer in the Sysselmannen office, read (in translation): "FOUNDATION SITE—Russian. Thick stone walls with a little turf on top. Inside are the lower remnants of upright boards. Seems to have been burnt." Careful measurements of the hut's dimensions followed, but nothing to explain the labeling of the ruins as Russian. In fact, contradicting that claim, the last line of the survey notes read, "Could be Karl Møller's cabin from 1898." This we knew to be fallacious, for we had found Møller and Fladseth's hut, along with their common grave, right beside Bjørneborg.

During that first visit on August 23, I had paced off the outer dimensions of this apparently very old "Russian" hut. I came up with a rough nine by five yards, or about twenty-seven by fifteen feet. This was less than two-thirds the size given by Le Roy, which was thirty-six by eighteen feet. In front of the rectangle of collapsed stone walls, we saw a squarish depression in the tundra that did not look like a natural feature. Could it have marked the outlines of a vestibule such as the one described by Le Roy? Still, the apparent size of this "Russian" hut failed to jibe with the academician's account. The clincher was the simple fact that this hut lay only a stone's throw from the sea—not two thirds of a mile to a mile inland. In fact, it was obvious that the small, shallow cove before the hut, formed by a semicircular indentation of coast facing northwest toward Edgeøya, made as perfect and protected a harbor as could be found on Halfmoon.

During the subsequent days, however, we had brooded on this hut, about which Rossnes's admittedly unreliable guide to Norwegian overwinterings made no reference. From the rudder of the *lodja* or *kotch* I had found, to the walrus-killing ground Mats had pointed out, to any number of very old pieces of wood (shipwreck debris?) joined by wooden pegs rather than nails and apparently shaped by axe, to the twelve graves at Dianahamna, we had discovered abundant evidence of Russian hunters on Halfmoon. (On Edgeøya itself, we would find not a single verifiably Russian artifact.)

The breakthrough in our thinking came thanks to a brilliant hunch of Mats's. One day in Bjørneborg, as we discussed the puzzle of Le Roy's insistence that the Mezeners' hut lay a mile inland (or "*un quart de lieue*" in the French edition—between seven tenths and nine tenths of a mile), he made a suggestion. "What if the ship was stuck in ice on the outside of Halfmoon Island?" Mats asked. "Then the sailors, they go on land, and they walk *across* the island to find the hut they know about."

"My God," I muttered. "It's perfect. Depending on where they hit the outer coast, it could have been between seven tenths of a mile and a mile's walk to reach the hut."

Vaughn jumped on our deductive bandwagon. "Yeah. Le Roy

doesn't quite get the picture. The Inkovs tell him they walked a mile inland, or whatever, but he doesn't realize they find the hut on the opposite shore."

"We have to go back and have another look at that hut," I vowed.

On August 28, then—our seventh day on Halfmoon—we set out once more toward the western end of the island. The wind was down and the rain had settled into a fine (though annoying) spray, but we were still enshrouded in thick fog. As the day progressed, the fog thinned, and we sensed that the sun, which we had not seen in six days, was about to break through, but in the end it only tantalized us, failing to burn off the vapors.

Mats loaded the Zodiac with camera gear, tools, a stove, and food for a hot lunch and motored solo down to the end of the island. It was his intention to build a makeshift scaffold to take the best possible picture of the ruins of the hut from above. The other three of us chose to walk to the cape along the beach on the northwest shore, which we had not combed on our first outing.

We took our time, looping often from the water's edge up to the top of the small cliff that fronted the sea to make sure we missed nothing. Vaughn had resigned himself to the painful grind of a daily hike, whose toll betrayed itself, despite his stoic silence, in a slight limp. Binoculars dangling from his neck, he paused every thirty or forty yards to search for bears.

About a mile down the beach, we came to a solitary grave. Laid across the mound of stones was a weathered board, with a faint inscription in black paint that I finally deciphered as "N R 1L S B." (Later we found two or three other boards with similar inscriptions, scattered across the island, none of the others associated with a grave.) Unlike the "GTS" carved in the board on the other lone grave, these characters did not seem to commemorate a dead hunter. Perhaps these boards were early Norwegian survey markers of some kind. We never learned anything more about them.

Another few hundred yards to the southwest, we came across a low structure built out of stones, enclosing two corridors that formed the shape of a capital L. "It looks sort of like a duck blind," ventured Vaughn. Mats would insist, however, that Svalbard hunters never used duck blinds. Two days later, on Edgeøya, Mats would discover an identical L-shaped structure on a cliff overlooking the sea. One more artifactual puzzle to add to our collection of ambiguities.

After a two-hour stroll, we reached the Russian hut. Mats was busy nailing driftwood logs together to make a shaky platform from which to photograph the site. Vaughn had brought along a tape measure that he used on his occasional work on archaeological digs in Utah. He and I now made a precise survey of the ruins (see diagram on page 256).

The interior measurements of the hut were 243 centimeters by 280—in feet, only about eight by nine. A very cramped living space, indeed—a mere seventy-two square feet, about a fourth the size of the interior of Bjørneborg as built in 1906. If eight people had managed to winter over in that latter hut, it seemed unlikely that the one we were now measuring could have accommodated more than two.

Remodeling huts over the years, however, seemed a common practice on Svalbard. Scattered across the tundra around the hut was a variety of objects. Mats identified several old nails, the handle of a coffee grinder, pieces of a sizable iron vessel with feet. He guessed that this stuff was Norwegian, dating from before the Second World War.

Other debris, however, looked older—particularly a squarish chunk of wood, coated with green lichens, with a wooden peg embedded in a round hole, as well as an eleven-foot-long timber lying atop the ruin, with very old axe marks conspicuous along its trunk.

Mats snapped away from his platform while Vaughn and I continued to measure the ruin. Now we noticed something we had failed to discern on our first visit. Just outside the girdle of piled stones, faint trenches hinted at what archaeologists call the "shadow walls" of an otherwise vanished structure. We measured these at 400 by 490 centimeters, or about thirteen by sixteen feet. This still got us nowhere near Le Roy's dimensions, but if we assumed the depression in front of the ruin adumbrated a vestibule, that added almost seventeen feet to the building's length. If all these speculations were valid, an original hut in place here (from which had been remodeled a much smaller shelter) would have stood about sixteen by thirty feet. We were now in Le Roy's ballpark.

I was keenly aware of just how procrustean such thinking might be. I was in danger of cutting off our sailors' feet to make this hut fit Le Roy's bed—or, more aptly, of cutting off the academician's appendages

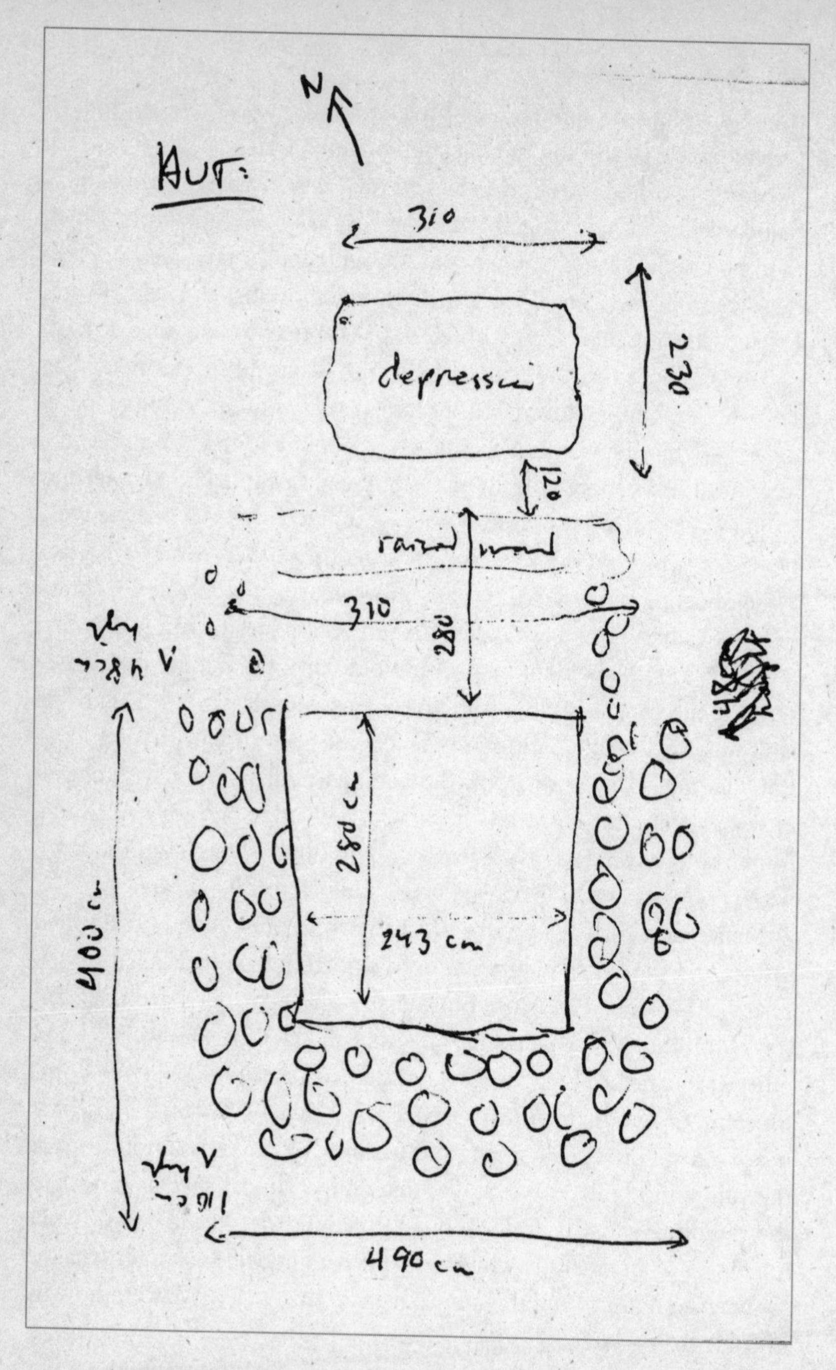

Floor plan of the ruins of the eighteenth-century Russian hut on Halfmoon Island that might have been the one in which the sailors lived from 1743 to 1749. (Courtesy of the author)

to fit the shadow walls along which we laid our tape measure. From my very first reading, I had been troubled by the dimensions Le Roy had given for the hut. So focused had I been on the outlandish height of eighteen feet, that it had taken me a while to be bothered by its eighteen-by-thirty-six-foot width and length. Those measurements gave a hut of nearly 650 square feet—almost three times as large as the original Bjørneborg. On the other hand, we had no idea how many Mezeners had wintered over in the hut that Aleksei Inkov had known about by hearsay. Had they comprised a sizable party, those Mezeners might well have built a spacious shelter. A century before, the Dutch at Smeerenburg had carried timbers to construct veritable factories and warehouses on Svalbard shores.

The timber lying across the ruin was the most provocative piece of debris. Could this, by some wild stretch of the imagination, be the remains of the promise cross Aleksei Inkov had erected before his hut?

Twenty yards in front of the ruin, a little above the high-tide line, we found an unmistakably man-made mound of stones. It looked like another grave. Could this, by an equally wild stretch of the imagination, be the resting place of Fedor Verigin?

The fog would not clear off, and now a nasty east wind had sprung up, blearing our faces with rain. We huddled in the lee of the hut while Mats cooked up another hypothermic lunch. The possibility that this structure was the very place where our half-mythic saga had taken place two and a half centuries before hung over our spirits, haunting the forlorn landscape. But our wishes were not horses: the hypothesis was unprovable.

Later, back in the U.S., two archaeologist friends asked me why I hadn't pried loose a few splinters of wood to take with me, for radiocarbon dating in an American lab. But on Halfmoon Island, I was heedful of the strictures imposed by the Sysselmannen. My permit defined as protected any historical sites dating from before 1945. "Protected historical artefacts," read the contract, "must not be removed from the place they were found." These included even the debris around the spring-gun traps. It was against the law to take home the tiniest bone of a bear slaughtered before 1945 as a souvenir.

Quite aside from the letter of the law, Vaughn and I felt that we had no business collecting anything from the ruin. The same self-taught ethic that allowed us to pick up and examine the drabbest gray Anasazi potsherd in a Utah ruin, but dictated putting it back in the dirt where we found it, now precluded our prying loose the smallest splinter from what might have been Aleksei's promise cross. We were not archaeologists. We were fortunate just to be able to roam Halfmoon and marvel at the desolate detritus of human hopes and fears we found scattered everywhere.

That night, back in Bjørneborg, Mats wakened suddenly to an unfamiliar noise. Jumping out of his sleeping bag, he seized his revolver and flare gun and went out in the yard, in the dim light after midnight, to look for a bear. "Then I realized," he told us in the morning with a wan smile, "it was only snow sparrows on the roof."

August 29 dawned once more to thick fog. Again we could see nothing of Edgeøya. We had hoped to make our second boat journey over to the mainland, but now we postponed it in favor of another Halfmoon loop, this time to the northeast point of the island, which we had not reached on August 26. Once again, Mats took the boat directly to the point, while Vaughn, Michel, and I crossed the island to the outer coast, then meandered northeast toward the cape. We found a number of pieces of possible shipwreck debris, festooned with ancient-looking iron bolts and wooden pegs in lieu of nails. And we found more spring-gun traps, littered with the bones of their victims.

As Mats had pulled his boat onto land near the northeast point and hiked up a nearby ridge, he had spotted another bear, the sixth of our trip. He and the bear had stared at each other for several minutes, in a standoff, before the animal ambled off to the south. "A very dirty bear, not too big," he told us when we had joined him. "So I think not the same as the other two we saw here on Halfmoon." Before our reunion, he radioed us over the walkie-talkie to warn us about the bear, so that we didn't blunder upon it in the fog.

Even before that call, this day Vaughn had seemed to me more apprehensive than ever. The occasional involuntary wince as he put his weight on his left leg revealed that he was still in considerable pain. Now Vaughn raised his binoculars to scan our surroundings more frequently than he had on other walks, and kept looking behind him, like a man who thinks he is being followed. Guessing that he felt, in Mats's absence, a heightened responsibility as the only true marksman in the company of a pair of Zouaves, I reassured him, "I'm confident you could stop a bear if he charged."

"I'm not," he said.

That evening in the hut, Vaughn fondled the cup-shaped lamp he had fashioned out of the clay I had scooped up near Dianabukta. In four days of sitting on the stove top, it had hardened nicely. Now he poured an ounce of olive oil into the vessel, laid a twisted piece of string in the oil as a wick, and lighted the lamp. Soon a clear yellow flame licked upward from the cup. We stared at Vaughn's experiment, half expecting the clay to crack or dissolve. Ten minutes later, the light was going strong. In fact, the lamp burned steadily for two hours before it flickered out, having burned the last of the oil.

Vaughn's lamp worked so well, in fact, that it raised yet another perplexing question about the Pomori's experience. If clay of this quality was readily available on the coast of Edgeøya—clay that didn't even need to be properly fired to serve in an efficient lamp—why had the Russian sailors had so much trouble getting their own clay, found "nearly in the middle" of their island, to work, succeeding only after boiling a flour paste inside the vessel? Was this a further argument for Halfmoon as the sailors' home, since the clay Vaughn had first worked with, gathered on our island, had produced only a crumbly patty?

I made a crude calculation. If the Pomori had kept their lamp going for six years and three months continuously (as Le Roy insists they did), how much reindeer fat would that have required? Supposing that reindeer fat burned only half as efficiently as olive oil, they would have needed an ounce for every hour, or a quart and a half per day. Over 2,280 days, that calculated as 3,420 quarts of fat. A quart of water weighs two pounds; for the sake of argument, I assumed a quart of reindeer fat weighed about the same (fat tends to float in soup, as Arthur Oxaas had noted). So the Pomori would have needed almost 7,000 pounds of fat to burn in their lamp during their long exile.

The sailors, Le Roy tells us, killed a total of 250 reindeer. Thus they needed to get 28 pounds of fat from each kill. If the average reindeer weighed 160 pounds, including antlers, hoofs, and bones, that meant that nearly 20 percent of each animal had to be rendered into lamp fuel. I had no idea what percentage of a reindeer was fat; but here again, the feat required of the hunters seemed barely doable. If they had turned 28 pounds of each reindeer into lamp-burning fat, how much fat was left to eat, with its antiscorbutic boon?

I put aside my calculations. Like our hunches about the hut on the southwest point of Halfmoon, they incorporated so many untestable assumptions that they were a priori suspect. But the fiddling with numbers had served another end: I felt all the more awe for the sailors' survival skills.

The lamp experiment brought home forcefully another facet of the Pomori's experience. During the two hours while our olive oil was burning, twice or three times, when someone opened the living room door, a gust of wind nearly blew the flame out. How the sailors must have disciplined themselves to prevent such a catastrophe!

It was hard to feel in your bones just how long a span six years really was. At one point, I asked each of my companions what they had been doing six years ago. As their memories sifted back to 1995, each of my friends burst into surprised laughter. So many things had happened to us in the last six years. . . . For the Pomori, only the same few things had happened, again and again in monotonous repetition, in the same monotonous place, every one of them a matter of life and death.

So our days on Halfmoon slowly passed. The absence of the sun, the eternal fog and rain, the misery of our luncheon bivouacs, the nagging worry about bears, began to approximate a minor ordeal. Yet always we had to remind ourselves that nothing we put up with could touch the extremes of the Pomori's exile.

So rich had been our finds on Halfmoon Island, so ubiquitous the fog and wind, that day after day we had put off further examination of the shores of Edgeøya. Now, however, we were running short on time. On August 30, despite the fact that the mainland was almost invisible—we caught only glimpses of gray ridges as the mist billowed open and shut—we prepared the Zodiac. During the previous days, we had admired Mats's competence with the boat, as he commuted to either end of the island. But now, in a sheepish confession, he completely undermined our faith in his nautical expertise.

Each time he took a ride in the Zodiac, Mats slipped our emergency locator beacon into a pocket of his jacket, then zipped the survival suit closed. Now, he acknowledged, it had suddenly occurred to him that if the boat flipped and we lay floating in the ocean, there would be no way to get his hands on the beacon to trigger its signal without unzipping the survival suit—which would mean certain death by drowning.

At this revelation, Vaughn and I stared at each other in something like horror, as we imagined the four of us floating in the icy sea, awaiting our hypothermic demise simply because of Mats's elementary mistake. How much experience could the man really have had with this sort of exploration by Zodiac, if so basic a precaution had escaped his grasp? It was one thing to taxi tourists to shore for brief promenades, under the watchful eye of the waiting cruise ship. It was quite another to be on our own, motoring across tricky seas with no backup.

Later I would wonder why Mats had confessed his oversight—would he not have saved face simply by starting to carry the beacon in an outside pocket of the survival suit, its cord clipped to a D-ring, as he henceforth did? In a private moment, reflecting on that worst-case scenario of the flipped Zodiac, Vaughn drawled, Swedish-rancher-style, "Guess we'd of just hadda rip open Mats's suit to get at that there beacon."

Now we decided to head straight across the two-mile channel to the nearest point of Edgeøya, a shallow cape called Lønøodden, after Odd Lønø. Mats laid out the map, got a latitude and longitude for the cape, and plugged the coordinates into his GPS. Distrustful as ever, I took a compass bearing on Lønøodden, then, as we rode northwest across the water, clutched the compass in my hand.

Sure enough, halfway across, the fog shut down tight and Edgeøya disappeared. I had navigated by compass through many a dense forest, across many a desert plateau, and now I disagreed with the bearing on which Mats was heading. "More to the right, Mats!" I shouted over the engine. He smiled condescendingly and held his course.

It turned out, when the gray cliffs once more coalesced out of the fog, that I was right. Without acknowledging his error, Mats corrected his course and skirted the coastline eastward toward Lønøodden. I resisted blurting out an I-told-you-so. It was not that the GPS had failed to work: more likely, Mats had slightly misread the map, plugging in coordinates that were off by a mile or two.

Vaughn's and my apprehensions during every boat ride were of course principally the product of our lifelong aquaphobia. At the same time, these waters were genuinely treacherous. Mats had told us that Gustav Rossnes, for all his experience boating around Svalbard, had flipped his Zodiac off Negerpynten sometime in the 1980s, and would have died but for his crash beacon launching a bold helicopter rescue. I recalled a pithy passage from *Yachting in the Arctic Seas,* the memoir of that blithe Victorian sailor James Lamont:

> The strength of the current here renders it by far the most dangerous part of Spitzbergen. At Halfmoon Island the flood tide runs north and the ebb south, at six or eight miles an hour. This tide, laden with icebergs from the great glacier before described [Edgeøyjøkulen], and with pack-ice which creeps round the south-east corner of Edge Island, oscillates backwards and forwards between the group of islands known as the Thousand Isles, and between them and the mainland. Where the channel is narrow the current is so swift that I have been sometimes unable, with a good crew, to row against it. I have seen the sea densely packed with ice in the morning, and by night a vessel could sail unhindered where a few hours ago a boat had been dragged over the ice for miles.

(The last sentence uncannily mirrored the conditions—an ice-choked sea one day, all the ice gone the next—that had caused the loss of the Pomori's ship in 1743, stranding the four castaways on land. Could this testimony be mustered as a further argument that the whole episode had occurred somewhere in the vicinity of Halfmoon Island and Negerpynten?)

Now, as we approached the cape, we got a firsthand taste of the treachery of this coast. Waves crashed against low cliffs and broke over the menacing edges of submerged rocks. The fog limited our ceiling to about a hundred feet. At a safe distance, we puttered east, looking for a sheltered cove, and finally found one.

We had no sooner pulled our boat up onto the stony beach than Vaughn quietly said, "There's one, up on that cliff. Just staring at us."

The bear was almost invisible in the mist, but through binoculars presented an alarming spectacle. The biggest we had yet seen, ghostly white, the beast stood motionless atop a brow of rock some three hundred yards away. Because of the noise of our engine, he had detected us long before Vaughn had spotted him. (It was indeed a male bear, Mats now averred.) The bear remained motionless, face turned toward us as perhaps he tried to catch our scent. As the fog swirled, he vanished into the shrouding grayness, only to reappear seconds later, towering like some guardian monster over our cove.

Mats had a hard time masking his disappointment that someone other than he had discovered our seventh bear. Had I not known Vaughn so well, on the other hand, I would have failed to detect the gratification he felt at his feat of spotting, beneath the nonchalance with which he camouflaged it.

Here on the shore of Edgeøya, with a fearless bear nearby, it was simply too risky to leave the boat unguarded, even surrounded by trip wire. Should the bear attack and ruin the boat, we had no way to get back to Bjørneborg, no emergency gear with which to endure the next several days. So Mats volunteered to stay with the boat, firearms ready, while the other three of us prowled the shore—to the westward, of course, in the opposite direction from the creature that lurked over our landfall.

It was a spooky hike. Only twenty yards away, Vaughn or Michel was reduced to a silhouette in the fog. We walked slowly across a spongy headland some hundred feet above the sea, waves crashing noisily below us every few seconds. There were bear tracks everywhere. On ground where our boots made no impact, we followed rows of oval depressions printed three inches deep in the mud and moss.

On every other point of cliff above the sea, we found an old collapsed fox trap, eight in all. It was puzzling that so far we had seen not a single fox. Except for the L-shaped stone structure Mats stumbled upon as he guarded the boat, we found no other signs of human visitors. The cliffs above us, all but lost in fog, were the homes of nesting birds, which explained the fox traps. But this shore seemed all but uninhabitable: poor in driftwood, deficient in harbors, exposed to the south and east winds. Perhaps such hunters as Odd Lønø or Arthur Oxaas had laid these fox traps, coming regularly to check them from their huts on Halfmoon or in Dianabukta.

Utterly sick of the fog, I was seized with the conviction that if we climbed the slope above us, we might break out of the murk and bask in sun for the first time in eight days. I talked my companions into the effort. It was miserable going, up a steep and endless cone of sodden scree, slipping half a foot back for every foot laboriously gained. Vaughn felt the ligaments in his damaged knee stretch in newly painful ways. After four hundred feet of ascent, we gave up, sitting to catch our breaths on a small ledge while we munched candy bars in silence. *This is indeed,* I thought again, *the most godforsaken place I've ever been. It's so ugly, it's almost beautiful.*

Back at the boat, we found the bear still in place in his cliff-top vigil. "What keeps him from just coming over to check us out?" I asked Mats.

"Bears can be attacked by other bears. He may not be sure what we are. Or he just doesn't like the feel of this cove."

I felt a sudden longing for the comfort of Bjørneborg, out there across the water. That touch of homesickness gave me a glimpse of how the sailors must have felt about their own hut. I could even empathize with the feckless Verigin, unwilling or unable to go out of doors.

We relaunched the boat, then motored four miles southwest at a distance from the coast. At the mouth of Negerdalen, Mats knew, stood a twentieth-century Norwegian hut. As we glided along, we scanned the shore in our binoculars, finding nothing of interest, until at last we spotted the boxy-looking cabin. Only a shallow, sandy underwater shelf stood between us and the hut. It looked like an easy landing to my untutored eye, but Mats declared it fraught with peril. "It is not hard to land," he said, "but it can be very hard to get off again." It was near here, Mats went on, that Rossnes had gotten stuck in the shallows, only to have his Zodiac flip as the tide came in. We contented ourselves with that binocular view of the lonely shelter.

The fog had thickened; Halfmoon Island was no more to be seen. We motored home, trusting to Mats's GPS, which once more brought us straight into the harbor in front of Bjørneborg.

The next morning, I woke from another sound sleep and peered out the window. "Foggy for a change," I muttered in disgust.

"But you can see the land on the other side of the bay," Mats countered.

"Good."

"Only it's disappearing fast."

Despite the conditions, we launched another Zodiac probe in the late morning. Speeding north, we passed through the waters off Dianabukta and came to shore at its eastern arm, where we had landed for our very brief reconnaissance on August 25. Our plan was to push from here along the beach that arrowed up toward the icecap of Edgeøyjøkulen, the northeasterly most possible habitation ground on the whole south coast of Edgeøya. Once more the wind was strong out of the east, though the fog had risen to hover as a thick leaden ceiling almost a thousand feet above. The universe was a gray swath of beach sand and talus hillside.

We had walked only a few hundred yards when we saw, all of us at the same time, our eighth bear, ambling down the beach straight toward us. So far, it seemed, the creature was oblivious to us. We conferred. Unless we chased the bear away, we would have to abort our day's hike. We continued until we were within 150 yards of the bear, which we could see was another giant. It had paused, still unaware of us, to sit on its haunches, as if contemplating a nap.

Mats whistled shrilly, to get its attention. The bear's head swiveled. Mats jogged closer and suddenly fired his flare gun. The animal jumped to its feet, ran a few yards away, then stopped to peer back at us. Mats started running, and we trotted after him. Was his machismo, I wondered, getting the better of him? Was he playing Hemingway in the Arctic? Mats fired again; this time the shell landed at the bear's feet. It ran a little farther, stopped, stared at the lunatics who were tormenting it, then, to our relief, started climbing the hillside to the north. We watched for half an hour, snapping distant telephoto shots, as the bear made a long angling detour up the hillside, obliquely skirting us as it climbed toward a hanging valley. A pair of reindeer appeared on the brow of the horizon. When the bear headed toward them, they trotted casually away. At last the bear vanished.

Mats was pleased with himself. "Sometimes you fire a flare," he said, "and the bear just sits there. That's when it's time to go back to the boat."

We walked the shore for hours, finding nothing of human origin but the usual tide-washed junk. Once more, there was a paucity of driftwood. Here was the bleakest coast we had yet hiked. The edge of the icecap still lay some eight or nine miles ahead, but we could see much of the intervening beach, which seemed to stretch blank and featureless into the distance. At last we turned and headed back to the boat.

A few hours before, however, on our way to the Edgeøya landing, we had made the strangest discovery of our whole journey. The mouth of Dianabukta is sprinkled with eleven tiny islands, known collectively as Abbotøyane. As we motored past one, I had peered hard at its crown, where an assemblage of rocks seemed to me to have an unnatural look. I persuaded Mats to land so we could investigate.

The pile of rocks, located directly at the center and highest point of the round island, was clearly some kind of man-made structure, though so crude, it was hard to judge what it had once been. Among the rocks, Mats found a nest with several Arctic tern chicks in it. He picked one up and held it, trembling, cupped in his hand, while its mother screamed from the sky and strafed us. "It's too late in the season," Mats murmured. "They aren't going to make it."

Wandering nearby, I spied another assemblage of stones. "Look at this, guys," I said. "I think it's a tent ring."

A circle of about a dozen stones, deeply imbedded in the soil, about six yards across, centered upon a hollow that suggested the site of a campfire. Wandering about the tiny isle, we found two other nearly identical structures.

What might they have been? Vaughn and I had seen tent rings left by Indians in the American West, all that remained to indicate the temporary shelters of nomads (Ute, Apache, Navajo) who had used the stones to anchor hide teepees or brush wickiups. Tent rings bedevil archaeologists, for they are almost impossible to date or to attribute to a specific people. Mats wondered whether these rings and the anomalous structure on the crown could have marked the temporary camps of Dutch or Russian whalers, who had perhaps set up their cooking and cooling vats here. But why on such a miserable hump of an island, barely two hundred yards in diameter, utterly bereft of driftwood? And, as Vaughn pointed out after scouring the place with his eagle eye, there was not a single piece of metal to be found—no spent cartridges or twists of wire or square-headed nails such as we found everywhere on Halfmoon.

The Sysselmannen survey earlier in the summer had missed this site. Mats suspected that no other modern visitors had ever beheld it. There seemed no good reason for Russian or Norwegian hunters ever to have paused here, and those men were not known to pitch round tents—if indeed the stone circles indicated tent rings. My fondest fantasy—so far-fetched I hardly dared to mention it to my comrades—was that we had found the elusive traces of the same prehistoric peoples that scholars such as Hans Christiansson and Povl Simonsen had argued for on the basis of stone tools. If the depressions in the centers of the rings indeed covered ancient campfires, some day archaeologists might be able to date this site, and perhaps demonstrate for good the existence of Neolithic hunters who had followed the reindeer to Svalbard, only to vanish completely millennia before the first Icelanders or Russians or Dutch had arrived. If so, perhaps the reason that those long-lost men and women had chosen the barren isle for refuge was safety—against the polar bears that even in the Stone Age had roamed Edgeøya.

On the first day of September, the weather was the same—fog and an east wind. The temperature had dropped. Mats said, "In a few days, it will start snowing."

By now we had scouted most of the southeast coast of Edgeøya—the shore that Starkov had told me was the place to look for vestiges of the Pomori—and found nothing but a bunch of fox traps and a relatively recent Norwegian cabin. We had dearly hoped to round the cape of Negerpynten and push north to Andréetangen, where the Sysselmannen survey indicated a Russian hut, but in such weather, the journey would have been too dangerous. Meanwhile, for all the barrenness of the Edgeøya shore, Halfmoon Island teemed with the remains of human endeavor.

Michel and I hiked a four-hour loop to check out the extreme southern shore of Halfmoon, which we had not previously scouted. It was the first time we had gone out without one of our two bona fide hunters as bodyguard, so we clutched our Mausers a little less casually than before, and I swept the horizon scrupulously with my binoculars. We found more spring-gun bear traps, and another weathered board with a black paint inscription, "N R 3. S. B."—but nothing that looked really old. Standing on the very southern shore, we watched the waves break savagely on the low sea cliffs. Here, the land was exposed to the full power of the Barents Sea. Somewhere out there, at that very moment, Russian divers were attempting to raise the submarine sepulcher of the *Kursk*.

The next morning, I was awakened suddenly by Mats pounding on the wall of the hut and screaming. I sat up and put on my glasses, only to see the frame of the rear window, just seven feet away, suddenly fill with the face of a polar bear.

Only a few minutes before, at 6:30 A.M., Mats had been kneeling on the floor, blowing the fire in our stove to life, when suddenly the stove pipe began shaking. We later figured out that the bear, attracted no doubt by the first wisps of smoke, had climbed the stone girdle on the back wall of Bjørneborg (Bear Castle, indeed!), laid his forepaws on the roof for balance, then seized the stovepipe where it protruded from the roof.

Mats grabbed his flare gun and his revolver and headed out the front door. Before he could circle the hut, Vaughn loaded his own flare gun, stepped into the small work room annexed to the hut's back wall, opened the loophole, and fired point-blank at the bear. Nothing happened. It was only the second time in Vaughn's hunting career that his weapon had misfired. In other circumstances, this could have been a perilous mischance.

From the back corner of the hut, Mats fired at a distance of a mere ten yards. The bear, still perched on the stone wall, gazed at Mats in puzzlement. It took another flare to drive it to the ground, and two more before the animal lumbered off to the north, though at its own leisurely pace.

Mats came back inside, still panting. "We may have more problems with that bear," he said. "He wasn't scared."

Now I cursed myself for not having seized my camera, which lay on the dining table, and snapped a portrait of the bear's head framed by the window. Instead, I had leapt out of my sleeping bag and fumbled to load my own flare gun. "That was right, David," Mats reassured me. "The bear, he does not know what a window is. He could come right through."

To our relief, Bear Number 9 made no more appearances at our hut. If we had needed a vivid demonstration of the necessity of boarding the place up every time we took a short stroll—a chore that sometimes felt like a fussy nuisance—we had just received one in spades.

Only an hour after this encounter, Vaughn looked out the front window to see a pair of walruses lolling a few yards off shore. We walked down to the beach and spent a half hour photographing these beasts, which, rather than spooking, came within a few feet of land to satisfy their own curiosity about the strange two-legged animals that had invaded their domain.

On land, walruses pose little threat to humans, but in the water or on ice floes, they can be dangerous. Valerian Albanov and his men, crossing ice and open leads on their desperate march toward Franz Josef Land in 1914, had several times been attacked by walruses, which they concluded were even more dangerous than polar bears.

Assuming that Sergei Terent'ev, the historian I had met by accident in Arkhangel'sk, was right, the whole purpose of the Pomori expedition in 1743 had been to hunt walruses. The method of the day was either to harpoon them in shallow water from boats, or to shoot them with guns if the animals were found basking on shore. It is striking that Le Roy recounts not a single walrus killed by the four sailors during their long stay on Edgeøya. Once the men had used up their twelve musket balls, of course, their rifle was useless as a weapon. The lances with which they killed ten polar bears became (after the deliberate killing of the first) strictly implements of self-defense. A bow and arrow was no match for a walrus. The sailors might have slain these amphibious beasts with their lances, but the catch, in meat, would hardly have justified the risk—especially with reindeer in such abundance on their island.

We had toyed with the idea of spending the day—the last before our scheduled pickup by the Norwegian research ship, the *Lance*—on one last Zodiac excursion to Edgeøya. But the eternal fog had descended once more, the mainland was invisible, and to make matters worse, the swell in the bay was the highest it had been since August 27. Mats speculated that a storm over the Barents Sea might be sending big waves surging toward the southern shores of Svalbard. "This is not good for our pickup," he muttered darkly.

So we spent September 2 in the hut. On a manic jag of nicotine withdrawal, Michel had been having a hard time sleeping. Now he sawed driftwood for hours, building the stack inside the hut considerably higher than what we had found upon our arrival twelve days before. Mats had started shamelessly bumming Vaughn's Norwegian chewing tobacco; fortunately, Vaughn's stash of Skoal was holding out. At dinner that night, we would drink our last two bottles of wine.

Through a good part of the day, we endlessly discussed what our wanderings around Edgeøya had taught us about the Pomori's elusive ordeal. Their antique tale was like some rare stone we had found—a meteorite, perhaps—that we kept passing to one another and turning over in our hands, as we sought to divine its true nature. And then, in the middle of what seemed like yet another rehash of old speculations, we made the critical intellectual breakthrough of our trip.

I had read Le Roy's narrative, in both French and English, at least a dozen times. Yet only now did I put several facts together to link a chain of logic that should have smitten me on first reading. We know that the two Inkovs and Sharapov were rescued on August 15, 1749, Old Style (August 26 by our modern Gregorian calendar). We know that they had spent six years and three months on their island. Thus their ship had been lost at the end of May 1743, or in early June at the very latest.

The question was now obvious. "Where is the ice at the end of May?" I asked Mats.

A fire lit in his eyes, as he seized a scrap of paper and pen and drew a quick map of Edgeøya. "I was here, cruising on the *Explorer* just this July," he said. "And here was the ice." He drew a swooping curve to mark the edge of the pack, then hatched in the space between that and the coast, indicating landfast ice.

Michel and Vaughn were peering over Mats's shoulder. The conclusion was ineluctable. In July 2001, at least, the ice had lain in a thick convex bulge protruding from the south coast of Edgeøya. All of the Tjuvfjorden was encased in pack. There were only two places where a ship could have approached Edgeøya from the south—at Hvalpynten, the southwest cape, where Keilhau had found the big Russian settlement in 1827, and just off Halfmoon Island. In July, Andréetangen, where the other Russian hut that I had hoped to investigate stood, had been more than twenty miles from the edge of the ice.

I felt electrified. "If this is the same pattern year after year," I blurted out, "if this was how the ice formed in the eighteenth century, then there are only two places where the Pomori's ship could have been driven close to Edgeøya in May." I pointed to Hvalpynten and Halfmoon on Mats's sketch. "But Keilhau said the hut was definitely not at the Russian settlement near Hvalpynten, and besides, they've done excavations there. That leaves Halfmoon. And Keilhau thought Halfmoon was the place."

We threw in the obligatory demurrals. "We don't know the ice formed the same way back then," somebody said. "We don't know that Le Roy got the length of time right," said someone else.

I wanted, however, to believe. In my notebook, as I recited them out loud, I jotted down all the reasons for Halfmoon as the place of exile:

1.) The shape of the ice pack in late May.

2.) According to Le Roy, the island "has no river, but a great number of small rivulets."

3.) The sailors found their clay "about the middle of the island."

4.) Aleksei Inkov named the island after himself—too grandiose an appropriation, one would think, for Edgeøya, which already had a Russian name.

5.) The sailors seemed to know every nook and cranny of their island.

6.) There is plenty of driftwood on Halfmoon, but a relative scarcity on the shores of Edgeøya that we had scouted.

7.) Halfmoon lies smack on the main bear migration route, and the sailors were forced to kill nine bears in self-defense.

8.) There *is* an apparently Russian hut on the southwest cove on Halfmoon.

9.) If the ship had been stuck in ice on the outer coast of Halfmoon, Aleksei and his three comrades might well have walked between seven tenths of a mile and a mile inland to reach that hut.

The single line in Le Roy that seemed to mitigate against Halfmoon was the description of "many mountains and steep rocks of a stupendous height." But if the sailors had been alluding to Edgeøya as seen from Halfmoon, the description fit perfectly.

I looked at my comrades. They all had smirks on their faces. In that moment, we could believe that our quest had succeeded.

• • •

Later, of course, the doubts would creep back. The argument was completely circumstantial. It was not as if we had found an old spoon with the name "Inkov" engraved on it. And the argument was procrustean in the extreme. I was desperate to make the "facts" fit our experience. The truth, however, was that, thanks to our short stay, thanks to the fiendish difficulty of exploring Edgeøya's shores, we had really covered only a small fraction of the terrain that a thorough search would demand.

As soon as we woke on September 3, the vigil began. It was foggy again—we had not seen the sun now for twelve days—and the ocean swell, if anything, was rougher than the day before. "Not good for the pickup," said Mats once more.

The arrangement Mats had made with the *Lance* was simply that sometime on the 3rd, the ship would gather us up. Because of its tight schedule, we had to be ready to go the minute we got the signal. We had already begun packing our belongings the night before; now we finished the chore, hauling our duffel bags down to the shore, and Mats disassembled our garbage bag toilet.

The day before, Mats had raised the possibility that, given the poor weather, the *Lance* might anchor at some distance from Halfmoon and send the helicopter it carried parked on deck to pick us up. This speculation had the baleful effect of making us strain our ears, minute by minute, for the distant drone of a chopper. Vaughn and Mats, in fact, had had trouble sleeping, convinced time and again that they heard the blissful whine of the engine.

Now, on the 3rd, it did not seem likely that the research vessel would just pop into view in the harbor before Bjørneborg, yet each of us kept peering out the front window in hopes of just such an apparition. More likely, we would get a call on our two-way radio, which Mats had turned up loud and hung from a rafter nail over the dining table.

"It's kind of like sitting in a duck blind," said Vaughn in midmorning.

"At least you know the ducks are there," I rejoined.

"Sometimes you go a whole day and don't see one."

About a dozen times, at the ends of my Alaskan expeditions, or anticipating crucial airdrops, I had waited like this for the bush pilot to appear, with no means of communication to let me know he was on the way, but only a date agreed upon weeks before. It had always been a cruel psychological trial. One learned to feign indifference, pretending that it was a privilege to have these extra hours in the wilderness, going off on short hikes as if that counter-magic might help speed the plane's advent.

Several times in Alaska, the plane had come two or three days late. Once, in the Revelation Range, our party of climbers had waited for a week, only to learn that our pilot had been killed in a crash in the Chugach, leaving his partner to fly an unfamiliar ski-wheel craft and find us from the X on the map of Alaska that had been the dead pilot's only record of where he had deposited us a month and a half before.

Here on Halfmoon, we had plenty of food left, a snug cabin, and a foolproof backup plan. If the *Lance* failed to show up by September 6 (three days after our scheduled pickup), a friend of mine in the States would call the Sysselmannen office and demand our evacuation. Yet for some reason, the wait this time, as we pretended to read our books on September 3, seemed as agonizing as the most prolonged of my Alaskan vigils. Only Michel, *branleur* to the end, remained genuinely laid-back about when and whether the ship would pick us up. Mats was eager to get back to his wife and children, and for all I knew, he was heartily fed up with our prickly company. Vaughn had no idea whether his father was still alive.

There was one crucial difference between this pickup and all my Alaskan expeditions. From my base camps on those unexplored glaciers, I had always plotted an emergency hike-out route. It might mean sixty or seventy miles and several dangerous river crossings, but I had made it a precondition of all my Alaskan forays that, if the plane failed to show up, I could hike out to Farewell or Allakaket or Talkeetna.

There was no hiking out from Halfmoon Island. Mats had joked about taking the Zodiac all the way to Longyearbyen in an emergency, but I doubted that we could have pulled that off, even if we had managed to carry enough gas for the voyage.

There was another difference, as well. During our thirteen days on Halfmoon Island, despite how well I had slept, I had been plunged into intimations of my own mortality. Perhaps this was because so much of the day-by-day routine in Svalbard reminded me of those months in my twenties and early thirties spent on the Tokositna or Gillam or Peters glaciers. Then, the future—in the shape of unclimbed mountains—had seemed to stretch limitless and joyous ahead of my steps. Now, at the age of fifty-eight, I could no longer cherish that romantic illusion. Most of my life was over, and it was the past, haunted with regrets, that seemed to stretch beyond the front door of Bjørneborg, not the future.

In a meditative moment, I had shared these feelings with Michel. At once, he repeated for me a striking *pensée* he had heard from the lips of a woman friend in her eighties, the widow of a famous French climber who had been killed decades before by a falling rock: "When one is young, the circle around one's life is the whole world. In maturity, it becomes your village. In middle age, your house and your garden. And then, when you are old, your bed."

The mountain ranges of Alaska, even at their most malevolent, had always seemed majestic and beautiful. I had chosen my expeditions for aesthetic reasons, seeking out soaring walls of granite rising from untrodden glaciers. But I had not chosen Edgeøya—rather, it had chosen the four sailors who had had the misfortune to be shipwrecked here.

It was too soon to gauge what the personal impact on me of having spent a mere two weeks where the Pomori had survived for more than six years might mean. In my prime in Alaska, I had had reason to believe that on unexplored mountain walls in the subarctic, I plied my craft of ascent almost as well as anyone in the world. Here on Halfmoon Island, however, juxtaposing our well-supplied summer lark against the ordeal Aleksei and Khrisanf Inkov and Stepan Sharapov had undergone, I had to concede that I was a mere beginner in the art of survival. In this lost and godforsaken corner of Svalbard (yes, the adjective was apt, whether or not the God the sailors believed in exists), despite a year of obsessing about their six-year exile, I sensed that I had not come close to fathoming its transcendental depths and heights.

At 3:09 P.M., the radio abruptly crackled to life. Mats seized the walkie-talkie, strode out into the yard, and spoke in Norwegian to the captain of the *Lance*. Because of the bad weather, the vessel had paused some eight miles to the west, well beyond the southwest cape of Halfmoon. It was our job to get there by Zodiac, as fast as we possibly could.

We nailed Bjørneborg shut, then divided all our gear into two immense loads. Mats took off in the Zodiac with Michel. Vaughn and I sat by our gear and waited for twenty, thirty, forty minutes, until we began to wonder whether something had gone wrong. The whole time, Vaughn clutched his Mauser, which he had not fired since our first day, when we had lobbed practice shots out over the water.

Alongside the ship, we later learned, the Zodiac had bobbed in the heavy chop as crew members lowered a rope ladder over the edge. Michel was so eager to get on board that he started climbing the ladder before the crew could tie it off. Shouts in English and Norwegian finally straightened out our addled Frenchman.

Then, on the return trip to pick up Vaughn and me, Mats came close to disaster. With no cargo aboard, the Zodiac started to bounce wildly as it sped across the whitecaps. On one such ricochet, it almost flipped. Mats had to abandon the tiller and throw himself headlong into the bow to keep the boat from capsizing. He told us this only hours later.

At last, to Vaughn's and my unspeakable relief, Mats motored into sight. We loaded up the last of our duffels and headed west across the turbulent water. I took a last glance back at Bjørneborg, wondering how long it might be before anyone else would spend the night there. In the rain and fog, I caught a premonition of the winter that would soon seize the land.

Half an hour later, we were on board the *Lance*. The crew winched our Zodiac out of the water, Mats standing proudly in the center of it like a skipper going down with his ship. On deck, lurching with the swell, we stripped out of our survival suits for the last time and left them puddled at our feet. Almost instantly, Vaughn began to be seasick.

Mats turned to the captain and asked, "Got a cigarette?"

Epilogue

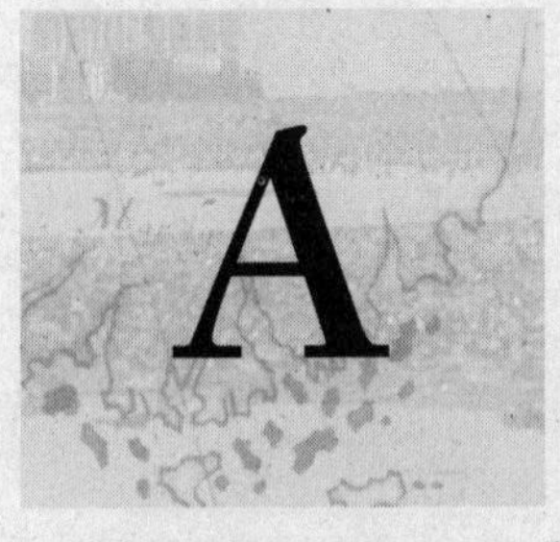

As we pulled into the harbor in Tromsø two days later, we were greeted by Mats's wife and children. They were used to his prolonged absences in Svalbard, but now their fervent embraces mirrored, I guessed, their own awareness that this trip had been more serious than Mats's usual cruise ship milk runs.

The next morning, as the three of us prepared to head to the airport, our parting hugs with Mats were heartfelt. For all the man's disorganized planning, for all his autodidact's contempt for authority—even for all his bumming of cigarettes—our guide had taken care of us. We had gotten through two weeks in an unmistakably dangerous wilderness with no mishap more serious than Vaughn's injured leg. About bears and Zodiacs, the two most critical aspects of our journey, Mats had seemed to know what he was doing.

Vaughn, Michel, and I spent a single night in Paris before they headed home, by plane and train, respectively. We had a last dinner at my favorite restaurant in the neighborhood, the Brasserie Balzar, where we got gloriously drunk, toasting one another like heroes returned from Odyssean trials.

I lingered on in Paris for several days. Emotionally exhausted, I did not even seek out the company of my several Parisian friends, but spent each day walking the streets and sitting in sidewalk cafés, sipping Sancerre while I gazed at the beautiful women parading by. A thing so simple as the fact that the trees were green with leaves filled my throat with joy. It seemed a rare privilege to be allowed to hang out, with no obligations, in the most civilized city in the world.

Vaughn and I had agreed that no incentive could ever be powerful enough to lure us back to Edgeøya. But when I eventually put together a slide show for friends, most of them reacted positively to the images of Halfmoon and Edgeøya: as one of them put it, "Yeah, it looks pretty stark, but it's beautiful too, isn't it?" I wanted to say, "You just don't understand. . . ." A few teased me: "How come you didn't do it right, and stay through the winter?" I could only shudder.

Michel's reaction was different from Vaughn's and mine. A week after returning to Chamonix, he thanked me over the phone for "the best vacation I've had in at least ten years." But then, in subsequent months, he slipped into a depression that could only partly be blamed on cigarettes and business snarls.

Vaughn's father had hung on to life during Vaughn's month in Europe. In Fort Collins, they had a moving reunion and an irreplaceable last few days together. When his father died in early October, Vaughn was guiding clients in Grand Gulch. Surprisingly, after a week of rest, Vaughn's leg had recuperated sufficiently so that it was almost as good as new. Whatever damage the surging Zodiac had done to his ligaments, they had healed by themselves.

I too went through a depression on returning home. I could not stop thinking about Edgeøya and the Pomori, but I felt powerless to sort out the meaning of my long wild-goose chase. What had I learned in libraries, in Russia, in Svalbard about the nearly lost story, and what lay forever beyond my grasp?

A wild-goose chase, of course, need not be a waste of time. Dozens of books have been written about Coronado, the Spanish conquistador whose grand *entrada* from 1540 to 1542 opened the American Southwest to Europeans. Several of these works (two of which I had read with pleasure) purported to retrace Coronado's route, by horse, foot, and automobile, even though we have only a vague idea where the expedition went, and only a few pieces of junk from any of its campsites have ever been conclusively identified—itself a startling fact, given that Coronado rode with three hundred soldiers on horseback, accompanied by hundreds of slaves and Indians, driving herds of cattle, sheep, and pigs.

For that matter, authors such as Tim Severin and Thor Heyerdahl launched best-selling careers by chronicling voyages in putatively authentic boats, claiming to have retraced journeys that we have no hard evidence ever took place—those of Irish monks to North America in the sixth century, of South American rafters to Polynesia long before the time of the conquistadors. A good wild-goose chase is an exercise in experiential empathy: by undergoing a research journey that at least parallels the flight of the wild geese one knows about from rumor, one catches glimpses of their passage, even of their very essence.

Upon my return, friends asked me if I had found the sailors' hut. I could only say, "I think there's one chance in three we found it." But even that estimate sounded like an arrant boast, once I had uttered it. Two archaeologists I had consulted before my journey had wondered whether anything might remain on Svalbard of a hut erected before 1743. Though preservation is excellent in the Arctic, it cannot match the pristine conditions that obtain in Anasazi sites inside sandstone alcoves in the Southwest, where mud-and-stone dwellings erected more than seven hundred years ago look as if they had been built yesterday. On the other hand, the site of Barents's overwintering on Novaya Zemlya in 1596–97 has been located, and excavations have commenced.

It is entirely possible that the Russian hut we studied on the southwest cape of Halfmoon Island is not the one the Pomori lived in, but that we were correct in identifying Halfmoon as the place of exile. Having covered every square foot of the island, we had found no traces of another pre-Norwegian structure; but that does not mean the Mezeners' hut had not once stood on the island. Both Russian and Norwegian hunters seem to have been demons for scavenging materials from one ruin to erect what would eventually become another.

In other ways, on Halfmoon, we had approached the sailors' experience. We had crafted a working lamp out of native clay that must have been similar to theirs. We had tasted the scurvy grass that might have kept the Inkovs and Sharapov alive. I had crept within a well-aimed bow-and-arrow shot of five reindeer. We had found anonymous graves that served as a memento mori of just how hard it was to winter over on Svalbard. In only thirteen days, we had seen nine polar bears, four of which we had had to scare off with our flare guns. We had listened to the tormented call of the red-throated loon, had counted waves crashing on shore, had stared through fog for a glimpse of land, had walked across the slimy basalt with the rain and wind lashing our faces.

Thanks to my research and trip to Svalbard, one dramatic insight forced itself upon my attention. As all mountaineers tend to do, I had unconsciously subscribed to an old fallacy of history-as-progress as it applies to terrestrial exploration. Climbing the Whitney-Gilman route on Cannon Mountain in New Hampshire, I had said to myself, "Pretty damned good for 1929" (the year of its first ascent)—even though the route was a piece of cake for me. In mountaineering, it is indeed true that advances in technique and gear and training, coupled with the taming of the unknown by sheer familiarity, result in a relentless upping of standards of difficulty. The hardest short rock climbs in the world in, say, the 1960s, which only the crème de la crème of the day's experts had solved, can now be knocked off by thousands of casual devotees. As Alfred Mummery, the great Victorian mountaineer, ruefully observed, the "most difficult ascent in the Alps" eventually becomes "an easy day for a lady."

In terms of the kinds of survival skills the Pomori possessed in 1743, history has meant little or no progress. It could even be argued that the opposite is true, that we know *less* about survival in the Arctic than we did 250 years ago. On first reading Le Roy, a friend of mine, himself a veteran mountaineer, had underscored this point, saying, "A hundred years later, and they wouldn't have made it." The Industrial Revolution, my friend argued, had robbed the common man and woman of skills and know-how that had been second nature for millennia. By 1843, perhaps, Le Roy could no longer have claimed that "all Russian peasants are known to be good carpenters: they build their own houses, and are very expert at handling the axe."

This truth came home to me in the recognition that, for all my wilderness experience, had I been faced with the conditions that ensnared the four sailors in May 1743, I could not have survived even a few months on Edgeøya. Vaughn, Michel, and even Mats readily concurred. Whether such resourceful hunters and overwinterers as Odd

Lønø or Per Johnson could have lasted six years under the terms of the Pomori's vigil, I could not say for sure. But I doubted it—not without guns, rowboats, matches, and waterproof clothing.

While we were still on Halfmoon Island, Michel and Vaughn had each come up with a pithy summation of the Pomori's achievement. For Michel, the sailors, in the course of surviving so long in one of the most inhospitable places on earth, had enacted, as he put it, "a résumé of humanity. All by themselves, they rediscovered the stages of human evolution."

It was an appealing, thoroughly Gallic notion, I thought—but in the end a little too pat to be true. Yes, Paleolithic hunters had invented lances not unlike the two the sailors had fabricated, with which over the eons they may have hunted the mammoth and the saber-toothed tiger to extinction. Yes, later, in the Neolithic, all over the world men had independently invented the bow and arrow, just as women had learned to make pots and lamps from clay.

Yet the Mezen men had not truly reinvented these critical implements out of a conceptual vacuum. Rather, they had known that such things as the lance, the bow and arrow, and the clay vessel had once been vital to human existence, and they had possessed the skills to make workable replicas out of the appallingly scarce and limited materials at hand (including polar bear tendons!). At one point, Vaughn had raised the intriguing and probably unanswerable question of just what crafts and techniques the Pomori might have learned from their Samoyed neighbors. Vaughn knew enough about hunting, for instance, to comprehend just how hard it would have been to find a piece of driftwood with the right arc and springiness to serve as a decent bow.

The other problem with Michel's clever aperçu was that, alongside the Stone Age know-how that seemed to emanate from their fingertips, the sailors carried in their heads all kinds of baggage from the Russian eighteenth century. In particular, they were devout Christians raised in the Orthodox Church. It seems undeniable that their faith had much to do with keeping them alive, for in the obligation the men felt to keep the saints' days, the bargain with God that compelled Aleksei to erect his promise cross, lay the coal of glowing hope that sustained the sailors through all their months of otherwise hopeless waiting.

Vaughn's own summing up of the Pomori's feat was less apotheg-matic than Michel's, and maybe thus a bit truer. "In six years here," he mused during our last day in Bjørneborg, "those guys went from surviving to simply living. By the end, they had this place figured out." I had to agree. By 1749, the sailors (but for Verigin) had ensured a steady diet adequate to keep them healthy; from hides they had made clothing and boots that kept frostbite and hypothermia at bay; and they had solved the problems of heating and lighting their hut. They could have gone on living, Vaughn implied, on their desolate island indefinitely.

In recent decades, anthropologists working in Australia have over-turned the old received picture of "wretched aborigines," arguing instead that the native hunter-gatherers had figured out their environ-ment so well that they may have needed to work as few as fifteen hours a week to ensure survival, leaving them free for endless bouts of story-telling, singing, and painting on rock walls. They lived, according to these revisionist scholars, in a state of "aboriginal affluence."

The phrase seems apt for the sailors on Edgeøya, too. "Aboriginal affluence" was the reason that, when they were rescued, they had two thousand pounds of reindeer fat stored away, and more reindeer and bear pelts than they knew what to do with. Perhaps Le Roy obliquely reflects this achievement in a sentence I had read over and over again: "Excepting the uneasiness which generally accompanies an involun-tary solitude, these people, having thus by their ingenuity so far over-come their wants, might have had reason to be contented with what Providence had done for them in their distressful situation."

Had the same shipwreck and survival befallen English sailors rather than Russian, I believe, their story would be as famous as *Robinson Cru-soe.* Why had the Pomori's tale become so obscure? The isolation of Russian history from the culture of western Europe has much to do with that neglect, as well as the stoic nonchalance about suffering and ordeal summed up so trenchantly by Masha Gavrilo, on my first trip to St. Petersburg: "We are Russian. We have many stories like this."

Gavrilo is wrong in one sense. There is no other survival story in Arctic or Antarctic annals that even comes close to the Pomori's, in terms of men beset by fatal dangers beating the odds for so long a spell through sheer resourcefulness. Sir Ernest Shackleton's rescue of his shipwrecked men in the Antarctic in 1916, so deservedly celebrated both at the time and in recent years, was an utterly brilliant performance combining open-boat navigation with self-taught mountaineering, but the men left behind on Elephant Island were well provisioned, and had to endure "only" four and a half months of winter tribulation.

The two most famous accounts of shipwreck and survival on a deserted island—both novels—are *Robinson Crusoe* and *The Swiss Family Robinson.* Both are also among the most popular children's books ever written. There seems, in fact, to be an intrinsic appeal for young audiences in such stories. The homiletic retelling of the Pomori's saga by the early-nineteenth-century German children's author J. H. Campe in his *Polar Scenes* has already been noted. I had also come across a 1953 Russian novel, called *The Way to Grumant: A True Pomor Tale,* by one K. Badigin, that had apparently enjoyed some success as a children's book. In it the four sailors are named Aleksei, Stepan, Vanya, and Fyodor: instead of the "fat and lazy" Verigin, this last character has been transformed into a plucky teenaged boy. Along with killing polar bears in self-defense, the castaways tame a bear cub and keep it as a pet.

Why should stories of shipwreck survival lend themselves so readily to children's literature? *The Swiss Family Robinson,* to be sure, reads like a children's book, and it had its origins in the yarns a Swiss pastor, Johann Wyss, liked to spin out to entertain his four sons. But *Robinson Crusoe* was manifestly not intended by Daniel Defoe to be a book for children. Its tone and language are adult, and the central conception of the narrative is a cautionary tale about the evil fate that results from the protagonist's failure to heed his father's advice to rest content with "the blessings attending the middle station of life."

Both *The Swiss Family Robinson* and *Robinson Crusoe* are first and foremost novels of adventure, and thus belong to a genre that has always been popular with children and adolescents—vide such books as *Ivanhoe, The Count of Monte Cristo, Kidnapped,* or *Around the World in 80 Days.* But the extraordinary popularity of Defoe's and Wyss's parables of survival, almost three and two centuries, respectively, after they were first published, derives from a quasi-Edenic fantasy that lies at the heart of each: the notion that resourceful Europeans, cast away on a desert island, can impose, with only their wits and their bare hands, a civilized, Western order upon the chaos of the wilderness.

The true story of the Pomori on Svalbard could hardly be further from the fictions spun by Wyss and Defoe. The Inkovs and Sharapov survive in a landscape that is Stygian rather than Edenic, only by adapting to it utterly. They never presume, as Crusoe and the Robinsons do, to conquer or domesticate nature: on Edgeøya, nature rules in all its implacable severity, and the sailors survive by fitting their lives to its demands. As such, the Pomori's story would seem ill-suited to moralistic fantasy, yet such authors as Campe and Badigin managed to turn it into children's adventure tales, replete with instructive lessons.

It is worth remembering that the Inkovs, Sharapov, and Verigin set off for Svalbard in 1743 not to seek adventure, but to make a living, presumably by killing walruses. Theirs was a dangerous and exciting profession, but in the Pomori context, a job all the same. It would no doubt have greatly surprised Aleksei and Khrisanf had Le Roy asked them, "Well, what did you learn from your amazing adventure?"—nor does the academician ever seem to have proferred such a query. The single overarching moral he draws from the tale—that necessity is the mother of invention—comes to Le Roy not from the sailors' lips; rather he imposes it on the narrative, steeped as he is in the rational optimism of the Enlightenment.

As a foil to the fantasies of Defoe and Wyss, we might reflect on the true story of "shipwreck" and survival that, it could be argued, has most captivated the public imagination during the last half century. That would be the plane crash in the Andes in 1972 chronicled in Piers Paul Read's classic account, *Alive.* The surviving passengers, mostly Uruguayan rugby players from the lowlands, knew nothing about the mountains in which they suddenly found themselves marooned. In their plight, they proved as helpless and inept as the Pomori were tough and resourceful. Paralyzed by superstitions about avalanches and snow conditions, they did little more than huddle in the broken fuselage and pray to be rescued. Only after the two most able survivors finally hiked out to a mountain refuge that they could have easily reached in the first days after the crash were their companions eventually found and saved.

No children's book, *Alive.* The sensational revelation that pushed

Read's account to the top of the bestseller list was the news that, in their extremity, many of the survivors had resorted to cannibalism. Those who could not bring themselves to eat the flesh of their dead companions died themselves. Intriguingly, it was by appealing to the analogy of the Catholic sacrament of eating the body and blood of Christ that these desperate men and women overcame their repugnance and rationalized the gruesome deed that kept them alive.

No easy or homiletic lessons seemed to percolate out of the Uruguayans' ordeal. At first, rather than being regarded as heroes, the survivors were vilified as barbarians. It was only thanks to Read's clear-eyed and unjudgmental telling of their story that its shape as tragedy emerged, finally winning the victims the sympathy they deserved.

Survival stories, in general, promise to tell us something basic about the human condition. From them, we earnestly attempt to wring some insight into "the meaning of life." And bad movies and potboiler novels only too willingly oblige, offering trite upbeat formulas by which their protagonists vow to live out the rest of their days, or supplying saccharine evidence that God will answer our prayers in the darkest of predicaments.

It is the need to believe that suffering has a transcendent meaning that has turned Anne Frank's complex *The Diary of a Young Girl,* with its precocious meditations on evil, its exploration of her own budding sexuality, into the homiletic melodrama of its stage adaptation, reduced to a pious fantasia on her most famous line, "In spite of everything I still believe that people are really good at heart." It is the same impulse that accounts for the popularity of Viktor Frankl's courageous effort, in *Man's Search for Meaning,* to extract from his harrowing experience as a prisoner at Auschwitz an existential understanding of the value of that suffering.

In this context, the will to survive itself is regarded as a virtue. Yet is it, in the long run, anything more than an animal instinct—the wolf chewing off its own foot to escape the trap?

In *The Myth of Sisyphus,* Albert Camus wrote, "There is only one truly serious philosophical question, which is that of suicide. To decide that life is not worth living is to answer the fundamental question of philosophy."

It had occurred to me to wonder whether what really happened to

Fedor Verigin on Edgeøya was that he gave up on life. I believe that his illness was real and terrible, but the conjunction of that and the apparent hopelessness of his fate may have filled his heart with terminal despair. Perhaps Michel's mordant little ditty on *"le pauvre vrai Guérin"* had hit the nail on the head, in its last line: "And who wanted only to die."

The homilies of survival literature would have us believe that Aleksei Inkov's reaction to his plight on Edgeøya—never giving up hope of salvation, observing the saints' days, erecting his promise cross—is the noble and admirable one. But in the situation, would not despair have been an equally human response? As Le Roy himself writes, of the moment when the sailors returned to the shore to find their ship forever lost, "This melancholy event depriving the unhappy wretches of all hope of ever being able to quit the island. . . ."

In both Catholic and Russian Orthodox theology, suicide and despair are mortal sins. Traditionally in Russia, suicide victims were not allowed to be buried in the same cemetery as the other Orthodox dead. The sin of despair is regarded as a deeply serious one because it implies, in the words of one theologian, "the voluntary and complete abandonment of all hope of saving one's soul"—hence, a denial of God's grace.

Yet viewed from a skeptical, agnostic perspective, the Church's stern stance on suicide and despair betrays a terror of the counter-possibility: that suffering is meaningless, that life has no teleological purpose. Camus is right: whether or not life is worth living is the fundamental question.

For me, for about fifteen years, from age seventeen to thirty-two, mountaineering seemed to give my life a coherent meaning. It was not simply that the ascent of unclimbed walls in Alaska was the most important thing in life—it was that everything else was subordinated to it. Each summer's expedition defined my goal. The months between were all off-season, as I slogged through college and graduate school, then taught English in a small private college.

Yet when I inevitably tailed off as a mountaineer, when climbing ceased to give shape to my yearly round, I found that nothing I had learned on those expeditions had taught me any wisdom about how to get through "ordinary" life. Whatever meaning climbing in the wilderness had seemed to impose on my life, it evaporated in captivity. For that reason, I have always been skeptical about such movements as Outward Bound, founded on the dogma that outdoor challenges can change your life, as I am about the deeply ingrained Romantic idea of nature as a school of character.

Several times, hiking down to the lowlands after more than a month on an Alaskan glacier, I had been moved to tears by the smell of the tundra, or had plucked willow leaves and stuffed them in my mouth to reconnect my senses with the living world. It was the same reawakening to the beauty of the ordinary I had felt in September, sitting in the outdoor cafés in Paris after only two weeks on Halfmoon Island, finding joy in the sight of ordinary leaves on ordinary trees. Herein lies one of the most often cited "meanings" of suffering and ordeal—that after months or years of deprivation and danger, one can never again take for granted the ease and beauty of everyday life. But of course this epiphany never lasts. The ordinary resumes its ordinariness.

One would give anything to know how the matchless ordeal undergone by the Inkovs and Sharapov changed their subsequent lives. Le Roy gives us only two homely details: that after six years of drinking only water, the sailors could not "bear any spiritous liquors," nor could they get used to eating bread again, because "it filled them with wind." The chronicler, of course, is recording the Inkovs' reaction a mere four months after their return to Russia. I doubt that Le Roy bothered to stay in touch with the sailors after they went home to Mezen.

Our only other clue to the aftermath of the exile is the poignant fact that in 1778 Khrisanf Inkov died on Novaya Zemlya with his two sons, trying to overwinter once more in the high Arctic. On first learning of that denouement, I had found it unfathomable that after Edgeøya, any of the three surviving sailors would ever have gone back to the Arctic, let alone to overwinter. But I remembered the several times on big mountains that I had been caught in a predicament that it would take all my skill to escape. Each time, in the midst of the agon, I had sworn to myself that if I got off the mountain alive, I would never go climbing again. Of course, I never kept my resolve.

I can see now that my year-and-a-half-long obsession with the Pomori's story was born of a hunger to discover not only their hut, but the kernel of meaning that must lie at the core of their experience—to find some sense of purpose to replace the structure I had lost when Alaskan mountains ceased to be the most important thing in life. In that sense, finding the sailors' hut was an over-literal goal. What if the ruined structure on the southwest cape of Halfmoon proved indeed to be the Pomori's shelter? Did that really tell me anything more about the meaning of their trial in the wilderness?

In the end, the value of my wild-goose chase was simply to bear witness to the sailors' feat of survival. The incredulity that every cab driver or casual acquaintance voiced when I told him the outlines of the story bespoke its dazzling uniqueness. What the Pomori had accomplished on Svalbard was not some instructive lesson in the virtues of faith, perseverance, or ingenuity. It was a work of art.

For me, the most sublime works of art ever conceived are the late compositions of Franz Schubert. Although reams of nonsense have been written about the "meaning" of a string quartet or cello suite, one cannot translate music into words. Listening to Schubert's piano sonata in B flat major (Opus Posthumous), I do not ask myself what the piece means. I simply sit transfixed, suffused with joy that a thing so beautiful can exist, stunned at the mystery that a young man dying of syphilis in Vienna could have created it.

Likewise, the Pomori's six years and three months on Edgeøya. I will never fathom the "meaning" of their survival, if it has any. The men themselves will never emerge as more than shadowy ciphers in my imagination. But that they did what they did matters to me. Beholding the work of art they wrought by clinging to life, I am flooded with a feeling like joy, deepened by astonishment that human beings were capable of such a creation.

Acknowledgments

My initial debt is to Christian de Marliave, connoisseur of all things polar, whose resurrection in France of Valerian Albanov's classic Arctic survival narrative, *In the Land of White Death,* gave me the first inkling of the extraordinary drama that had played itself out on the shores of Svalbard between 1743 and 1749. On my reconnaissance trip to Russia in the fall of 2000, Victor Boyarsky, director of the Arctic and Antarctic Museum in St. Petersburg, proved not only an enthusiastic host but also an invaluable liaison to other experts. Boyarsky's erudite staff greeted me with hearty (if occasionally puzzled) cheer; in particular, Masha Gavrilo became a constant ally as I pursued the knottiest research problem of my life.

In Cambridge, I was lucky enough to enlist Julia Bekman Chadaga for my first four months of tracking down the shipwrecked sailors' elusive story. A brilliant graduate student at Harvard, bilingual and conversant with all kinds of intimidating Russian sources, Julia guided me through the first dozen bends of my historical labyrinth. Her place was taken by Hugh and Masha Olmsted, who not only dug deeper into those sources, but accompanied me to St. Petersburg, Arkhangel'sk, and Mezen. Without their interpreting and their scholarly acumen, I would have been utterly lost in Russia. In St. Petersburg, Hugh and Masha's colleague Aina Luibarova performed many a valuable research service.

The staffs of Widener, Tozzer, Houghton, and Lamont libraries, as well as of the Map Collection, went out of their way to aid my search among Harvard's incomparable research holdings. Later, I received equally gracious help at the Bibliothèque Nationale de France, the Société de l'Histoire de Protestantisme Français, and the Bibliothèque de la Généalogie in Paris; at the British Library in London; and at a half dozen libraries and archives in St. Petersburg. In Arkhangel'sk, I found invaluable new material in the Maritime Museum and the Arkhangel'sk Area Archive, whose savants went to great lengths to lend a hand to a fumbling American visitor. In that northern city, I was fortunate to bump into Sergei Terent'ev, whose matchless knowledge of eighteenth-century Russian Arctic sailing and exploring vastly deepened my understanding of the castaways' story. In Mezen, Vasily Ivanovich Drannikov opened his solid little local museum to my perusal; another Vasily (our chauffeur) drove us all over town and to Pogorolets, where the farmer Ivan Mikhailovich hosted our visit. Most precious of all was the time I spent in Mezen with Elizaveta Aleksandrovna Inkova and Nina Fedorovna Inkova, the last in the proud Inkov line, whose comprehension of the old story passed down from one generation to the next made for a fascinating counterpoint to Le Roy's unreliable narrative of the four Pomori's astounding saga.

Other scholars and experts in various disciplines who came to my rescue included Aleksei Kasparov, Nikolai Vaisilievich Shulgin, Peter Boyarsky, Viktor Derzhavin, and Polina Viira (who guided me on a delightful day tour of Novgorod) in Russia; Hallvar Holn, Kolbein Dahle, Elizabeth Cooper, Ann Balto, and Per Johnson (one of the last of the great Svalbard bear hunters) in Norway; Dieter Füngerlings in Germany; Dr. James Levine in Boston; Canadian biologist Andrew Derocher; and astronomer Tom Bogdan in Boulder, Colorado. Tove Hellerud made felicitous translations of several Norwegian texts, including Arthur Oxaas's vivid account of his 1906–07 overwintering. Fellow author and Arctic aficionado Larry Millman gave me valuable hints where to look, and my friend Matt Hale perused some old German texts to sort out arcana beyond my ken. During the last stages of my writing, another brilliant bilingual Harvard student, Inna Livitz, came up with some startling new insights into my half-lost story.

In Svalbard, the crews of the *Professor Moltanovsky* and the *Lance* made our getting to and escaping from Edgeøya possible. Mats Forsberg, our guide throughout the journey, handled the two greatest threats to our safety—voracious polar bears and treacherous ocean channels—with professional aplomb. Mats got involved with my quest in a fashion that went well beyond the call of duty, and provided several of the key breakthroughs in comprehending the Pomori's plight.

My French publisher and friend, Michel Guérin, the self-styled *branleur* on our four-man expedition, was an ideal companion on Halfmoon Island: his insouciance quelled any number of my anxieties, and his intellectual scrutiny of the half-mythical sailors' tale gave me new hope in understanding it. My other crony on Edgeøya, Vaughn Hadenfeldt, proved once again not only why he is in my estimation the finest wilderness guide I've ever met, but why in a tough or dangerous situation he's among the two or three partners I'd be most grateful to have at my side.

Finally, my canny agent, Stuart Krichevsky, and his barefoot associate, Shana Cohen, believed in this book from start to finish, and helped untangle many a contractual or editorial snag. At Simon & Schuster, Gypsy da Silva and Gabriel Weiss copyedited my text with their usual perspicacity, and Johanna Li performed her effortless magic as the project grew from nebulous idea to published book. And my longtime editor, Bob Bender, unerringly steered me past the seductive booby traps and cul-de-sacs that strewed my narrative path. That rarest of modern-day phenomena, a veteran of the publishing wars who still loves books enough to make them as good as they can be, Bob gave me ample reason all over again to rejoice that he is my editor.

Index

Page numbers in *italics* refer to maps and illustrations.